ROCKY FORD, COLORADO
A WALK PAST LOCAL DOORS

From the Air

Rocky Ford, Colorado 1936   Courtesy, *Denver Public Library Western History Collection, X-13204*

ROCKY FORD, COLORADO,
A Walk Past Local Doors

Businesses and Residences from the Fairgrounds to Reservoir Hill, US 50 Curve to Curve

First business block in Rocky Ford, c 1886   Photo courtesy of *Rocky Ford Public Library*

David J. Muth

Glacier View Meadows
Livermore, Colorado

Rocky Ford, Colorado—A Walk Past Local Doors:

Businesses and Residences from the Fairgrounds
to Reservoir Hill, US 50 Curve to Curve

Published by:
Iron Gate Publishing
P.O. Box 999
Niwot, CO 80544
www.irongate.com

All rights reserved. No part of this book may be reproduced or transmitted in any form or by any means, electronic or mechanical, including photocopying, recording or any information storage and retrieval system without written permission from the author, except for the inclusion of brief quotations in a review.

The Publisher of this book makes no representation that it is absolutely accurate or complete. Errors and omissions, whether typographical, clerical or otherwise do sometimes occur and may occur anywhere within the body of this publication. The Publisher does not assume and hereby disclaims any liability to any party for loss or damage by errors or omissions in this publication, whether such errors or omissions result from negligence, accident or any other cause.

The author has used his best efforts in collecting and preparing material, including obtaining permissions for photographs for inclusion in *Rocky Ford, Colorado—A Walk Past Local Doors: Businesses and Residences from the Fairgrounds to Reservoir Hill, US 50 Curve to Curve,* but does not warrant that the information herein is complete or accurate, and does not assume, and hereby disclaims, any liability to any person for any loss or damage caused by errors or omissions in *Rocky Ford, Colorado—A Walk Past Local Doors: Businesses and Residences from the Fairgrounds to Reservoir Hill, US 50 Curve to Curve*, whether such errors or omissions result from negligence, accident or any other cause.

Copyright © 2016 by Iron Gate Publishing

Printed in the United States of America
    ISBN   1-68224-025-8   ISBN 13   978-1-68224-025-0

Cover photo, 1897 Recker's Hall. See p, 132 for details.
Photo courtesy *Rocky Ford Public Library*

For the People of Rocky Ford

Acknowledgments

Since 1871, and with the first use of *'rocky ford'* to describe the location of a prominent river crossing, there have been many to thank for their pioneering contributions. They are the people whose names appeared in private letters, early editions of the town's newspapers, or the public record somewhere for the rest of us coming later to know. Soon after the formal beginning of Rocky Ford in 1878, many others came with their hopes and talents, using them in their effort to build a town. I have written this narrative with what they have provided.

Thanks also to these thoughtful and accommodating citizens for their several forms of assistance during our letter correspondence, email, telephone conversations, and visits to the Arkansas Valley: **Donna L. Abert** for previewing the first draft of this book with an historian's eye, **Doris L. Baublits** and **Merle L. Baublits** for their extensive photo collections of towns, schools, and other historical materials of Otero County, **Leanna Chavez** for library assistance, **Sally Cope** for Chamber of Commerce historical items, **Maria Gauna** for photocopies in the library, **Fred Jaramillo** for his guided tour with brother Ken and my wife C J and me in the Bloomfield Usher Dye house, **Carol Gause** and **Don Gause** for photos and pleasant discussion of historical buildings and places, **Joan Gregory** for assistance in the Rocky Ford Public Museum, **Heather Maes** for directing me to materials at the Woodruff Library in La Junta, **Ruth Muth Grenard** for her photos and time spent driving me around town, **Sheila Henry** for copies of CDs in the Rocky Ford Public Library, **Bill Hodges** for assistance to items in the Rocky Ford Public Museum, **Susan Brown Holsclaw** for information of Memorial Bridge and help identifying building street addresses, **Judy Johnson** for her collection of prominent dates for the Centennial Calendar, my wife **C J Muth** for photos and patience following me all over town, my brother, **Ken J. Muth** for his memory of people and building locations, **DK Spencer** for his several personal observations and memories of some of the town's characters and history of the Santa Fe in Rocky Ford, **Laura Thompson** for suggesting persons to interview, and **Howard Winsor** whose work, apparent in many photos, is now in the library and museum.

Photo collections were the most valued resources for this book, freely offered, without reservation. Photos without citation are now found in public domain.

I am grateful for the patience of my wife C J and the expertise of our daughter Mary E. Crist who helped me navigate the tough times with many helpful suggestions using the indispensable electronic marvel known as the personal computer.

From the founder of Rocky Ford:

"The first Watermelon Day was in 1878. My crop for this year being very bountiful, I decided to invite all the people in the surrounding territory to partake in my crop. The country then being thinly settled the crowd was quite small, not more than 25 persons being present, and they being mostly from La Junta coming in a Santa Fe Caboose. I cut the melons on the grain door of a boxcar. Only one wagon load was required to feed the crowd and give all they wanted to carry home."
GW Swink

George Washington Swink Story, 1977, unpublished, John Doll.
Courtesy *Rocky Ford Public Museum.*
GW Swink served two terms as a Colorado state senator, 1892-1900.

From a First Resident of Rocky Ford

"If you of have any notion of coming west locate where you have a dependable source of water for irrigation. Don't waste your time 'dry farming.' The time is not far distant when the dependable water supplies will be taken up and only flood water available."
JM Hendricks

Letter in the *Rocky Ford Enterprise*, December 27, 1888.

Contents

INTRODUCTION	1
PART 1: BUSINESS CROSSROADS Our Walk on Main Street	3
PART 2: BUSINESS CROSSROADS Our Walk Continues on Elm Avenue	41
PART 3: AMONG THE CROSSROADS A Random Walk	51
PART 4: SELECTED ROCKY FORD HISTORY A Walk Through Old Town Site	91
PART 5: A PHOTO HISTORY A Walk Past Local Businesses	103
POSTSCRIPT Life of a Building, and of a Town	283
AFTERWORD Observations On Watermelon Day	284
THE AUTHOR Publications in Retirement Publications in Career	286 287
APPENDIX A. Chronology To The Centennial Year 1987 B. GW Swink, Founder of Rocky Ford	289 297
NOTES ON TEXT	301
SOURCES	305
NAME INDEX	307
GENERAL INDEX	315
ADDENDUM	327

Preface

Readers might ask *"Why write about the history of Rocky Ford businesses?"* There is much information available in local archives and online about growth of the town and of the Arkansas Valley. There were in Rocky Ford 14 individuals or real estate companies in 1911, 21 In 1914 and only three in the late 1940s. Although there was much business activity before and after those years, I expanded the text from there as the information was encountered.

Three significant periods of building construction have been identified*. Two were 1876–1887 and 1887–1920. The former was primarily adobe works along Railroad Avenue and Tenth Street. When Rocky Ford was re-platted in 1887 and Main Street moved one block west, frame and brick structures appeared with some adobes between Elm and Maple Avenues. The third period, 1895–1920, began during the second, and incorporated the system of *city block* construction using locally produced brick. These were on Main Street between Maple and Sycamore Avenues south of the railroad and north of the railroad, between Railroad and Catalpa Avenues.

The early 1910s, in second and third growth periods, were years of the automobiles, increasing success of the sugar beet industry, growth of a labor base, cattle and other livestock industry, increase of town and number of supporting commercial enterprises. Directory information revealed that addresses in the business district, primarily along Main and Elm, were residences and undeveloped lots. As businesses opened on Main, many north from the railroad to the fairgrounds, houses were replaced. South on Main from the railroad to Sycamore and the Rocky Ford Canal, businesses predominated. Residences were almost exclusively present from there south to Washington Avenue.

Development of businesses along US 50–Elm Avenue was different in how customers accessed them. The days of randomly tying up horses and carriages resulted in the first traffic jams and when auto traffic began in the 1920s the town required an orderly system to keep streets open. Diagonal and parallel parking were tried in the days of two-way auto traffic. City Council adopted a resolution in January 1935 restricting parking between Ninth and Tenth on Elm to one hour, exempting physicians. The development of the interstate system on Elm and Swink Avenues required all parking be parallel, thereby limiting access to some businesses.

* Richard F. Carrillo, Historic Site Surveyor, September 12, 1981

Early directories show some store fronts housed different businesses at the same address, true also of residences where persons with different surnames were living together such as in hotels, rooming or boarding houses.

Business people moved their businesses often, seeking improvement. The duty of the city clerk was important keeping address confusion minimal. A few businesses, such as *Mom and Pop* stores were listed by name or street, some without directory addresses or phone numbers. They were away from Main and Elm and were very popular until larger grocers offered more choices and volume in almost everything. Mom and Pops offered credit, such as at Maude and Bertram Beek's Grocery in my neighborhood. Cheese boxes held family charge books to record purchases. Each month on payday families paid their bills.

Since the days of the Mom and Pop, businesses of Rocky Ford have shown frequent change. I hope the reader finds interest in this kind of history.

Entrance to the Arkansas Valley Fairgrounds c 1880–1890s.

Introduction

Rocky Ford in 1911

Rocky Ford had a population of 5,500 citizens living in the Arkansas River Valley in one of the earliest irrigated sections of Colorado. Advertising in eastern states was directed to potential immigrants, enticing them to homestead and develop farm land. Promoters wrote of the climate that enhances farming success among a system of canals that delivered water from the river close by. Proponents claimed that the many vine fruits and vegetables were all sweeter, benefitting from an abundance of water, good soil, and sun. Wholesome living was to be experienced in a town not supporting businesses that drew the unseemly person. Neither was liquor allowed nor allowed to be produced by any person or business.

Instead, living in Rocky Ford, one would benefit from amenities such as the new $50,000 high school building just completed in 1908 and the five other schools in town employing 37 teachers who were mentors to 1,400 students. A new beet sugar plant was operating by 1900, starting its first campaign then and processing sugar beets which were sweeter, having been grown on the farms around Rocky Ford and in the Arkansas Valley. There was a Chamber of Commerce interacting with the town's businesses; a steam laundry, electric light and power plant, canning factory, creamery, and flour mill. The town's three newspapers, *Rocky Ford Tribune, Enterprise,* and *Gazette* printed the news.

Church-going faithful would find Presbyterian, Baptist, Lutheran, Methodist, Catholic, Christian, Congregational, Dunkard (Church of the Brethren), and in 1916, Christian Science meeting regularly. A library was new, built in 1909, and four banks were doing business. There was also an opera house and several theatres of the kind that offered readings, plays, and public discussion.

Parts of the Rocky Ford Ditch—later called canal—had been completed during the summers of 1873–1874 by men using shovels and hard labor. By 1880 it was nearing its Timpas Creek terminus. By April 12, 1887 water was running to each town lot during the first lot sale.

Twenty-four years after the town site was platted and when the lot sale was held, investors were busy building on their lots and raising their orchards and other crops. Main Street was lined with cottonwood trees and had open ditches running water to smaller ones just inside properties to trees and lawns. At far north of Main Street lay George W. Swink's timber claim, now the area of the Arkansas Valley Fairgrounds.

Information for year 1911 contributed by the *USGenWeb Archives Project, usgwarchives.net.*

Rocky Ford in 1914

A directory was published this year by FA McKinney that included much information. City officers, committees, schools, newspapers, churches, halls, public buildings, and political boundaries were listed. This directory also listed street addresses, names and occupations of residents, and names of businesses. The town had grown with many changes; fifteen miles of sidewalks were completed and Main Street was paved by 1925 (see p. 302, *Notes on Text*).

Businesses of many kinds were on Main Street, Elm and Swink Avenues, and a few on other streets. Some were short-lived, others continued for years. Today, there is another generation of businesses, store fronts, and residents. They are indicated in the text as *future home of* or *eventual site of*. A person walking along Main, Elm, or Swink past each address and business in the early 1900s, must have been pleased at the variety of businesses ready to meet their needs.

N Main and Fairgrounds Entrance

Several houses and lots were on N Main before being developed for businesses. Some of them belonged to people related and living under the same roof. Boarding houses were filling the need for those who needed meals and a place to stay.

The 100 block began north of the railroad and Central Park or Railroad Park; the 700 block of N Main ended at the fairgrounds; . For this narrative, even-numbered addresses on the right-hand text pages are on the east side of Main; odd numbers are on the left-hand pages. Businesses are highlighted in bold print on the pages they are discussed. Where no directory entry existed for an address, a note is made of future names of businesses or residents at the site when known. Many of these are from the directory printed ca. 1945–1948. *Publisher or printer unidentified in the directory but the likely provider was Rocky Ford Tribune.*

Entrance to the Arkansas Valley Fair Grounds c 1920, below, was into part of George W. Swink's timber claim donated so that the annual celebration would have a permanent location. Many trees are visible in the background providing shade for the thousands of visitors to the fair each year. The arched gated entrances were removed long ago partly to accommodate large vehicles. They stood at the northernmost end of Main Street. Adobe walls later extended from each gate toward the east and west fairground boundaries.

Image from tinted post card.

Rocky Ford Magazine v.1, no. 1, Summer 1998.

Part 1: Business Crossroads

Our Walk on Main Street

Arkansas Valley Fairgrounds to Beech Ave, odd	4	Front Street to Walnut, even	21
About city streets and addresses	4	Govreau Grocery & Meat Market	21
Arkansas Valley Fairgrounds to Beech Ave, even	5	Walnut Avenue to Maple, odd addresses	22
Author's comments on text	5	City Council actions	22
Beech Avenue to Catalpa, odd	6	City Directory ads c 1945-1948	23
City Council actions	6	City Council action	23
Beech Avenue to Catalpa, even	7	Block 300 S Main	24
City Council actions	7	Walnut Avenue to Maple, even	25
Catalpa Avenue to Chestnut, odd	8	Maple Avenue to Sycamore, odd	26
The Berkeley and El Capitan	8	Bloomfield Usher Dye House	27
Catalpa Avenue to Chestnut, even	9	Horse Carmon	28
Cartwright Building	9	Maple Avenue to Sycamore, even	29
Chestnut Avenue to Swink, odd	10	Sycamore Avenue to Locust, odd	30
WR Gibson's Racket Store	10	Ad block from 1945-1948 City Directory	30
Chestnut Avenue to Swink, even	11	Sycamore Avenue to Locust, even	31
B&AIE	11	Rocky Ford Ball Club	31
Swink Avenue to Elm, odd	12	Locust Avenue to Pine, odd	32
Boompa's Country Collections	12	Arkansas Valley Fair Racetrack and Grandstands	32
Swink Avenue to Elm, even	13	Locust Avenue to Pine, even	33
Tabernacle	13	Block 300 N Main	33
Elm Avenue to Railroad and Front Street, odd	14	Pine Avenue to Spruce, odd	34
Al's Goodie Shop on Front Street	14	Ad block from 1914-1915 City Directory	34
Elm Avenue to Railroad, even	15	Pine Avenue to Spruce, even	35
Rocky Ford State Bank, 1900	15	Spruce Avenue to Willow, odd	36
Railroad Avenue to Central Park (Railroad Park)	16	Exaggerated Postcard, 1908 Cabbages	36
Frank Boraker and shop	16	Spruce avenue to Willow, even	37
Railroad Avenue & Central (Railroad) Park, even	17	Produce Men	37
Jackson & Lawson Transfer	17	Willow Avenue to Washington, odd	38
Wig-Wag Signals and Crossing Signs, Central Park	18	Ad block from 1914–1915 City Directory	38
Railroad Avenue to Front Street	19	Willow Avenue to Washington, even	39
Santa Fe Depot	19	Early Water Mains	39
Front Street to Walnut, odd	20	Epigraphs: William C. Steele, 1917	40
Council action, 1902 and Ballot issue, 1896	20	LeRoy Elser, 1955	40

Arkansas Valley Fairgrounds

Begin walking south past odd numbers, west side of Main Street:

719 N Main, Wyatt, John H, Carpenter, job work, door and window screens a Specialty, All Kinds of, home, (Mary J); Haley, Clay, horseman, residence; Haley, Walker, carpenter, ABS Co, residence.
717 N Main, Barnett, Lizzie S, (widow, Danl), home.
715 N Main, Poole, G. Arzo, laborer, residence; Poole, J. Frank, section foreman, home, (Minnie). Later home of Carl Leeman.
713 N Main, Smith, Mrs Annie, home; Martin, Elizabeth V, (widow. Wm), home; Martin, Ernest, laborer, residence.
711, 709, 707
705 N Main, Stockstill, Mary E. (widow Richard), residence; Stockstill, John A, rancher, home, (Edna).
703
701 N Main, Price, John R, repairer, Railroad Ave E of Main, home, (Etta).

Beech Av. Intersection

About city streets and addresses: Throughout these pages Italicized numbers indicate no residences or businesses listed in the directories consulted. Absences of directory entries indicate undeveloped lots and some numbers appear to have not been used at all during the years 1911–1915. Several businesses also had used more than one address on a block where there appeared to have been moves or reassignment of numbers to accommodate multiple enterprises.

More developed lots were close to the center of town, nearest the intersections of Elm and Swink Avenues with Main Street. Addresses begin at 100 near the railroad for both North and South Main and increase as one walks to the north or south. West Elm and West Swink Avenues begin with 100 and increase as one walks east to the curve and the original entrance to town from that direction. In the 1914–1915 directory, the easternmost numbers ended with 1500.

Attempts to determine street addresses from vintage photographs for either businesses or houses were not always successful. City directories provided some, old newspapers others, yet properties were often identified only by street, avenue, or by an intersection. Throughout the city directories used for this narrative, address numbers were the responsibility of the city clerk. These were assigned by twos, odd on one side, 101-103-105-107-109, even, 102-104-106-108-110 the other side of streets to the end of a block. Many house or building numbers were not prominently displayed or visible. Added notes of interest are City Council actions appearing on some pages as footers, printed as they were recorded.

Our Walk on Main Street

Arkansas Valley Fair Grounds

Walk south past even numbers, east side of Main Street:

722 N Main, Rickey, Wm B, agent, home, (Rebecca J); Barrow, Frank M, clerk, home, (Nell F).
720 N Main, *future* location of Colorado National Guard Armory.
718 N Main, Rowe, Thos, Veterinary Surgeon, home 704 N Main (Almira).

716, 714

712 N Main, Martin, Le Roy, laborer, residence.

710, 708, 706

704 N Main, Peterson, Jas Oscar, ranch head, residence; Peterson, Mrs. Lottie F, home; Rowe,
    Thos, veterinary surgeon, home, (Almira).
702, 700

Beech Av. Intersection

Author's comment on text: Text narrative relies on historical events and personal recollection. Factual errors in interpretation or judgement are mine. Text is not exhaustive of the business community or of the succession of businesses over the years at any business address. Directories were not all-inclusive, only representative of Rocky Ford businesses. The business community enumerated at this writing by *manta.com* lists 471 individuals and companies in 39 categories with businesses within the city or close by. Abbreviations used in the directories were preserved in this text.

    Because I have only visited and not lived in Rocky Ford since 1954 it was important to have the insight of one who has been a permanent resident. Donna Abert well addresses this concern and as one knowledgeable of the history of Rocky Ford has offered much in detail of the business community as it has changed over the years. The text is benefitted by her review.

    Text pages contain citations for narrative where appropriate. Citations of publications and titles are in *Sources*, page 306. Some photos of buildings and activities are placed randomly throughout the pages and may not be illustrative of nearby text.

    This narrative is written from my perspective growing up in Rocky Ford, 1936–1954 and as a frequent visitor since. More than five years—1948–1952—as a *Gazette-Topic* carrier helped me gather knowledge of the streets, alleys, and avenues of town from my bicycle seat.

Beech Av. Intersection

623 N Main, Hoover, B Frank, laborer, home, (M Ella); Hoover, Delbert J, laborer, residence; Hoover, Diana, (widow John), residence; Hoover, Ralph W, laborer, GE Bryant, residence.
621
619
617
615
613 N Main, Snider, Ed, cement worker, home, (A Nora).
611 N Main, Marlow, Wm, laborer, home in rear; Davenport, Blanche, clerk, residence.
609
607 N Main, Pierce, Jas (c), porter; Jos Winiger, home; Jefferson, Elsie (c), residence; Moore, Carl, (c), laborer, residence. [The meaning of (c) is not given].
605
603
601 N Main, Kaplan, Nathan, clothing, 313 N Main, home 600 N 10th, (Anna); Moore, Al, clerk, Rocky Ford Grocery Co, residence; Moore, Eliza J, (widow Alfred L), residence.

Catalpa Av. Intersection

City Council actions, as recorded:

Apr. 14, 1908 Ordinance entitled "An ordinance regulating and licensing the use of automobiles and motor vehicles." Passed

Jan. 18, 1938 Moved that a caretaker at city dump be paid $150 per annum and be paid semi-annunally. Carried.

Beech Av. Intersection

622 N Main, Reeves, Bud W, restaurant, 956 Elm Ave, home, (Mabel)

620

618

616 N Main, Turley, Rachel T, residence.

614

612 N Main, Barker, Sylvia A, (widow Jas), residence; Woods, Alfred W, (Rocky Ford Bottling Co), home, (Marian Alta).

610

608

606 N Main, Carroll, Mrs CE, home; Cramer, Ben , rancher, home (Temperance).

604

602

600

Catalpa Av. Intersection

City Council action, as recorded, December 4, 1893:

Special police reports that he has been waiting on people quarantined [scarlet fever]. That there is only 1 house (Mr. Laramore) within the Town who are now quarantined.

News Item

Workmen and spectators gathered at Nepesta November, 1899 to witness construction of Pueblo - Rocky Ford Toll Line. Colorado Telephone Company completed four lines to La Junta from Pueblo in 1896, enabling four people to talk at once. An operator would ring each party's phone listed by name. Numbers were assigned when more customers subscribed.

Catalpa Av. Intersection

519 N Main, **The Berkeley**, (boarding house), Mrs Viola Farris proprietor, Farris, Dick (Rocky Ford Sanitary Plumbing Co), home, (Viola); Moore, Ralph B, bookkeeper (RF Sanitary Plumbing Co), residence, Dobbins, Robt Gaston, head bookkeeper ABS Co, boards. *Future* residences of Virgil V. DeBolt; William Longden.

517 N Main, *future* Pilgrim Holiness Church, Gandara Mercantile, p. 142.

515 N Main, McKenzie, Frank W., agent Singer Sewing Mach Co, home, (Cora E).

511–513–515 N Main, *Future site Plews Ford Motor Co.*

509, 507, 505, 503

501 N Main, Davy, Thos H, prop. **El Capitan Hotel**, residence. *Later*, the Chic Paree Beauty Shop operated within followed by Eve Fleet Dancing Lessons.

The Berkeley, seen at >200 magnifications of the *Frontispiece* photo p. ii. The roof of the El Capitan is visible at the frame's bottom. Because of the acute angle, the El Capitan appears very close but in fact there were several lots and at least one home at 515 N Main between them. Enlarged from *Frontispiece*

Vintage postcard photo c 1935–1940 courtesy *Rocky Ford Public Library*

The first hospital in Rocky Ford was Dr. RN Pollock's, built in 1907 at 915 Chestnut, far left in the photo. Both the 1900 Hotel El Capitan and hospital building are extant. The latter served town until the Drs. BB and BF Blotz Physician's Hospital was built at 803 Maple in the 1920s. Note, p. 302

Concrete light pedestals were immovable obstacles in a collision.

Chestnut Av. Intersection

Catalpa Av. Intersection

520, 518, 516, 514, 512, 510 were not listed in the 1914–1915 directory.

508 N Main, lot does not appear in 1914–1915 directory, the *future* site of Baughman's Garage.

506 N Main, Miller, Jacob L, Sec. Otero County Agricultural Assn, Correspondent *Rocky Mtn. News* and *Pueblo Chieftain*, Tel West 9, home, Tel West 24 (Cora F). *Future* office of WN Hull, Osteo. Physician, ph. 505.

Note: The countryside of Otero and neighboring counties was home to so many magpies in the late 1940s that they were deemed a nuisance for several reasons. Dr. WN Hull, a member of a local sportsman's club, used his property on the alley-side between Main and 10th to set up barrels for the reception of magpie eggs and hatchlings. The club advertised 3 cents per egg and 5 cents per hatchling to any and all who would bring them in to be counted. The project was well-served by scores of kids who climbed the cottonwoods to rob nests. Dr. Hull soon had to rely on the honesty of those bringing in eggs and young for the count when the barrels he set up were overflowing.

504 N Main, Graves, John D, Wagon Maker and Repairer, Second Hand Buggies and Wagons for Sale, Carriage Trimming and Painting, home same (E. Louisa).

502

500 N Main, Amos, Horace, (S Anne) Amos, Linn, Amos & Co, home.

Cartwright Building of 1910, was designed to appear as an automobile front at 421 N Main. Chestnut Avenue entrance had the same appearance, p.112. Proprietor Charles Cartwright's Reo dealership preceded Gene Shelton's Buick dealership. Roxy Theatre operated there c 1930s until a change in ownership; it was then Rex Theatre. Otis Love bought the building after the Rex could not be sustained. Contractor Lester W. Burchett leveled the sloping floor with sand and covered it with concrete for a skating rink. Skating did not remain popular and a teen center, The Oasis, p. 144, was established there until heavy snow damaged the roof. The building was demolished in 1980.

Photo, *Rocky Ford Daily Gazette Centennial Recollections* April 10, 1987

Chestnut Av. Intersection

Chestnut Av. Intersection

423 N Main, J. Wood Peery Cash Grocery, p. 112, home 502 N 9th (Anna L); Graham Hill, room. *Future* site of North Side Cut-Rate Package & Liquor Store and Pool Hall, Raul and Zack Jr. Hernandez, prop, followed by Hair Affair.

421 N Main, does not appear in 1914–1915 directory, *future* site of Roxy Theatre May 1934 and Rex Theatre Sept. 2, 1938, ph. 303-J, *future* site of Lee's Barber Shop in left entrance.

419 N Main not in 1914–1915 directory, *future* site HP Talhelm Bakery & Grocery, Henry's Cleaners.

417 N Main, Rumsey Grocery & Bakery, p. 278, Central Meat Market, CS Bailey & JE Umbarger, proprs.; Bailey, J Edd., residence (Rosa), *future* site Cut & Style.

415 N Main, Farris, John, manager R. Farris, residence, (Mrs R) Farris, R, general merchandise, *future* site of Hoff Plumbing & Heating; Pat's Beauty Salon c 1960s.

413 N Main, does not appear in 1914–1915 directory; *future* site of Rocky Ford Tribune.

411 ½ N Main, Masonic Hall, p. 110.

411 N Main, Beymer, Arthur S, Realtor (real estate), home 401 S 8th 1(Emma J), *future* site of Casebeer Produce Co., Pott Electric c 1960s.

409 N Main, Otero County Agricultural Assn, OW West president, CF Burke vice-president, JL Miller secy., HA Ball treas., Tel West 9, *future* site Ebbert Seed Co., Star Theatre June 3, 1911.

407 N Main, Rodeck, Louis L, Billiards, home 300 N 11th.

405 N Main, Burrell, Delavan V., Propr. Rocky Ford Seed House, p. 107, Tel West 50, home 404 N 10th, Tel Ford 117 (Maude), *future* site the Burrell Seed Growers Company.

403 N Main, Fenton Drug Co. (p. 107), Palace Drug Store, WC Fenton president and Treas, Tel White 651; Physician and Surgeon, Office 403 N Main, Hours 8 to 11, 1 to 3, Tel White 651, home 900 Swink Ave, Tel White 652 (Nannie A), *future* site Electric Shoe Shop.

401 N Main, K of P (Knights of Pythias) Hall, also 917 Swink, (p. 108). *Future* site of George Aldis Food Market; Post Office, Wm J Brown Postmaster; JC Penney Co., and Lewis Furniture. WR Gibson's Racket Store was located here in the 1900 photo below.

Swink Av. Intersection

WR Gibson's Racket Store

Thompson-Claypool Undertakers were at one time occupants of the Knights of Pythias Hall—see ad, p. 329. The service was entered from Swink Avenue at left. Upper photo, p.108, shows entrance corresponding to 917 Swink, as in the ad. Photo, p. 33, has their ad painted on the side of 315 N Main facing the Knights of Pythias building.

Photo courtesy *Rocky Ford Public Museum*

Chestnut Av. intersection

422 N Main, Athey, Mrs Myrtle, residence; Moore, Mrs Merle, home; 420–422 N Main, *future* location of Amos Hardware, ph. 310, Speed Queen Laundry.

420 N Main, Gorsuch, Eula, bookkeeper; J Wood Peery, residence; Gorsuch, Lucas B, Propr. The Union Cleaners and Pressers, home, (Della). 420–422 N Main *future* site of Amos Hardware.

418 N Main, Keck, Paul P, Veterinary Surgeon, home 602 N 13th (Emma I); McGee, Jas M, *rancher*, home, (Mary E); McGee, M. Mabel, residence. *Future* site Wilson Plumbing & Heating (also once to Railroad Ave., p. 189).

416, 414

412 ½ N Main, Koontz, Jesse J., apprentice RF Garage, home, (Mary), Produce Co, (EW Casebeer).

410 N Main, Horn, Coleman, laborer, residence; Palmer, Mrs. Hillie, home.

B&AIE Center *rockyfordcolorado.net*

408 N Main, (did not appear in the 1914–1915 Directory). *Future* site of Templeton-Bush McCormick-Deering Implements. *Future* Donk's Furniture address 404–408. *Future* B&AIE Center at 408.

406 N Main, Lumbar, Jas K, proprietor Rocky Ford Garage, residence; Lumbar, WD, assistant, R F Garage, residence; [Previous business Dodge Brothers Garage c 1914. See also business at 419–421 S Main, p. 132, Banta-Smith Auto Co. It is not clear which site was original place of business for James K. Lumbar]. *Future* site June Chevrolet Company 1936–1939, p. 198.

404 N Main, Hall, Mrs Effie, home; Stephenson, Chas, laborer, rooms; Dessie), Luth, LW, molder, rooms; Gunther, A., meat ctr. Stauffer Meat Market, rooms; Nichols, Al M, painter; CL Lawrence, rooms. *Future* site of McClelland Motor Parts, Donk's Furniture..

402

400 N Main was not identified in the 1914–1915 city directory. The front corner of the building, built Jan. 4, 1900 by George Higgins, is visible in the cover photo on the NE corner of Main and Swink. *Future* site of B & M Implement Co., p. 128, 245; Culligan Soft Water Service.

Swink Av. Intersection

Note: N Main at 400 was location of a large brick livery west of the new Liberty School, p. 237, built to the east across the alley on Tenth Street between Swink and Chestnut Avenues, former location of Little White School before it was moved, p. 166. Liberty School was later razed for construction of Nava Manor at 965 Swink Av. and CSU Extension Service 411 N Tenth Street.

Swink Av. Intersection

315 N Main, Funk, Henry, Confectioner, home 506 N 10th (Alice J); Crystal Springs Bottling Co, rear. Site of Funk's, pp. 107, 249, soda fountain, 1914, and Bruse's Variety Store, p. 128.

313 ½ N Main, Rogers, Lynn H, mgr. West. Union Telegraph Co, home, (Rose A).

313 N Main, Van Skike, Richard H, Furniture, home 1015 Chestnut Ave (Nackie R). *Future* site Nathan Kaplan Clothing, Well's Confectionery and Lunch, ph. 675; Love's Shoe Store.

311 N Main, Economy Variety Store, pp. 107, 249, AL Moody, prop.1913, moved from 202 N Main. *Future* site of Don's Mens Store, p. 141.

309 N Main, Kimsey-Cover Block. , Joseph H. Price Dry Goods, Ladies Furnishings, Etc, Tel. Ford 12, home 503 N 8th, Tel. West 161 (Carrie E). *Future* site of Fraser Dry Goods; Smith's Department Store; Harris Pharmacy.

307 ½ N Main, does not appear in 1914–1915 directory. *Future* site of JH Samuel, Dentist, ph. 107-J; Ward C. Fenton, Phys-Surg, ph. 680.

307 N Main, Funk's, soda fountain, Henry Funk, prop., in 1908. Business moved to 312 N Main 1911–1912 and 315 N Main in 1914. *Future* site Evalynn's Dress Shop

305 N Main, not in1914–1915 directory. *Future* site JC Penney Co., Inc; Athalie's Dress Shop, Madonna's Towne Shoppe, JC Mercantile, Boompa's Country Seconds.

303 N Main, Hardey Dry Goods Co, Henry Hardey Sec and Treas, Dry Goods and Shoes, Tel. West 53; *future* site of Richard Van Skike, Furniture.

301 ½ N Main, Hale Block, pp. 133, 279, North, Paul M, Lawyer, Notary Public, City Clerk, Hale Block, Tel West 290, home 511 S 5th, Tel Ford 578 (Stella G).

301 N Main, Morse, Harry C, Jeweler, home 209 N 8th (Monnie E).

Elm Av. Intersection

Boompa's Country Seconds at 305 N Main Street

Courtesy rockyfordcolorado.net

Our Walk on Main Street

Swink Av. Intersection

312 N Main, Bruse, Henry, prop. Bruse's Variety Store, p. 128, home 306 N 12th (Katherine).

310 N Main, Nishimura, Sam, Ichi Ban Restaurant, p. 127, residence same (Shizu), moved from 202 N Main.

308 N Main, Cline, Ella, milliner, home 300 S 6th.

306 N Main, Overbagh, Henry A, High Grade Work Clothes, Shoes, Hats, Gloves and Furnishings, home 411 N 12th (Georgia B). *Future* site Carousel, p. 187; Global Treasurez in combined 304–306 address.

304 N Main, not in 1914–1915 directory. *Future* site of Hested Stores Co., p. 268, ph. 217-W.

300–302 N Main, Godding Block, p. 108, RH James, Seeds, Lewis Bros & Johnson Merc. Co, Mrs W D Lewis president, AS Johnson Sec and Treas, Hardware Furniture and Implements, Tel Ford 20; *future* site of Beman Building at 300 N Main. (See upper photo p. 116.) *Future* site La Frances Dress Shop; First Industrial Bank; First National Bank (Ordway); First National Bank (Las Animas), pp. 187, 213.

Elm Av. Intersection

Tabernacle Interior—right—of the long building above with high clerestory windows was site of a revival gathering. The location was 508 S Main south of Rocky Ford Ditch, future site of two tennis courts in 1932, p. 31, and three city wells in 1934. During February and March 1914 this building housed the Hart-Magann (sic) Revival. [H. Hart Hagan was associated with the 1859 Southern Baptist Theological Seminary, Louisville, KY, possibly linked to this revival].

Patriotism was a theme evident at this event before WWI began in Europe in July as seen above. The building was erected expediently by the community for the single purpose of the revival. The wood-framed building was covered with tar paper held by lath strips and was taken down soon after event conclusion.

Courtesy *DK Spencer* and *Rocky Ford Public Library*.

Elm Av. Intersection

209 ½ N Main, Lawson, John A., physician, also at 924 Elm Avenue (both entrances to the same building), corner Main Street and Elm Avenue.

209 N Main, Rexall Drug Store, p. 109, JC Braden prop., Tel Ford 119. *Future* site of City Drug Store, Blinn, JJ, Auto Baggage Truck No 1 Stand at JC Braden's Drug Store, Phone West 217, Junior Towne Shop, Arnie Olson's TV Repair, Erlinda's Salon, Coffea Shop.

207 N Main, Fleak Clothing Co., HI Maxwell president, LD Fleak vice-president, WM Maxwell secretary and treasurer. *Future* businesses, Donk's Variety & Radio; Antiques, Hamilton's Variety & Gift Store, Colorado Originals, Joan Smith, Norma and Kevin Lindahl, proprietors.

205 N Main, Rocky Ford Grocery Co., Chas. Recker president, TH Stratton vice-president and manager, Tel West 90. *Future* site of HD Garwood Seed Company, Baker Jewelry (p. 276), Western Auto.

203 N Main, Golden Rule Department Store, p. 113, MJ Herz, prop., Clothing, Dry Goods, Shoes and Furnishing Goods, Tel West 167. *Future* business, Holland Drug Store, p. 157.

201 ½ N Main, *future* site of American Fruit Growers, Inc., Paul P. Edwards, prop., ph. 165.

201 N Main, Rocky Ford State Bank. *Future* site Rocky Ford National Bank, pp. 129, 157; Community Banks of Rocky Ford, Crosswhite Realty.

Railroad Av. Intersection

Railroad Park (Central Park). East of the Santa Fe Depot in the sidewalk near the street is an iron cover marked *Water*. It is the location of Rocky Ford's first artesian well, pp. 62, 63, drilled in 1895 and used by townspeople and their animals who had until then been using ditch water. The well casing remains in place.

There were four other wells of various flow capacity, p. 90. One was in Garden Place, one on Play Park Hill or Reservoir Hill as many knew it. It was the poorest producer at about 10 gallons per minute. Gravity fed water to mains and smaller pipes to users from two 100 barrel tanks nearby. Another well was on the town lot on Front and Eleventh Streets and another private one was drilled west of town on property west of the junction of State Highway 71 and US 50.

Front Str. Intersection

Al's Goodie Shop, 105 S Main Street, a one-man business, was on the south side of Railroad Park, located near the sidewalk on the SE corner of the park. Mr. Goeringer used crutches since his childhood and was able to drive his car. He sold news, magazines, candies, pop, tobacco products, and punch-board chances. He followed this business at the same address with a realty and insurance business that was eventually moved to 901 Swink Avenue, c 1960s.

Town Nuisances
People mentioned these items at one time published in the *Enterprise* c 1897–1898: Russian thistles [tumbleweed], alkali, English sparrows, lack of school room, hail, and saloons.

Elm Av. Intersection

208 N Main, Wood, Geo T, proprietor The Central, furn. rooms, (Maggie); Guynn Mercantile Co., Kaplan Mercantile Co., p. 268, here later. Site of Mint Saloon, burned in 1898.

206 ½ N Main, absent from 1914–1915 directory. *Future* home of Mrs. Addie Dye.

206 N Main, Shelton, EC & Son, (EC and GM Shelton), Grocers, Tel Ford 17; Buck & Pap Grocers, Tel Ford 17; Wm. F. Gerbing Meats, home 515 Elm Ave (Emma P). *Future* site of Hardt Hardware, pp. 236, 269.

204 ½ N Main, Frame's Studio, Mrs. OL Frame prop., Artistic Photography; residence 911 S Main; Burnett, Erwin F, Optometrist, Tel West 241, home 1610 Pine Ave (Carrie C); Maier, Frank W, Physician, home 1004 Swink Ave.; (Matilda E); Maltby, RC Drug Co., BL Lawrence mgr., proprietors City Drug Store (p. 127), Tel. West 55.

204 N Main, Kreider, Eugene T, Jeweler 204 N Main, home 804 S 14th (Emma C). *Future* site of Gambles, p. 236.

202 N Main, Moody, AL, Economy Variety Store in 1912, from 900 Elm to 311 N Main in 1913; formerly City Drug Store, p.127.

200 N Main, George Maxwell Clothing; *future* site of Fashion Center, ph. 374, Walker's Men's Wear, Jess's Barber Shop c 1960s.

Railroad Av. Intersection

Rocky Ford Centennial Recollections April 10, 1987.

Rocky Ford State Bank in 1900, to be Rocky Ford National Bank, at 201 N Main. Bank is directly north of Railroad Park across Railroad Avenue. This building is located diagonally from Jackson & Lawson office at 110 N Main, p. 17. Street and sidewalk improvements eventually required removal of many remaining trees. (See also p. 129 for another view of this building.)

Railroad Av. Intersection

Early in the control of Main Street traffic, especially during a sugar campaign, the Santa Fe RR placed a small kiosk, large enough for a man to stand in between the tracks just off street on the east side of Main. Mr. BR Buis of 400 S Thirteenth spent his days in the area, either in the kiosk or on Main among the tracks with a hand-held stop sign. Traffic of the sugar factory switch engine and the main-line required vigilance by Mr. Buis to stop Main Street auto traffic. He was empowered to issue traffic citations to those who would not heed his stop signal. [DK Spencer relates Buis, the directory spelling, was pronounced by his friend emphasizing the *i* as in *Bius*].

Railroad track intersection-Central Park (Railroad Park)

Frank H. Boraker's Shop, was a small building across the street from Rocky Ford National Bank on the NE corner Railroad Park. Mr. Boraker was blinded in an industrial accident in Indiana where he lived prior to Rocky Ford. He sold confectioneries, newspapers, tobacco products and dispensed good will. His home was 713 Walnut. Photo courtesy *Rocky Ford Daily Gazette*

Frank Boraker on a winter day, 1942. On a warmer day benches would attract many friends, visitors, and story-tellers. Business is visible at extreme left of winter photo p. 81.

Often observed passing front of Boraker's one would see a stately-appearing, brown-skinned man in a suit. He walked with purpose, erect. He wore a turban headdress as would a person from India. My friends called him "The Indian" or "The Hindu" but none of us ever knew his name or where he was from. As kids, none of us dared ask this man our questions, p. 302.

Railroad Av. Intersection

110 N Main, Johnston & Govreau (Fred L Johnston, CB Govreau), Coal, Grain, Transfer, Water, Tel Ford 122. Later businesses Claude Silvers Coal; Frank G. Hough & Co. Beans, Heil Bean, Inc. Jackson & Lawson, photo below, preceded the above businesses.

108 N Main, *future* site of Bish Hardware & Furniture Company.

101–108 N Main, Rocky Ford Trading Co, SA Mathews president, HW Lance Sec. and Mgr, Hardware and Implements, home 801 Walnut Ave, Tel Ford 114, (Ione C.) 101 N Main. *Future* office of AT&SF Railway, ph. 8, Double R Automotive, Carquest, and Absolute Automotive.

100 N Main, Texas Co. Oils, Rocky Ford Trading Co agents, AT&SF.

Front Street Intersection

Central Park-Railroad Park-AT&SF Tracks

Photo from *The Story of Early Rocky Ford,* John Doll.

View c 1914 of the fair parade from Railroad Av. and Main Street. Jackson & Lawson Transfer at 110 N Main dealt with coal, grain, hay and feed from the SE corner of this intersection. Future location of Frank Boraker's business is directly across Main Street. Photo was taken from the roof of 200 N Main, Maxwell Building, p. 157, and George Maxwell Clothing.

Chariots pulled by four white and four black horses (drivers in costume) predate the 1925 silent movie *Ben Hur.* There was a Roman show with chariot races during the 1926 fair, p. 302.

By the tracks

Wig-Wag signals, at left, were placed at Main Street in 1921 and Tenth Street in 1923. They incorporated a light and bell in addition to back-and-forth arm movement. Both were removed with much effort about 1980.

trainweb.org

Crossing signs were wooden and triangular, right, in use before much automobile traffic. Driver attention was better attracted to both light and movement of the wig-wag signal.

Denver News

Railroad Park, below, from near Front Street on the south, shows young trees and a fountain similar to that in Library Park. Mayor RM Pollock had convinced Santa Fe Railway officials to move the lumber yard north of the depot to a location on Ninth Street. Grass and trees were planted extending the park from Front Street, across the tracks past the depot to Railroad Avenue.

Photo courtesy *Rocky Ford Public Library*

Scene in 1910 of Railroad Park with the 1907 depot having replaced an 1887 one, p. 19, moved to a N Ninth Street location. Wells Fargo Co. built a red brick building west of the depot at 100 N Ninth Street, the site later taken by the Railway Express Agency (REA), p. 302.

Railroad Av. Intersection
Santa Fe Railroad

100 S Main, Vaughn, John C, "The Transfer Man," Office, Flagman Station, Tel Ford 505, home 522 N 6th, Tel Ford 580 (Mattie).
102 S Main, JL Bass & CF Summers, Transfer & Storage, Office with Geo. Bryant, Tel West 62, Res Phone West 624; Bryant, Geo E, Coal, home 802 S 13th (Mabel M).
104 S Main, English, RW, Lumber Co, HA Dawley general manager. *Future* site Sharp Image Styling Salon, Carol Weiss, prop..
105 S Main, Al's Goodie Shop, *future* Goeringer Realty Co. c 1960s, and Santa Fe Depot.
106 S Main, Bish Brothers, ph. 370.

Front Str. Intersection

Railroad or Central Park appears on the west side of Main opposite the above addresses. Business addresses begin again to the south with the small one-man business, Al's Goodie Shop, p. 14, 105 S Main Street on the SE corner of the park.

Santa Fe Depot, built in 1887 was replaced in 1907 with a brick structure. A lumber yard on the north edge of the park between the depot and Railroad Avenue was moved to Ninth Street. Grass and American Elms were planted to expand the site. Three years later the park appeared as in the photo, p. 18. Mayor RM Pollock at this time was also responsible for landscaping the Reservoir Hill and Library Park sites. Along with elm trees the Library Park was planted with a number of walnut trees along the eastern border on Eleventh Street that attracted many squirrels.

Courtesy, *History Colorado, Fred Mazulla Collection, 10024501.*

Front Str. Intersection

201 S Main, First National Bank, MD Thatcher (Pueblo) president, HE Allderdice Cashr., John Richert, Asst Cashr., Tel Ford 58.

203 S Main, Shaw Clothing Co. (p. 132), Jas H. Shaw, president, Florence C. Shaw, vice-president, AF Anderson, secretary and treasurer. *Future* site Pott Electric; new city administration building.

205 S Main, Western Hardware & Furniture Co, JB Nichols, president, WL Smith Sec. and Treas., Tel Ford 93.

207 S Main, Harry J. Black's Jewelry, home 701 Chestnut Ave (Eva A). Clark Music Co, CO Clark president, WW Thomas v-president, LR Fenlason secretary and treasurer. Kellogg, Seay Moore, Osteopathic Physician, Graduate American School of Osteopathy, Office Hagen-Recker Block, upper floor, Tel Ford 64, home.

207 ½ S Main, Hagen-Recker Block; Wolfe & Smith Block, Wolfe & Malty Block.

209 S Main Grossarth, Wm., Jeweler, home 404 S 13th (Etta S). *Future* site of Red Cross Pharmacy; Williamson, Oliver M, clerk, GA Blakely, proprietor. *Future* site of Rocky Ford Trading Co., ph 526-W; Spencer's Restaurant, Sylvan 'Cecil 'Spence' Spencer, prop.

209 ½ S Main, Arkansas Valley Business, Chance & Collection Agency, Earl V. Minor Sec., Tel Ford 216; SL Fielder, room, ph. 93; Barbour, Llewellyn P, Physician, residence 511 S 12th. Chritton, Jas M, Justice of Peace, home 801 S 8th (Mary). Savage, S Hubbard, Physician, home 501 S Main (Bertha). Brown, Walter G, Propr. Palace of Sweets, Savage, Tel Ford 247, home 402 S 13th (Crystal).

Block, as used in this text, could mean an area bounded by streets or buildings on four sides or the distance along one side of such an area. Often one building in Rocky Ford was considered a Block, usually with dated entablature and name of owner/builder on its facade. Buildings adjacent, erected at the same or later time by others, by convention would often be known by the Block name.

Walnut Av. Intersection

Ballot Issue, 1896: The Anti-Saloon Party wanted to vote to remove saloons from town but failed to do so when the Business Men's Party, consisting of the mayor and three councilmen, contended, that without the $2400 they receive from the four saloon licenses, they would have to raise the town's taxes. Vote failed.

Dec. 12, 1902, Attorney Beall dealing with court cases: ... 3 cases were docketed in county court on appeal from Police Magistrate Court in cases selling liquor on Sunday. Attorney ask (sic) for instruction as to prosecuting the cases. On motion the attorney was instructed to prosecute all these cases in which there would be reasonable prohibition of securing a conviction.

[Instruction to the prosecuting attorney in the liquor cases appears to be *'Don't convict'*].

Front Str. Intersection

200 S Main, IOOF Hall (p. 78), Bonta, John L, Bonta Mercantile, home 402 N 14th (Carrie). *Future* site of Woodside Seed Growers Co., ph. 26 c 1940–50s.

202 S Main, Hall, Ruth E, Art goods, residence 905 S Main; Taylor, Chas W, Notions, home 407 S 12th (Clara B).

204 S Main, Govreau Grocery & Meat Market,* Chas L. Govreau, prop., home 1002 S Main [near the city water works] Alice M. *Future* site of Fiesta Café, Pantoya family prop.

206 S Main, Big Four Cash Grocery, (J W Leesing, J W Rex). 600 S 13th, Tel West 61 (Katherine). *Future* site of Smith's Cafe, The Toggery, Men's Clothing and Furnishing. (See p. 83 for interior view of Smith's Cafe.)

208 S Main, McDermid, Alex, Tailor, residence Elk Hotel; Winiger, Jos, Barber, home, 505 S 13th (Flossie A). *Future*, Bill & Bob's Super Service [first location], ph. 153.

210 S Main, not listed in early directories. Future home of Johnny's Auto Service c 1960s.

* "JC Gacy's building south of the Odd Fellows' building will soon be completed. It will be occupied by Young and Govreau [204 S Main] who plan to stock it with groceries and meat." *Enterprise,* March 10, 1898

Walnut Av. Intersection

Govreau Grocery and Meat Market

Recollections, Rocky Ford Centennial, Daily Gazette, April 10, 1987.

Walnut Av. Intersection

301 S Main, People's Home Bank, AH Bushey, president, AD Isherwood V-President, CC Coffman Cashier, TE Coffman Asst Cashier, (former site of Farmers and Merchants Bank), *future* site of Ruth Café, JJ Steir, prop., ph 382, Rocky Ford Drug Store, Rudy Sutherland, prop., Lighthouse Church, and Movie World, Juan Lucero, prop.

303 S Main, Smirl, TJ & Son (TJ Smirl and RJ Smirl), Grocers. *Future* site of Carman & Sons Plumbing & Heating, ph. 658.

305 S Main, Jones, Mrs Eva F, Milliner, res. Washington Ave 1 Block East Main.

305 ½ S Main, Garity, Francis E, cleaner and presser, home 303 S 12th (Audrey J).

307 S Main, Black, Arthur W., contractor, home 410 S 9th (May N). Hill, Thos J, Agent Mehlin & Sons, Bjur Bros and Ivers & Pond Pianos and Columbia Grafonolas and Records and Musical Merchandise, 404 S Main, after Nov 1st 1914, home 511 S 11th (Ella L).

307 ½ S Main, Loback, John H, Barber, home (Hattie M).

309 S Main, Ferril, C. Otto, Clothing, Shoes, Mens and Boys' Furnishings, Dundee Suits, Made to Your Measure $15, Tel West 121, 310 S Main, Holsun Grocery, Geo. R. Daring prop. *Future* site of Doc & Bonnie's Café, p. 53.

311 S Main, Bostwick Bros, Confectioners. *Future* site of Jenner Plumbing & Heating; Econo-Wash, Shuey Bakery.

311 ½ S Main, Corcoran, Mrs Alvia, propr. Elk Hotel, Tel Ford 121.

313 S Main, Rodeck Billiards, (name uncertain). *Future* site of Chamberlain Realty, p. 212; Christian Science Reading Room.

315 S Main, Claude's Shoe Shine Shop, p. 212, Claude Tyler, prop. *Future* site Home Realty c 1960s.

Maple Av. Intersection

City Council business, as recorded.
January 20, 1894: Moved that the health officer be authorized to investigate the healthfulness of hogs being slaughtered and offered for sale within the Town and to take any action they find necessary. Carried.
    March 5, 1894: Mr. Dennes reports he and Health Officer reports that they went to meat market and found no mutton on sale. They took no further action.
    September 3, 1894: Marshall reports that calaboose [200 block S Eleventh] needs clearing out and also needs 2 locks. Moved that marshall be authorized to purchase a jail lock for the calaboose. Carried.

Our Walk on Main Street

Three Businesses advertising in the City Directory circa 1945–1948—see preceding page 22.

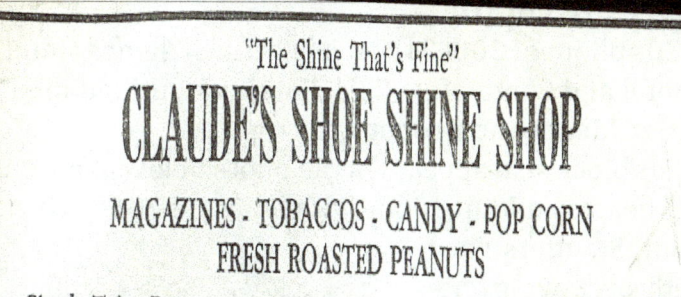

Note: Burnt orange was the cover color and of some internal ad pages of the c 1945–1948 City Directory, p. 314.

City Council business, as recorded:

```
Apr. 12, 1890 --   On motion "The Watermelon" became and be the official
                   organ for all publications for the town or issuing
                   year.
```

Rocky Ford Magazine vol. 1 no. 1

Block 300 S Main

A 1920s photo of 300–316, above, with St. James Hotel at 300–302. White or painted brick mark the hotel and Cantaloupe Café. Four unidentified men stand front of Gem Theatre, next door to **Stauffer Meats** and **Grocery,** far right.

This block also appears in the photo below at another time. Stauffers eventually occupied the Gem Theatre building, along with others at 306–310 in 1914 when the business moved from 917 Walnut. Stauffers was already occupying one building right of the white door, above (Stauf ... on the canopy) and expanded into the other addresses later.

Distinctive keystones are above windows of the **St. James**, **Cantaloupe Café**, and the **Gem Theatre**, especially visible on the Gem.

Photo courtesy *Rocky Ford Public Library*

Walnut Av. Intersection

300 S Main, *Rocky Ford Tribune* (Weekly), Int Stanley & Sons Publishers, Tel West 10, (Int L. Thiers, Dean and Bryan Stanley), publishers. *Future* site of Citizen's Utilities Co., ph. 46; original site of St. James Hotel in 1888, later site of Public Grocery & Market June 18, 1897. *Future* site Hancock's Men's Wear at 300–302.

302 S Main, Palace Of Sweets, WG Brown Propr, Manufacturers of Ice Cream and Fine Candy, Tel Ford 247, Cantaloupe Café.

304 S Main, Delmonte Grocery, (JS Denny, SA Lopez), grocers. *Future* site of LL Marsh Jeweler; RH James Seeds, ph.650-W.

304 ½ S Main, St. James Hotel, second floor of Cantaloupe Café; MG Miyama, rooms, ph 752-W.

306 S Main, Gem Theatre, TR Gilmore proprietor. *Future* 306–310 S Main site of Stauffer Food Co., Rhoades Food Store c 1960s.

306½ S Main, McMahan, Frank H, home (Edith M); Morris, Newton C, teacher High School, residence, (Elmira E), Rooms over the Gem Theatre (doorway left of the men on p. 24).

308 S Main, Arlington Cafe, GM Hooper Propr, Open Day and Night, Tel West 505, Hannon, Jos, dishwasher Arlington Café, residence; Tel West 505 (Mary Anna); Snow, Cecil V, cook Arlington Cafe, residence.

310 S Main, *future* site of Dairy Bake Shop, ph. 500, Holsun Grocery.

310 ½ S Main, Asher, Mrs Florence A, Propr "Ma's Place, Regular Meals and Short Orders, Fine Chili," home 302 S Tenth.

312 S Main, McColm, Edw B, Confectioner, home 205 N Seventh. *Future* site of Model Dry Cleaners, ph. 200; Dairy Bake Shop, Mr. & Mrs. JK Montgomery, prop., ph.500.

Maple Av. Intersection

This group is assembled at a S Main Street address when board walks yet fronted businesses. Common in the 1890s, boardwalks on Main Street were gradually replaced with concrete sidewalks by 1925.

Men, women, and children are present indicating an event of interest to all. Several public meeting places were on S Main. Several men's hats hang inside on a wall behind man number 17.

Courtesy *facebook.com/Rocky-Ford-Colorado*

Maple Av. Intersection

401 S Main, St. John Building, Van Antwerp Sanitarium, Van Antwerp & Van Antwerp (HS and HE Van Antwerp), Chiropractors. Sherman, Henry C. Confectioner, Bingham S., Washington Ave (Grace S).

403 S Main, Lawrence, Chas L, Wall Paper and Paints, Tel Ford 133, home west-side 12th 1 Block South Washington Ave, Tel Ford. *Future* site of JH Langford, Used Furniture, ph.143-W.; Elizabeth Guyton, attorney, Dog House, Evan's Jewelers.

405–407 S Main, Opera House Block, Beaty, Robt. R, electric supplies, residence Manzanola. *Future site* of The Grand Theater in 1935 at 405, ph 108.

407 S Main, Grand Opera House 1900–1935, J W Todd Mgr; *Rocky Ford Gazette-Topic*, (Semi-weekly), J B Lacy Publisher, Tel Ford 134. *Future* site Beauty Nook, ph. 143-J., Chic Paree.

409 S Main, undeveloped lot until the future A&W Root Beer. *Future* combination of 409 with 411 would become offices of Atty. Elizabeth Guyton, then, Tri-County Family Care Center.

411 S Main, Cleveland, WJ, DVM, Veterinary Surgeon, Tel Ford 613 (E Faye); Lovejoy, HE, Physician and Surgeon, Tel Ford 190, Hours 8 to 12, 1 to 5, evenings by appointment, home Willow Ave; Lowther, WA, rancher, home, (Anna)., 413 S Main, DD Potter, residence ph 299, *Future* site of Shorty's Tavern.

413 S Main, *was not identified as an occupied address in 1911. Future* site of Dr. CR Schuth.

415–417 S Main Ebbert Seed Co, AW Creager president and Mgr, Seeds of All Kinds, Baskets, Boxes and Crates, Tel Ford 137; Van Buskirk, H. Seed Co, PJ Reifel manager. Claude Frantz, ph. 183-J; *future* site of DV Burrell Seed Growers Co., ph. 330; *future* site of Freeman's Fine Pastries at 415.

415 ½ S Main, Scribner, Jerry B, principal Scribner's School of Dancing, (Nora H). Scribner's, Social Dances each Tuesday and Saturday Evenings, Tel Ford 103.

417 S Main, Bijou Amusement Hall.

419–421 Walter Cheek Block, p. 126. Rocky Ford Garage, James Lumbar, prop; Banta-Smith Auto Company.

423 S Main, Adams, Robt M, traveling agent, home (Ada B); McDermid, Mrs. M. Elizabeth, residence.

Sycamore Av. Intersection, and Rocky Ford Canal

City Council business, as recorded:

May 16, 1896: On motion the Marshall was instructed to enforce the Town's ordinance regarding the keeping of hogs within the limits of the incorporation. On recommendation of the Health Officer the Marshall was instructed to have all alleys east of Main Street well cleaned up at once.

December 28, 1903: Petition to forbid the re-establishing of the dairy operated by C. H. Long at South 13th Street & Pine. It was read, the committee is reporting unfavorable to the petition. Moved report be accepted.

Bloomfield Usher Dye House

Freeman's Fine Pastries at 415 S Main was a popular place for several years. Their cream puffs, favorite of many, were made only in winter to preserve the cream filling. The bakery was near the Grand Theatre on the west side of Main. Across the street on the corner with Sycamore is the large Dye House at 420 S Main. The house was built in 1900 while horses and carriages were still the transportation.

Mr. Dye's carriage house was behind his home entered from Sycamore Avenue where he kept at least one horse, a favorite which frequently pulled his carriage. A story, well-known when this author was growing up there was that he loved one particular horse and carriage so much that he expressed a desire that at his death he be buried with the whole rig, horse and all near Dye Reservoir.

This tale is lost to many. Mr. Dye was eventually buried in Valley View Cemetery, a Union veteran of the American Civil War who died in 1910. He was a private at enlistment and mustered out an artificer of the Michigan 1st Regiment Engineers and Mechanics. His home later housed a mortuary and eventually a home for at least two families. A large, ornate crest with the letters *BUD* remains on the house on the Main Street side, p. 121.

Town Tales

Royalty-free illustrations courtesy yahoo.com

Families living there often sat on the veranda watching events on Main as people went about their business. Three town characters, frequently together at their favorite watering hole were observed coming out of Freeman's bakery where they were after another favorite treat. They were known as 'Billy,' 'Runt,' and 'Toad,' mercifully protecting their real names.

Billy, trying to mount his bicycle, rode toward the Rocky Ford Ditch, but a few yards away. Runt and Toad walked with him but because of too much beer on board and concentrating on his bicycle, Billy headed for the ditch. He fell off in time to see his bicycle go into the water.

Billy was on the ground when one of the ladies living across the street saw that he might need assistance, not being offered by Runt or Toad. She walked across the street and asked Billy if he needed help. He replied that he wanted another beer. He received a kick as he lay on the ground and was told that he was a disgrace to the community. *Rocky Ford Daily Gazette* next day listing the previous day's police activities, noted that Billy had been observed a little out of control, was arrested on Main Street and cited for 'drunken crawling.'

Horse 'Carmon'

Horse 'Carmon' is shown to the State Board of Agriculture, 1905
Until the early 1920's, horses were the main means of personal transportation for the world. Breeding and care of these animals was a major industry, and was of prime concern for most people. In 1905, Colorado Agricultural College proudly showcased their work in horses bred to pull carriages. This photo was taken just outside of the massive College Horse Barn of "Carmon" and the State Board of Agriculture (now called the CSU Board of Governors). Standing behind "Carmon" from left to right are: Board President B.F. Rockafellow of Canon City, Mr. Harlan Thomas, two unidentified men, Dr. R. W. Corwin of Pueblo, Mr. B.U. Dye of Rocky Ford, Mr. Alfred Augustus Edwards of Fort Collins, and CAC President Dr. Barton O. Aylesworth. The College Horse Barn was located about where the Morgan Library and the Clark Building stand today.

BU Dye, third from right, among university officials and others interested in the breeding of fine horses, particularly for use in wheeled transportation of the times.

Colorado A&M Horse Barn below, 1919.

Photos courtesy Colorado State University Archives and Special Collections

Maple Av. Intersection

400 S Main, Garwood & Butterfield (p. 120), HD Garwood, Jas. Butterfield, Hardware and Furniture, Tel Ford 116. *Future* site of Geo. McKenzie Furniture & Music Co., ph. 137-J. *Future* Stormy's Second Hand Store.

400–402 S Main, Hagen Block.

402 S Main, Hagen, Mrs S L, Furnished Rooms, with Bath, Reasonable Rates, Tel Ford 266; *future* site of Grand Hotel, ph. 3360.

404 S Main, Hill, Thos J, Agent Mehlin & Sons, Bjur Bros and Ivers & Pond Pianos and Columbia Grafonolas and Records and Musical Merchandise, after Nov 1st 1914, (moved from 307 S Main), home 511 S 11th (Ella L); Morris, Anderson E, Shoemaker, home 411 S 13th (Nancy E).

406 S Main, Barrow, GE, Amusements, Carroms,* Cigars and Tobacco, Soft Drinks, Chewing Gum, Etc.,home, second floor.   * Billiards

408 S Main, Lyon, Chas R, Baker, home 607 S 11th (Edna).

410–412 S Main, Hotel Best, Mrs. CA Arnold Miller, proprietor ph. 115; Mrs. Myra Sanders, rooms.

414–416 vacant.

418 S Main, Dearing, Jesse M, insurance agent, home (Leona); Mina E. Gibeson, ph. 141.

Columbia Grafonola ad, 1914, courtesy popscreen.com

420 S Main, Dawley, Earl A, student, residence; Dawley, Hiram A, general manager RW English Lumber Co, home, (Myrtle B); Dawley, Richard S, rancher, residence; Otwell, Annie E, teacher, rooms; Weir, Addie, clerk, rooms; Booth, Ives, laborer rooms; Harry DuBois, residence ph. 270-R. House built by Bloomfield Usher Dye.

Sycamore Av. Intersection and Rocky Ford Ditch

R A McCart Pool Hall once occupied 406 S Main on this block. Trade token at left was then in use.

ebay.com

Sycamore Av. Intersection and Rocky Ford Canal

501 S Main, Siders, Mary L (widow John K), residence; Savage, S Hubbard, physician, 209 ½ S Main, home, (Bertha); Mrs. FR Kelley, home, ph. 240.

503 S Main, Hopper, Luta, residence; Hopper, Roland A, apiarist, home, (Caroline E); Hopper, V Orrell W, apiarist, residence.

505

507 S Main, John, Frank, warehouseman GE Bryant, home (Elva M); RL Parr, residence, ph. 657.

509

511 S Main, Fleak, L Dennis, v-president Maxwell-Fleak Clothing Co, home (Daisy); W. Lawrence Hammond, residence, ph. 351-J.

513 S Main, Ellis Auto Service,* ph 208, Ira B. Ellis, prop. Mae, Maedene, home 600 S Tenth, ph. 328.

515 S Main, Ira B. Ellis, Ellis Auto Service, home, ph.208. (See also p. 178 bottom.)

* Ellis Auto Service location is perhaps the only one on S Main to have first been a service station and later a home. The station was long ago converted to a home for a family but the appearance of a small drive-under front for automobiles yet exists. Another such business was 1100 Pine Avenue. Familiar to many neighbors as Beek's Grocery of the past, the building exists today.

Locust Av. Intersection

```
ELLIS AUTO SERVICE
           UNITED MOTORS
    CARTER - STROMBERG CARBURATORS
   DELCO - REMY              AUTO LITE
513 South Main                Phone 208
```

Rocky Ford Directory, 1945–1948.

Note: Town lot sizes in 1894 were reduced to try to accommodate the large number of people moving to Rocky Ford. This was especially true in Garden Place, south of the railroad and east of Fourteenth Street, where lots originally were 2 to 5 acres. Additionally, street numbers were assigned to businesses, until then hard to find for shoppers of the time.

Sycamore Av. Intersection and Rocky Ford Canal

500 S Main. Business district ends at Sycamore. Open space at 500 S Main between the Rocky Ford Canal and next residences at 512 and 514 to the south was site of two tennis courts with a high fence bordering the ditch. Field, right, visible in the lower right corner of the *Frontispiece,* was near site of a revival in 1914, p. 13. Both sites were eventually divided into more lots. B U Dye house at 420 S Main is visible at top bordered by trees.

Photo enlarged from *Frontispiece*

512 S Main, McDowell, Beulah, (widow Archie), residence; Phillips, Lulu (widow Geo), home; David J. Heckman, ph. 132-W.
514 S Main, Hopper, Bert W, apiarist, home (Ona P).

Locust Av. Intersection

Rocky Ford Ball Club 1907 team photo on the racetrack in front of roof supports and seats of the grandstand.

The players, back row (left to right), TY Northen, mgr., Kearney, 3b, DeWeese, cf, Hill, 1b, Ray, 2b, Caruthers, lf, FD Stoop, Pres. First row (left to right), Hendricks, rf and p, Moore, Capt. and ss, Rosson, c and rf, Love, c, Payne, c, Kearney, mascot (reclining). Team was pro or semi-pro based in Denver.

Courtesy *baseballhistoryblog.com*

City Council business, as recorded:

June 14, 1909: Moved that mayor issued and order prohibiting the playing of baseball within or near Rocky Ford Sunday. Carried. [No explanation given for the passing of the motion.]

Locust Av. Intersection

601, 603, 605, 607

609 S Main, Wolfe, Roy E, Physician and Surgeon, Office Hale Blk, Tel Ford 6, home, Tel West 6 (Jane M); Ted Eppinger, residence, ph. 307-R.

611, 613

615 S Main, Aulgur, Calvin A, barber, 954 Elm Ave, home (Gabie L).

617, 619

621 S Main, Coon, Arthur D, rancher, home (Lois L); Reynolds, John F, student, residence; Reynolds, Loren A, student, residence; Reynolds, W I, head plumber RF Sanitary Plumbing Co., home, (Clara E); LC Giffen, residence, ph. 251-J.

Pine Av. Intersection

Arkansas Valley Fair, Racetrack and Grandstands. Tinted post cards were popular souvenir items produced by photographers for general sale. Three separate grandstands are shown (right), attesting to the popularity of the Fair c 1920s. The near grandstand was the longest surviving until it too was replaced in 1970 after a 1968 fire.

Racetrack and horse barns were built in 1893 after several interested persons in horse racing bought part of GW Swink's timber claim for their idea. The first grandstand was built in 1895. One other that is described as '*open*' stood east of the one that burned.

Postcard photos, *coloradoplains.com*

Locust Av. Intersection

600, 602, 604

606 S Main, Weist, Philip J, deputy sheriff, home; Whitlock, D Thos, real estate, home, (Lulu M); *future* home Thomas C. Nichols, residence, ph. 304-W.

608 S Main, Daring, Geo R, proprietor Holsun Grocery, 309 S Main, home (Ada).

610 S Main, Voegtle, Robt, Propr Voegtle's Harness and Shoe Shop, home, Tel Ford 513, (Mabel).

612 S Main, Cheek, Fred W, contr, home (Nellie Mackin); *future* home Carolyn Killian, ph 168-J.

614, 616, 618

620 S Main, Mrs. GW Lewis, residence, ph. 724; *future* home Robert T. Babcock, ph. 313.

Pine Av. Intersection

General Blacksmithing *Rocky Ford Magazine v.2, no.1*

Current business site of Don's For Lad and Dad, Inc., at 311 on the left, Don's Mens Store as many know it. This building, with ornate center superstructure, is visible bottom photo p. 111 and at right in the photo p. 133. Blacksmith, A. McCormack, advertised *Plow and Buggy Work, Horse Shoeing a Speciality* in his ad, p. 328. His business once located at 1021 Railroad Avenue at Eleventh Street, on the original business block. Business services were *Harness and Saddles, Spring Wagons, Buggies and Wagons, Hardware, Furniture and Undertaking.* Near the white horse are ads for a hotel and Undertaking, for Thompson-Claypool, 917 Swink. Site at 313–315 N Main, above, eventually housed Well's Confectionery & Lunch, *future* Love's Shoe Store.

Pine Av. Intersection

701

703 S Main, Smirl* Callie E., clerk TJ Smirl & Son, (Emma A.), reidence; Smirl, Letha, student, residence; Smirl, Ralph J. (TJ Smirl & Son, residence. *Future* home of Hunter Cover, bank cashier, (Edith), Charles, ph. 361.

705

707

709 S Main, Arnold, Hobart M., waiter Arlington Café, residence; Arnold, Oliver F., insurance agent, home(Myrtle E.); Lawson, John A., physician. 924 Elm Ave., residence.

711 S Main, W. N. Deal, (Vitula), residence.

713

715 S Main, Lawyer, Bert L., Mgr City Drug Store, home, Tel West 638 (Helen N.); Taylor, Geo. H, home,(Bessie N.); Lee H. Cover, Durbin Cover, college student, ph. 695-R.

* The Smirls were in the dry goods, shoe, and garment businesses (I.L. Smirl), located at 200 S Main, the IOOF building. T.J. Smirl & Son operated a grocery with Callie E. Smirl, a clerk in their store, 303 S Main.

Spruce Av. Intersection

```
PHONE WEST 505                                    ROOMS

              The Arlington Cafe
                 G. M. HOOPER, PROPRIETOR

         REGULAR MEALS 25c AND SHORT ORDERS

                   OPEN DAY AND NIGHT
308 SOUTH MAIN                          ROCKY FORD, COLO.
```

City council action, as recorded:

April 21, 1904: Moved that Myrtle Dairy operated by C. H. Long at Ninth and Pine Streets be declared a nuisance and ordered abated. Carried.

Pine Av. Intersection

700 S Main, Boyd, Chas B, painter, home (Pearl A); Crans, Harriet, (widow Bartholomew M), residence.
702, 704, 706

708 S Main, JE Lewis, ph. 117-W.
710

712 S Main, Brannan, Chas O, teamster Johnson & Govreau, home (Effie Z).

Spruce Av. Intersection

Several cantaloupe crates (flats) are in this photo ready for transport. Known as a ***Shook***, the original packing crate is described p. 37. Many packing sheds were around the countryside where melons were the crop. They were also locations for handling cucumber, tomato, watermelon, onion, celery, bell pepper, chili, and other vegetables during harvest, sorting, grading and shipping operations.

Photo is identified as the **Frank Day farm** located south of US 50 and the area known as *Roberta*. The area had a small grocery and a few houses near the bridge over Timpas Creek. Timpas Creek is a tributary of the Arkansas River and is crossed by County Road 22.00 northeast of the terminus of the Rocky Ford Canal.

Frank Day's farm is believed to have been at the intersection of CR 22.00 and State Hwy 10.

Photos courtesy *Rocky Ford Public Library*

Spruce Av. Intersection

801 S Main, Haslett, John W, laborer, residence; St. John, Artis P, Vacuum Cleaning, Office and residence, Tel Ford 604 (M. Belle).

803 S Main, George A. McCormack, ph. 144-W.

805, 807

809 S Main, Palmer, Walton L, contr., home, (Belle L); George W. Forbes, residence, ph. 271-W; RJ Grenard, residence, ph. 726-J.

811 S Main, Petersen, August H (Petersen & Beck), home (Emma E); DF Beck, Contractors.

813 S Main, Cadwallader, Elmer E, manager Crutchfield & Woolfolk, home (E Elizabeth).

815

817 S Main, Love, Thos W, painter, home (Allie E).

Willow Av. Intersection

Postcards with exaggerated subjects, such as **Cabbages** by photographer WH Martin, proliferated in communities for advertising purposes. This photo from 1908 was used by Rocky Ford and other communities by changing the town and state locations in the subscript and on card reverse. This particular subject card was also used by communities in Oklahoma and Iowa.

Courtesy *Rocky Ford Public Museum*

The team is protected by a *fly harness*. Its many narrow strands of leather and their movement serve to discourage biting flies and mosquitos. Another example of such a postcard with a different subject is on p. 299.

City council business, as recorded:

December 13, 1904: Application of CW Jackson asking for license to conduct a bowling alley at No. 306 Main Street was read and on motion that license be granted.   [N or S Main Street is not specified.]

Spruce Av. Intersection

800 S Main, Owen Krueger, residence, ph. 327.
802, 804

806 S Main, Harry E. Ascherman, residence, ph. 755-W.
808 S Main, Harry Grimsley, ph. 104.
810, 812, 814
816 S Main, BE Mitchell, residence, ph. 734-W.

Willow Av. Intersection

Produce men. A team with a wagon harvest cantaloupe in the center background. This field appears near the cemetery, adjacent stone markers visible along the tree line.

In 1895 GW Swink devised a cantaloupe shipping container of cottonwood lumber to protect the melon en route. To this time melons were shipped in barrels, bushel baskets, peck containers and gunny sacks. His slatted container, 12 x 12 inches and two feet long would hold 45 average-sized melons, allowing air circulation and visual inspection by buyers. They also stacked well in rail cars. The ***Shook***, named by cantaloupe growers and buyers, greatly facilitated the cantaloupe industry. It was the original cantaloupe crate.

Truman Lusk later worked with Love Box Company to develop a container of waxed cardboard after wood became expensive.

Courtesy, *Rocky Ford Public Museum*

In 1898, a representative of the Western Game and Poultry Company of St. Louis contracted with the Rocky Ford Melon Growers Association for all the melons they could ship that year. The 800 members of the association were soon shipping 28 car loads by rail but the market became over-supplied and there was loss of much of 150 carloads that season. Major adjustments had to be made by growers, buyers and shippers, especially in handling and refrigeration.

Willow Av. Intersection

901 S Main, Johnston, Fred L, Johnston & Govreau, home (Jessie K), ph 516-J.
903
905 S Main, Hall, Melvin W, retd. rancher, home (Lurana B). Hall, Ruth E, art goods, 202 S Main, residence; AG Enderud, ph.250.
907, 909
911 S Main, Frame, Owen L, real estate, home (Olive B), Frame, Mrs OL, proprietor, Frame's Studio, 204 ½ N Main, MR Harrison, residence, ph. 684.
913, 915
917 S Main, Umbarger, Clyde S (Bailey & Umbarger), home (May E).
919 S Main, Stanley, Bryan (Int Stanley & Sons), residence; Stanley, Dean (Int Stanley & Sons), residence; Stanley, Int (Int Stanley & Sons), home, (Nora L), Stanley, L Thiers (Int Stanley & Sons), residence.
923 S Main, Shelton, Edwin C (EC Shelton & Son), home, Tel West 514 (Effie M), Shelton, Edwina, nurse, residence; Shelton, Garland M, (E.C. Shelton & Son), residence. *Future* home of HB Mendenhall, ph. 44.

Washington Av.

Frame's Studio
Mrs. O. L. Frame, Propr.

ALL THE LATEST STYLES IN FINE PHOTOS
SATISFACTION GUARANTEED
Kodak Developing and Printing for Amateurs

204 1-2 NORTH MAIN   ROCKY FORD, COLO.

Ad block from 1945–1948 City Directory

City Council business, as recorded:
October 17, 1910: The keeping of beet pulp within the city limits produce an unpleasant oder and so detrimental to the health of the people. "Be it resolved the city council that keeping in or keeping of beet pulp within the city hereafter is strictly for bidden."
[Many missed the odor of beet pulp after the ACSC final campaign in 1979.]

Willow Av. Intersection

900

902 S Main, Bass, John L, (Bass & Summers), home (Nora J); Cook, Geo T, rancher, home, (Mary F).

904 S Main, Boggs, Emery R (Latson & Boggs), home, Tel West 142 (Canna); Lawrence M. Kelso, residence, ph. 681.

906 S Main, Linn, Lewis C, clerk CL Govreau, home (A Gertrude).

908, 910, 912, 914, 916, 918, 920, 922

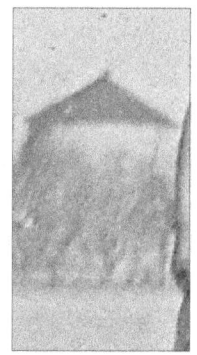

Author's collection ca. 1930s, *Storage Tank, Reservoir Hill*

Washington Av.

1000 S Main, City Water Works [south of Washington Avenue]

City Water Works was the final business our walk encounters at the southern end of Main Street according to the 1914–1915 directory.

Note: No businesses and few residences were south of Washington Avenue.

Early Water Mains

Repairs on Washington Avenue, c 1950 between Thirteenth and Fourteenth Streets, were made on a section of wooden water main laid in the center of the street. Pipe was formed of *staves* bound by metal clamps.

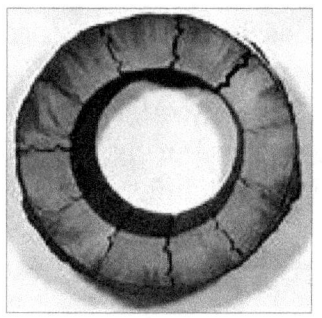

Photos courtesy wikipedia.org

The work was interesting to neighbors who wondered at the means of water delivery then. John Doll's description of the 1896 water system was of a six-inch pipe buried on Main Street to Swink Avenue conducting water from the first city well dug in 1895. Four-inch mains laid a block each way from Main to Swink, Railroad, Front, and Walnut completed the system then. Additional piping provided service as the town grew.

Railroad Town Company and the 1887 Town Plat

"For the first ten years the town laid out by Beghtol and Swink was the old fashioned cross-road type. When the Railroad Town Company was formed in 1887 Swink placed his land at the company's disposal. The original six block town site had long blocks that were divided into twelve blocks by dividing them with Elm north of the railroad and Walnut south of the tracks. The new Railroad Town Company laid out that area between the Swink timber claim and the Rocky Ford Ditch north and south and between Twelfth and about Fifth streets east and west."

William C. Steele
Letter, *Some Rocky Ford History*, published in *Rocky Ford Tribune*, 1917

From an Early Resident of Rocky Ford

"My family and the Charles Robbins family arrived in Rocky Ford March 2, 1889. ... As I recall the town in 1889, the business section consisted of two blocks each side of the railroad tracks on Main Street. Homes on west Swink Road, later Swink Avenue, were Geo. W. Swink, E. C. Gobin, C. C. Washburn, Capt. Rohn, Charles Daring, Sr., and Mr. Beghtol. On Elm and 9th Street, where the Elks Home was later built, Ed. Smith built a new home for his bride, Mame Gerst in 1889."

LeRoy Elser
Letter in *Rocky Ford Daily Gazette*, August 26, 1955

Part 2: Business Crossroads

Our Walk Continues on Elm Avenue

West Elm Avenue to First Street	42
Businesses west of city limits	42
First Street to Second, even	42
Farm Market	42
Second Street even	42
Third Street to Fourth, odd and even	43
Fourth Street, odd and even	43
American Beet Sugar Co. Corporate Cowboys	43
Fifth Street to Sixth, odd and even	44
Sixth Street, odd and even	44
Gobin Community Center	44
Seventh Street, even	45
Eighth Street, odd and even	45
Ninth Street	45
Gobin Block	45
Ninth Street to Main and Tenth, odd	46
Lunch counter	46
Ninth Street to Main and Tenth, even	47
Roy's Conoco	48
BPOE Lodge 1147	49
Trade token	49
Tenth Street, thru Fifteenth	50
Van Dyk Insurance Agency	50

West Elm Av.

An automobile ride from the west toward Rocky Ford is on US 50, a narrow two-lane concrete highway. Each section joint produced a rhythmic sound as tires rolled over them, especially audible at the much slower speeds people experienced in 1914–1915.

At the city limits US 50 is contiguous with Elm Avenue. Elm Avenue, as well as all streets in town, were unpaved in 1914. Numbers for homes and businesses increase toward the east. A walk beginning two miles out places us at the first businesses on the rural route to town. For reference in the text, some business names are placed where we knew them to be in the 1940s and 1950s but were not there 1914–1915.

The first two businesses west of town limits—in the 1945–1948 directory—were: Otis E. Adcock & Son, Apiaries, ph. 0180-J-1, R-2, 2 mi. west US 50, and Frank's Garage, ph. 0182–R-2. Ross Repair & Machine Shop on west US 50 operated much later. Templeton-Busch, Inc. would also, in the future, locate on US 50 west of town.

First Str. Intersection

First Street is among the shortest in town with its north end at Chestnut Avenue, then crossing Swink Avenue, ending at Elm Avenue or US 50. First Street, on maps today sometimes is called Market Street. This was the 1950s site of West Side Farmer's Market p. 221.

Courtesy Rocky Ford Public Library

114 Elm Av., *future* site of Coca Cola Bottling Company, ph. 301.
116 Elm Av., *future* site Nikkel's Superior Service, ph. 381, and of Johnson's Superior Station.
118 Elm Av., *future* site Easy Wash Laundry.

Second Str. Intersection

210 Elm Ave., *Future* site of Huri-Back Service Station, Enlo Henry, prop., ph.393. The short Elm Avenue extension is fixed between Second and Third Streets behind Huri-Back Service Station. Wimpy's or Huri-Back Lunch* located where this Elm extension joined US 50.
   *Many printings use a double-r spelling, but see *War Price & Rationing Board* form p. 84.

Our Walk Continues on Elm Avenue

Third Str. Intersection

Third and Elm Ave. *Future* site Silvers Westside Market.

301 Elm Ave, Enlo Henry, home, (Effie); Sheila, ph. 335-J.
302 Elm Ave, Conklin, Henry H, rancher, home (Rhoda A).
304 Elm Ave, Greer, John B, ranch head, home, (Hattie E).
306 Elm Ave, Newberry, Wm W, laborer, home, (Beulah A).

310 Elm, Future site of Bertha's Lunch, ph. 391, *future* site of Country Kitchen.
314 Elm Ave, Boley, Dora, dressmkr, residence, Boley, Fay Ellen, music teacher, residence, Boley, Lou, dressmkr, residence, Boley, Martha, (widow Ephraim M), home.

Fourth Str. Intersection

Fourth and Elm Ave, *Future* sites (in succession) of Finley Motor Company, ph., 214-W; Tom's Service Station, ph. 296; Holder's Service Station, ph. 377.
401 Elm Ave, Gibson, John B, laborer, home, (Vena). *Future* site of Otero Tire Co.
406 Elm Ave., *Future* home of Plant's Drive-In.

In 1893 a stock yard was built on the east edge of town east of Fifteenth Street to accommodate cattle loading and transport. South Fourth Street ended near the Santa Fe tracks where a small corral was located. This corral, built in 1902, was also used by local ranchers to facilitate loading cattle cars. Both increased in use after 1900 when the sugar factory opened and beet pulp was added to cattle feed as a supplement. Corrals remained in use until the 1960s, then removed.

Larger cattle feed lots just west of the factory were also maintained to feed pulp. These corrals were operated by Arlyn Samuel Kitch, a pioneer rancher in the Timpas area. The property was popularly known as the Kitch Feed lots but belonged to the American Crystal Sugar Company. Cowboys employed below were at one time herding cattle for the precursor American Beet Sugar Company. The use of these lots was also discontinued in the 1960s. Feed lot now owned by RJ Nelson and is called Ribeye Feed Yard.

American Beet Sugar Company Corporate Cowboys

Courtesy ABSC / ACS Company archives

Fifth Str. Intersection

501 Elm Ave, Elder, John H., laborer, home, (Belle).

502 Elm Ave, Dietrich, Jacob S., machinist ABS Co, home, (Hattie G.); Hayes, Maud S.

503 Elm Ave, Hamman, Ashley J., chemist ABS Co, home,(Jesse B).

515 Elm Ave, Gerbing, Leota, stenographer, residence, Gerbing, WF, meats, 206 N Main, home, (Emma P.).

516 Elm Ave, Hahn, Celia L., stenographer ABS Co, home; Hahn, Lottie M, residence.

524 Elm Ave, Coon, Harry J., machinist helper ABS Co, home.(Helen C.), Coon, Sarah A., (widow Hiram J.), residence.

527 Elm Ave, Gerbing, Fannie, (widow of Gustav T.), home; Holmes, Anna L., stenographer ABS Co, rooms. *Future* site Gobin Bookkeeping Service c 1960s.

Sixth Str. Intersection

600 Elm Ave, Tewes, Wm H., carpenter, home.

601 Elm Ave, *future* home of Chuck Wagon, Bob Sexton, prop; Tank 'N' Tummy.

602 Elm Ave, *future* parsonage of St. Peter's Lutheran Church.

604 Elm Ave, Brown, Clay D., molder, Goodner Pump & Mfg Co, home (Nellie O.), Brown, Geo. M., Mach helper ABS Co, residence, Brown, Eliza Jane, (widow Geo M.), residence, Brown, Ralph A., laborer ABS Co, residence, *future* site of St. Peter's Lutheran Church, p. 218, Rev. AP Bruenger, ph. 193. This was a house moved to this location and remodeled in 1925. Goodner's moved to Seventh and Railroad.

610 Elm Ave, *future* site of Veatch Market, ph. 339.

623 Elm Ave, *future* site of Amarine Radio Service, ph. 586-W.

Gobin Community Center

Center stands at 105 N Main Street on former site of the Railway Express Agency (REA) and is adjacent the Chamber of Commerce.

Courtesy *Rocky Ford Chamber of Commerce.*

Our Walk Continues on Elm Avenue

Seventh Str. Intersection

Elm Ave at Seventh, *future* sites (in succession) of Haley's Texaco Service, ph. 373; McCoy's Service Station, ph. 389.
700 Elm Ave, Miller, Mrs. Kate, home.

Eighth Str. Intersection

800 Elm Ave, *future* site of Easley Service Station, ph. 383.
807 Elm Ave, Herring, John, with Reliance Auto Co., home, (Anna E.).
810 Elm Ave, *Future* site Bill & Bob's Service.

Ninth Str. Intersection

Gobin Block, then and now at 900 Elm Avenue from Ninth Street. View is to the east on Elm with **Royal Hotel**. Photo (right) is from the 1940s showing parallel parking on two lane Elm Avenue, once tried on Main Street. There have been numerous business changes in the blocks between Ninth and Tenth Streets but the view is much the same as this modern view except for some trees, power poles and later model cars. (See pp. 134–135 for other views of the Gobin Block.)

Street signs of **Fairchild Floral** at 908 and **La Nortena** at 902 are visible at right of photo.

Upper photo courtesy Rocky Ford Public Museum. Lower photo courtesy facebook.com/RockyFordCO/.

Ninth Str. Intersection

From Ninth Street to Tenth, businesses and residences were concentrated on both sides of Elm Avenue. For this section only, odd numbers are separated in the text to the left (north), even numbers to the right hand pages (south).

901 Elm Ave, Rev SB Warner pastor, First Methodist Episcopal Church.

907 Elm Ave, *Rocky Ford Enterprise*, weekly, WR Monkman, publisher.

909 Elm Ave, Arkansas Valley Railway Light & Power Co, FS Johnson, plant super., 101 S Twelfth.

911 Elm Ave, Arkansas Valley Fair Assn, Loyd R. Pollock secretary grounds, N end Main; Fort Lyon Canal Co, B F Powell engineer; Hall, Gilbert M, receiver State Bank, home 300 S 7th (Flora J.); High Line Canal Co, Pollock, Lloyd R, Sec Rocky Ford High Line Canal Co, Sec Rocky Ford Canal Co, Office, Tel Blue 26-1, residence 500 N Ninth, Tel Ford 11; Rocky Ford Canal Co, LR Pollock Sec; State Bank of Rocky Ford.

913 Elm Ave, *future* site of Fenlason, Leon R., Real Estate, Loans and Insurance, Tel Ford 63, home 701 S Fourteenth, Tel Ford 141 (Nonette S).

915 Elm Ave, Anderson, Jonas, Merchant Tailor, Cleaning and Pressing, Tel 68, home 204 N 12th, Tel Ford 235 (Nannie I); Western Union Telegraph Co, LH Rogers Mgr, Tel Ford 128; *future* site of Love's Café, ph. 395.

917 Elm Ave, *future* site of Bennett's Liquor Store, ph. 121-W; Catlin Canal Co.

917–917 ½ Elm Ave, *future* site of Whittaker Agency, real estate and insurance, ph. 171-W.

919 Elm Ave, Tucker, Walter C, Barber, home 308 N Tenth, (Frances I.), 920 Elm Ave, Crutchfield & Woolfolk, commission mercts.

921 Elm Ave, *future* site of Baker's Drug Store.

Main Street Intersection

963 Elm Ave, Mountain States Telephone and Telegraph Co, EF Smith Exch Mgr.

965 Elm Ave, *future* site of Joe's Barber Shop.

Tenth Str. Intersection

Lunch Counter mystery. The austere appearance of this long, narrow dining area suggests cleanliness. The street address is not known, neither are the staff and patrons identified, but the photo was taken in 1914 Rocky Ford.

Courtesy *Rocky Ford Public Museum*

Our Walk Continues on Elm Avenue

Ninth Str. Intersection

900 Elm Ave, (Gobin Block, SE corner Ninth east to the alley),. Moody, AL, prop., Economy Variety Store 1912, later moved to 202, then 311 N Main in 1913.

902 Elm Ave, *future* site of Hi-Way Liquor Store, Glen Love, prop; Home Finance Co. c 1960s.

904 Elm Ave, Kerney, Rae C, Barber Shop, home 601 Swink Ave. (S. Abbie)

906 Elm Ave, *future* site Rocky Ford Enterprise, ph. 263; (209 N Main, Blinn, JJ. Auto Baggage Truck No 1), stand at JC Braden's Drug Store, Phone West 217, home 608 N Eighth

907 Elm Ave, *Rocky Ford Enterprse*, WR Monkman publisher (weekly), Tel West 263; *future* site Fairchild Floral.

908 Elm Ave, *future* site of Rector Hotel, ph. 196.

910 Elm Ave, *Future* site Betry Printing Co. (Street address not in early directories.)

912 Elm Ave, Gobin Billiard Hall, Fred Knause Propr, Billiards, Cigars and Tobacco; Gobin, Eva L, fancy work, residence 404 N Ninth, Knause, Fred, residence 506 S Ninth; *future* site Quality Market; *Rocky Ford Enterprise*; *Rocky Ford Daily Gazette*.

916 Elm Ave, *future* site of Mary C. Loring Ladies Wear, ph. 169-W.

918 Elm Ave, Ustick Undertaking Co, CM Ustick Mgr, Undertakers and Embalmers, ph. Ford 3. Eventually moved to 305 N Eighth Street.

920 Elm Ave, *future* site of Marticia's Gift Shop.

922 Elm Ave, home, Long, Fredrick C, insurance agent, 604 S Eleventh (Esther J); Postal Telegraph-Cable Co, Mary E Meyers manager; *future* site of Canterbury Barber Shop, Erlinda's Beauty Salon.

924 Elm Ave, Conquest, Mrs Nellie, dressmkr; Lawson, John A, physician, residence 709 S Main; (Dr. Lawson also at 209 ½ N Main), Rocky Ford Club.

Main Str. Intersection

954 Elm Ave, Aulgur, Calvin A, Barber Shop, home 615 S Main (Gabie L).

956 Elm Ave, Reeves, Bud W, Restaurant, home 622 N Main (Mabel).

958 Elm Ave, *future* Karl's Kafe, ph. 378.

960–962 Elm Ave, Rocky Ford Sanitary Plumbing Co, (Dick Farris), Tel West 249; *future* site of Spanky's Bar; Johnny's Bar.

966 Elm Ave, McKinney, Wm. B., Carpet Weaver, home 1110 Chestnut Ave (Jennie B); *future* home of June Chevrolet Co. & Wrecker Service, ph. 79-W.

Tenth Str. Intersection

Note: North-south alleyways intersect both sections of the 900 addresses east and west of Main. Directory information is lacking for the missing numbers but may be explained by undeveloped lots or long building sides of those facing Main in the calculation and setting of lot addresses for Elm Avenue.

Roy's Conoco

Roy Taylor's Conoco Service in 1929 was on the NE corner of Tenth and Railroad. Mr. Taylor is with Carl Gregg and an unidentified boy. The top left building in the background on the SW corner of this intersection was the carpenter shop of George O. Teats, later McDougal Farm Equipment John Deere agency. The Conoco site was the former location of Hotel De Seeley, p. 88.
See also p. 302 concerning this business site.

The Van Dyk Insurance Agency at 1006 Elm backs to this site. Part of an existing building was once a saloon facing Railroad Avenue. Its facade on Railroad Ave retains a nineteenth century appearance, p. 94.

Rocky Ford Magazine, v.2, no. 1, 1999

Our Walk Continues on Elm Avenue

Photo courtesy *Matt Mendenhall, Mike Budge, rockyfordcolorado.net*

BPOE Lodge 1147 at 301 N Ninth Street. Date of photo is not known. After their charter on April 8, 1909, Elks held their first meetings on the upper floor of the Masonic Lodge, 411 N Main, p. 110. A cornerstone was set in 1913 and first use of this building was May 1914. This location had been the home site of Mr. and Mrs. Ed. Smith, built in 1889.

Many newcomers to Rocky Ford viewed the lodge number sign, in the shape of a clock with hands pointing to 11:47, as the time of day. Viewed when obviously not correct, many thought the clock was in need of reset.

This building has housed many gatherings and meetings of large groups, providing food for banquets and parties. High School class reunions are frequently held in the building while enjoying the hospitality of Elks Club members. Directly across the street to the east was the First Methodist Episcopal Church at 901 Elm Avenue, pp. 79, 199.

Trade tokens were common among some businesses such as billiard halls. They were stamped metal or plastic with a face value higher than their real value. Many types appeared in the 1940s as a substitute for currency to save critical metals needed for the war effort. They were commonly used for transportation fare in small coin denominations and for taxes on a purchase when the tax was less than a dollar.

ebay.com

Tenth Str. Intersection

Tenth and Elm, *future* sites of Plews Motor Company, ph. 587; Schmidt's Conoco Service; Rocky Ford Service Station, ph. 164., Nelson's at 1000 Elm, and Swede's Conoco. Rocky Ford Filling Station preceded Plews Motor Co. at 101 N Tenth Street The station also had a small drive-in restaurant, the enterprise of Lloyd Nelson's grandfather, EA Hawthorne.

1006 Elm Ave, Van Dyk Insurance Agency, moved to 1601 Elm Ave.

1007 Elm Ave, Arkansas Valley Broom Factory, (Paul I. Gobin, Geo. R. Cameron).

1012 Elm Ave, *future* site of Ray's Auto Repair, ph. 204-W.

1014 Elm Ave., *future* site of Kitch Pontiac, Rocky Ford Family Health Center, LLC.

1021 Elm Ave. *future* site of O-Boy Market and Grocery, ph. 611.

Website photo, *vandykins.com*

Eleventh Str. Intersection

1106 Elm Ave., Vencill Leather Shop.
1120 Elm Ave., future China Kitchen

Twelfth & Thirteenth Str. Intersections

Twelfth and Elm Ave, *future* site Valley 66 Service Station.
Thirteenth and Elm Ave, *future* site of Dale's Texaco Service, Dale Amerine, owner, ph., 31-R.
1300 Elm Ave, site of the 1897 LW Babcock Creamery, first creamery in Rocky Ford.
1309 Elm Ave, *future* site of Meng's, Mixed drinks, beer and dancing. ph. 309.
    Possibly 1940s location of Tiny's Tavern.
1320 Elm Ave, *future* site of Sonic Drive-In.

Fourteenth Str. Intersection

Fourteenth Street and Elm Ave, City Ice Service, ph. 735-W.
1410 Elm Ave, Chase Auto Repair, ph. Res. 748-M, Bus. 735-R.

Fifteenth Str. Intersection

1500 Elm Ave, Hall Motor Freight Company, ph. 28; *future* site Arch Inn; Curve Motel, fully known as Curve Enterprises & Motel, ph. 203-J, and Berry's Super Service.
Among other businesses US 50 East from city limits were future location of Taqueria Mexico at 1720 Elm and Griffin, Holder, & Thomas Onion Shippers.
   Note: East of Hall Motor Freight Company our walk finds no other listings in the 1914–1915 directory. Streets 16 thru 19 were added later to city limits as businesses expanded to the east on Elm Avenue.

Part 3: Among the Crossroads

A Random Walk

Epigraph; Harry V. Alexander, 1887	52
More Businesses of Early Rocky Ford	53
Doc & Bonnie's Café, Grady's Grill	53
Businesses listed in the 1945–1948 directory	54
Alta Vista Mercantile	54
Businesses listed in the 1945–1948 directory	55
Howard Grocery	55
Businesses listed in the 1945–1948 directory	56
Rocky Ford Floral Co.	56
Businesses listed with incomplete address	57
Horton's Market	57
Arkansas Valley Broom Factory	57
Main Street at Swink Avenue, 1899	58
City Directory ad 1945–1948	59
A Bountiful Crop of Klondike Melons, 1920	59
Santa Fe Depot on Melon Day c 1904	60
City Map illustration	61
First Artesian Well, 1895	62
First Artesian Well, casing marker	63
Town Site, 1876	64
Six-block town site of William Matthews	64
Watermelon Day	65
Before The Feast; After The Feast	65
Sen. GW Swink and the Arkansas Valley Fair	66
US Timber Claim Certificate	66
Hon. Sen. GW Swink	67
Grand Opera House	68
Grand Theatre, 1949; The Grand today	68
W&W Root Beer	68
St. James Hotel	69–71
Public Meeting Halls, Hotels & Rooms 1914–1915	71
Businesses of 300 Block S Main	72
City Council business, 1934	72
Rocky Ford Police and Firemen	73
Jacob A. Kipper	73
Patrolman Louis Box	74
Clyde F. Summers	75
William M. Lueker	75
Early Fire Fighters	75
The Old Republic	76
Rocky Ford High School, 1908	77
Rocky Ford Public Library, new and 1909	77
Rocky Ford Public Museum	77
IOOF Hall	78
First Methodist Episcopal Church	79
Watermelon Day 1916	80
Rocky Ford Concert Band	80
A 1940s Parade	81
November 1930 Snowstorm	81
City Water Works and Dump illustration	82
Smith's Café, 1929	83
Huri-Back Lunch aka Wimpy's	83
Huri-Back Lunch, menu	84
Rocky Ford Obelisks	85
Leghorns and melon illustrations	85
Swink and Russell 1871 Store	86
The Ford	87
Earliest Rocky Ford Businesses	88
GW Swink's 1876 Adobe Store	89
Water, Artesian Style	90

Words from the first Newspaper Editor in Rocky Ford

"Rocky Ford the Queen City of the Arkansas Valley is the Pride and Wonder of All. Her Massive Blocks are Loaded from Cellar to Garret With the Different Branches of Trade, to Tell the Story of Her Success."

"What We Say of Rocky Ford Can Be Said Honestly Without the Fear of the Recording Angel Laying Up A Charge of Prevarication Against Us."

Harry V. Alexander
Rocky Ford Enterprise, August 11, 1887

Harry Alexander believed in advertising and was extravagant in praise of town and business.

More Businesses of Early Rocky Ford

Walt's Place c 1940
Doc and Bonnie's c 1940
Grady's Grill c 1945
Doc and Bonnie's c 1945
Ginger's Café, c 1963
    (daughter of Doc and Bonnie)
Doc and Bonnie's, 1963–1984

Doc and Bonnie Walker's Café served the community 44 years, finally closing in 1984. Five businesses (left) were successions of their enterprise at 309 S Main.

Grady's Grill
Courtesy, *Doris Baublits*

Courtesy, *Rocky Ford Public Library*

Several businesses they knew as young members of pioneer families were recalled by residents during interviews for the *Rocky Ford Centennial* in 1987. Some businesses not in directories were short-lived or did not advertise, but the enduring ones are familiar to residents today:

Wrangler Foods, 800 Chestnut Avenue, Lawrence Warehouse Co., Arkansas Valley Seeds, Twelfth Street and, Railroad, Paul Lee's Restaurant, Kriss Kross Grocery, 203 N Main, Rocky Ford Drug, 301 S Main, Park Hotel, 920 Front Street, Babcock's Creamery 1300 Elm, Govreau's Grocery, 204 S Main, Cartwright Building, 421 N Main, Spencer's Confectionery, 313 N Main, Harrison's Variety Store, TJ Smirl's Grocery Store, 303 S Main, IL Smirl's Dry Goods Store, 200 S Main, J. Wood, Peery Grocery, 423 N Main, Bradshaw's Emporium, 205 N Main, *(Ellen Bradshaw Donk's family)*, Jenny Gobin Cameron's Hat Shop, Mary Loring's Clothing Store, 916 Elm, Weid's Bakery and Lunch, 914 Front Street, Gorsuch Cleaning Shop, Hancock's Men's Wear, 300–302 S Main, Grimsley, White, & Co., 605 N Main, Jenner Plumbing & Heating, 311 S Main, Johnson's Superior Bay Station, and First Industrial Bank, 300 N Main (Beman Building).

Businesses listed in the 1945–1948 directory

Les's Garage, 967 Ash Av. (Thomas Addition), ph. 745-W.

CA Heskett Produce Company, 101 S Second Str., ph. 220.

Clark's Grocery & Camp, 208 N Second Str., ph. 691-W.

Engle Grocery, 301–303 S Third Str.

Goodner Iron & Pump, 100 N Seventh Street, ph.707.

CM Ustick Funeral Home, 305 N Eighth Str., ph. 3-J.

Leroy's Grocery, 723 S Eighth Str., ph. 704.

Railway Express Agency, Inc., ph. 125, 100 N Ninth Str.

G&K Company (Grimsley & Keck), ph. 211, 101 N Ninth Str..

G&K Onions, ph. 171, 101 N Ninth Str.

Farm & Home Supply, ph. 213-W, 201 N Ninth Str.

Jackson Storage & Transfer, ph. 202, 201 N Ninth Str.

Rocky Ford City Hall, ph. 101, 203 S Ninth Str.

Clyde F. Summers, city fire chief, ph. 114-W, 205 S Ninth Str.

Fire Department, ph. 741, 201 S Ninth Str.

Elks Lodge No. 1147, ph. 111, 301 N Ninth Str.

Rocky Ford Fair Assn., ph. 111, 301 N Ninth Str., temporary offices in BPOE Lodge.

Green & Babcock, Inc., ph. 222, 102 N Tenth Str.

Rocky Ford Service Station, ph. 164, 211 N Tenth Str.

John Deere Implements, ph. 170, 109 N Tenth Str.

E & M Music Company, ph. 204-J, 301 N Tenth Str.

Alta Vista Mercantile, Frank R. Gandara, proprietor. Frank and Dolores Gandara lived on West Washington Avenue. Alta Vista Camp was located west of the golf course, now the site of Rocky Ford High School at 100 W. Washington Avenue. Mercantile business was moved to 517 N Main Street, p. 142, when American Crystal Sugar Company razed the building.

Courtesy, *Rocky Ford Public Library*

Howard Grocery

Courtesy, *Rocky Ford Public Library*

Polar Ice & Locker Co., ph. 59, 100 S Tenth Str.
Hendrix Auto Repairing, ph. 110-W, 607 ½ S. Eleventh Str.
Howard Grocery, ph. 399, 410 N Eleventh Str.
Continental Oil Co. office, ph. 188-J, 100 S Twelfth Str.
Wolfmeyer Grocery, 500 S Twelfth Str.
Milburn, Inc. Beans, ph. 192, 100 S Thirteenth Str.
Law Motor Lines, ph. 654, 300 N Thirteenth Str.
Blotz Seed & Produce Co., ph. 157, S Fourteenth Str.
The Texas Co., Charles Tindall, consignee, ph. 186-J, 101 S Fifteenth Str.
Kay Kraig Ceramics, ph. 214-M, 605 Chestnut Av.
Harding Electric Co., ph. 177-W, 701 Chestnut Av.
Lawrence Robinson & Son, vine seeds, ph. 20, 1018 Chestnut Av.
Chuck Wagon, Bob Sexton, prop., 601 Elm Av.
Hi-Way Liquor Store, Glenn Love, prop., ph. 33-J, 902 Elm Av.
Quality Market, ph. 520, 912 Elm Av.
OD Koonce Model Shoe Repair, 913 Elm Av.
The Whittaker Agency, ph. 174-W, 917 ½ Elm Av.
Meng's, mixed drinks, beer, dancing, ph. 309, 1309 Elm Av.
Star Café, Fred Baca, prop., ph. 394, 916 Front Str.
Park View Hotel, ph. 398, 920 Front Str.
H & B Seeds, Inc., ph. 129-W, 966 Front Str.
Grapette Beverage Agency, 7-UP Bottling Co., ph. 670-W, Front and Eleventh Str.

Rocky Ford Floral Company

Courtesy, *Rocky Ford Public Library*

Rocky Ford Floral Company, ph. 286-J, 1415 Pine Av.

Pott Electric Company, ph. 526-M, 203 S Main 411 N Main in the 1960s.

Physicians Hospital, ph. 7, 805 Maple Av.

Variety Repair & Keys, ML St. John, prop., ph. 67-J, 920–922 Maple Av.

The Robertson Dairy, ph. 218, 963 Maple Av.

Beek's Grocery, ph. 711-J, 1100 Pine Av.

Goodner Iron & Pump Works, ph. 707, Seventh and Railroad Av.

Tex's Automagic Service, 809 Railroad Av.

Otero County Agricultural Agt., ph. 17, *and* Otero County Farm Labor Assn., ph. 207, 901 Railroad Av.

Foerster Refrigeration Service, ph. 99, 903 Railroad Av.

Pickwick Inn Restaurant, ph. 11, 909 Railroad Av.

The Fenlason Realty Company, ph. 63, 911 and 917 Railroad Av.

Elizabeth L. Guyton, Atty, ph. 6, 913 Railroad Av.

JI Griffin, Onions, ph. 287, 1007 Railroad Av.

The JC Robinson Seed Company, Howard W. Veal, mgr., ph. 297-J, Twelfth and Railroad Av.

Otero County Welfare Office, ph. 15, 915 Swink Av.

Knights of Pythias Hall, ph. 291, 917 Swink Av.

Hetty Roach Beauty Shop, ph. 67-J, 1017 Swink Av.

Chrane Service Station, ph. 323, 901 Walnut Av.

Anderson Motor Company, WL (Sid) Anderson, owner, ph. 597-J, 902 Walnut Av.

Reynold's Oil Company, Howard E. Reynolds, Mgr., Ph. 173-J, 963 Walnut Av. *and* Priscilla Stitch & Gift Shop, ph.173-W, 961 Walnut Av.,

St. John Body Shop, Tenth and Walnut Av.

Valley Concrete, 1443 Maple Avenue.

Valley Decorators & Builders, Edwin DeWeese, Claude Frantz, proprietors, 1015 Walnut Av.

Valley Laundries, 968 Front Street.

Businesses with Incomplete Addresses

Army-Navy Store, Hancock Bros., owners.
Valley Motor Co. ph. 41-J.
Bish Hardware and Furniture Company, Jay W. Tracey, ph. 49.
Bob's Food Products, Valley Chip & Supply Co., ph. 1190-J.
Braden's Drug Store, N Main, ph. 19.
Coca Cola Bottling Company, ph. 301.
Dairy Treet 209 N Fifth.
Daring Insurance Agency, ph. 522.
Don's Mens Store, N Main.
Douglas Market, ph.139-J.
F&J Scaff Bros., ph. 866.
Hoyt's O-K Rubber Welders, US 50, ph. 606.
Horton's Market.
Jackson Transfer & Storage, agents for Weicker Transfer & Storage.
Jennie Gobin Cameron, Millinery & Ready-to-Wear.
Karl's Kafe and Bar, ph. 378.
Law Motor Lines, ph. 654.
Leroy's Locker Plant, ph. 613-W.
Leroy's Market, ph. 704-705.
Marticia's Gift Shop, ph. 581-W.
NBC Insecticide Company, ph. 084-R1.
Plant Food Corporation, ph. 0284-J-4.
Polar Ice & Locker Co., ph. 59.
Rocky Ford Onion Growers Co-Operative Association, 101 S Tenth Street, ph. 93.
Shamrock Service Station, ph. 266-W.
Shuey Bakery & Confectionery.
Southern Colorado Power Company, N Main
Luetcke Pontiac Co. on US 50.
Arkansas Valley Broom Factory, 1007 Elm.
Standard Oil, IH Kouns, ph. 371-W.
Stout's Skelly Service, Elm Av US 50.
Tiny's Tavern, ph. 390.
West Side Market, Fruits & Vegetables, ph. 507.
Swink Recreation Parlor, Mike Miller, prop.
Taguchi Grocery, 200 S Eighth, ph. 302-W.

The Fashion Center, ph. 374.
The Toggery, Men's Clothing and Furnishing, ph. 36-J.
Valley Produce, ph. 721.
Veatch Market, US 50, ph. 339.
Well's Confectionery & Lunch, ph.675.
Valley Motor Co., ph. 41-J.

Horton's Market

Arkansas Valley Broom Factory

Photos courtesy *Rocky Ford Public Library*

Main Street at Swink Avenue 1899 Courtesy, *Rocky Ford Public Museum*

View to the south on Main Street. The building at distant center appears to be 209 N Main, *future* site of Rexall Drug Store and later, City Drug Store; left foreground this side of the crosswalk is 400 N Main. Regarding this site: "John Mitch and James K. Dye built a two-story adobe on Swink Road and Main Street for a saloon." *Rocky Ford Enterprise* December 15, 1887

A Random Walk

From City *Directory* c 1945–1948

HELP BUILD ROCKY FORD
By Spending Your Dollars
In Rocky Ford

A Bountiful Crop of Klondike Melons, 1920   Rocky Ford *Daily Gazette*, Centennial, 1987

The **Klondike** was a popular **DV Burrell Seed Growers Company** seed product. Many Rocky Ford fields grew this large dark-rind melon to great weight. Some grew to 80 pounds but the average likely was lower.

Part of the annual harvest formed the Melon Day piles at the Arkansas Valley Fair until they were replaced by smaller, more manageable varieties. This photo with unidentified field workers in a Rocky Ford field appeared during the *Centennial* celebration in 1987. The men were preparing the harvest for transport.

Santa Fe Depot on Melon Day c 1904

Photo courtesy Library of Congress, LC-USZ62-42276, call no. *SSF-Carriages and Coaches*.

This view toward the nearly treeless Railroad Park behind the train shows the north side of the 1897 Recker Hall on Front Street. The second Santa Fe Depot, above right, was built in 1887 and still had the Gibson Lumber Company, later, Newton Lumber Co. yard on its north side, far right center. Both depot and lumber yard were eventually moved across Ninth Street in preparation for building the third and present brick depot in 1907. The park was then made larger north of the depot with more trees and grass.

    The large white frame building in the distance at center may have been the Charles Recker bakery building. He had moved to the west end of Front Street from the NE corner of Main St. and Front March 1897 from his original two-story frame bakery and restaurant. He also added the Park Hotel to his new building. Historian John Doll described its location "across the street from the present fire station ... Front and 9th Streets."

City Map

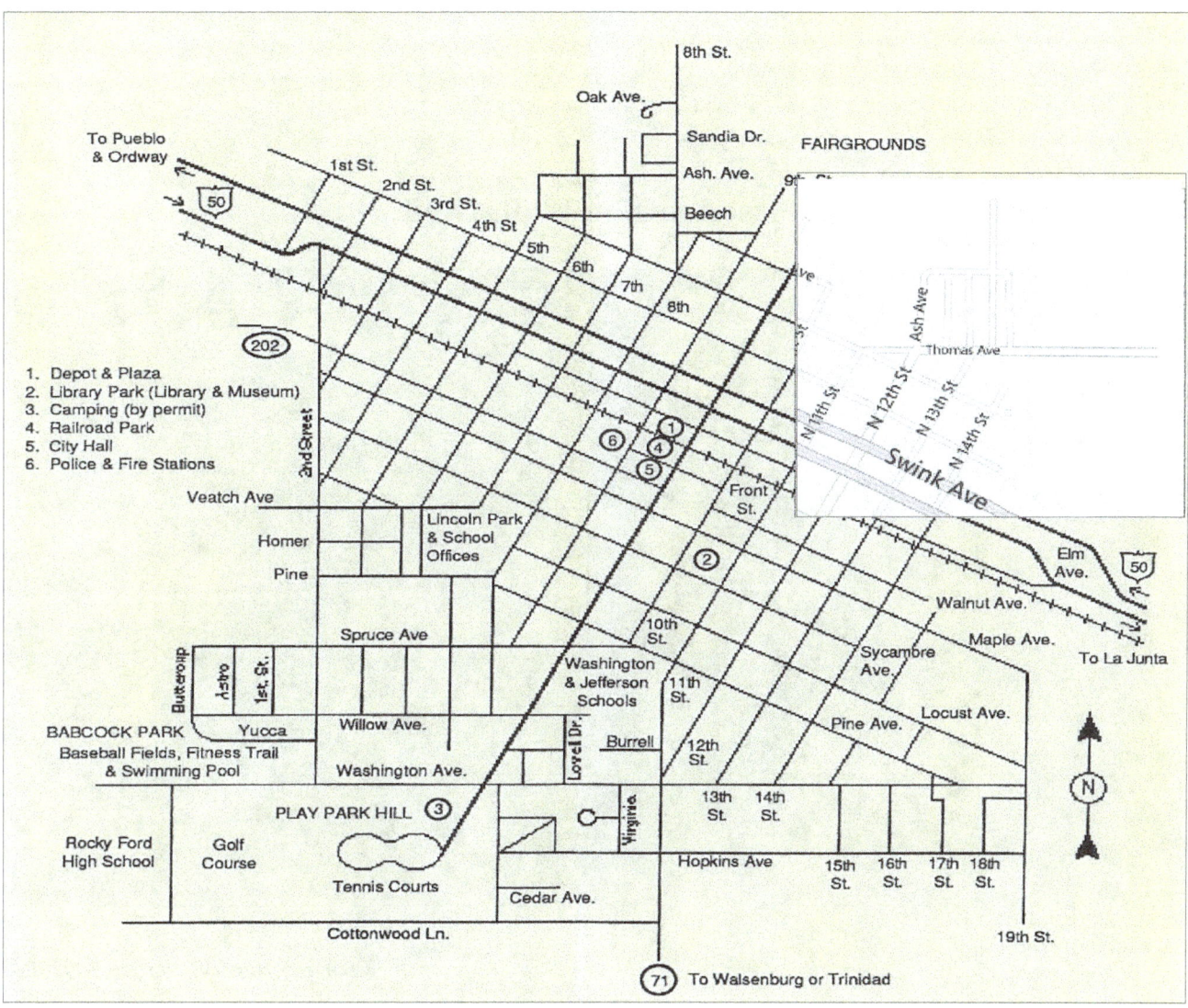

Courtesy *Rocky Ford Chamber of Commerce*

Thomas Addition, inset, is accessed thru Thomas Rd, 266 or CR 20, north off Twelfth and Thirteenth Streets. Original town plat, p. 64, was a six-block site, drawn by William Matthews and filed July 4, 1876 in the Bent Co. Courthouse. Part of Bent County later became Otero County. Original plat was not legal, lacking proper metes and bounds. A new plat was laid out, including the original, a lot sale was held April 12, 1887 and Rocky Ford began to grow.

First Artesian Well, 1895

Courtesy, *History Colorado, 10028849*

In 1894 the people in town asked their council to drill for water. To that time water was drawn from the Arkansas River through canals and used for everything, and as a result there were persistent cases of typhoid fever. GK Gilbert of the United States Geological Survey advised the council that water was there if the well went deep enough. He suggested Charles McVay, who had drilled for the Union Pacific Railroad, and who could use his oil well drilling rig and experience in the effort.

Money was raised and the derrick set up in Railroad Park across Railroad Avenue from the Rocky Ford State Bank, p. 14. Water was found at 790 feet with enough pressure to force it to the top of Reservoir Hill for storage and distribution. George W. Swink, a prominent investor in the venture, is standing, p. 62, in white shirt sleeves near barrels on a wagon. The inset marks the 1895 well casing in the sidewalk along Main Street east of the depot, now Chamber of Commerce.

Photo by C J Muth

A Better Source of Water

Happy citizens came with buckets to carry clean water home that had not come from the Catlin, Rocky Ford Canal or the river. However, at least one citizen previously cautioned by the medical community to boil raw water coming from river or canals stated "It tastes good enough for me raw." No doubt others among the community were reluctant to take this step to ensure safe drinking water.

The well provided water to be hauled by tank or barrels for distribution to customers. AM Jackson's [possibly Artesian Water Service] on the sign was providing this service and city council ultimately decided that water was to be distributed by a piping system. On Jan. 30, 1931 council resolution authorized RM Jackson [possibly related] to sell artesian water in tank lots.

Other wells were drilled in 1895–1897, one shown on p. 90. The second was on the town lot on Eleventh Street. The Town Lots were at Eleventh and Front Streets south of the railroad, granted by the Rocky Ford Town Company. The third well was drilled on George Swink's property near the storage tanks on Reservoir Hill but it had poor flow. Two 100 barrel* cement tanks were maintained there for gravity distribution into the town. Mr. McVay drilled a fourth well in Garden Place, somewhere south of the railroad, east of Fourteenth Street and a fifth privately owned well west of town where (Oliver) Steel Manufacturing Plant eventually located near the NW corner of State Hwy 71 and US 50.

Well water use in the growing town eventually resulted in decreased water pressure. Pumps were installed to draw water and force it to its storage. The city eventually was able to develop concrete-lined open settling basins on Reservoir Hill to replace the 100 barrel tanks. Water was then supplied by canals into setting ponds before treatment in the plant nearby.

*Standard barrel US measure = 31.5 gallons. One 100 barrel cement tank capacity was 3150 gallons. Water distribution by underground piping began with the success of the wells. The first rudimentary system is described on p. 39. (See p. 302 for ailments in addition to typhoid fever.)

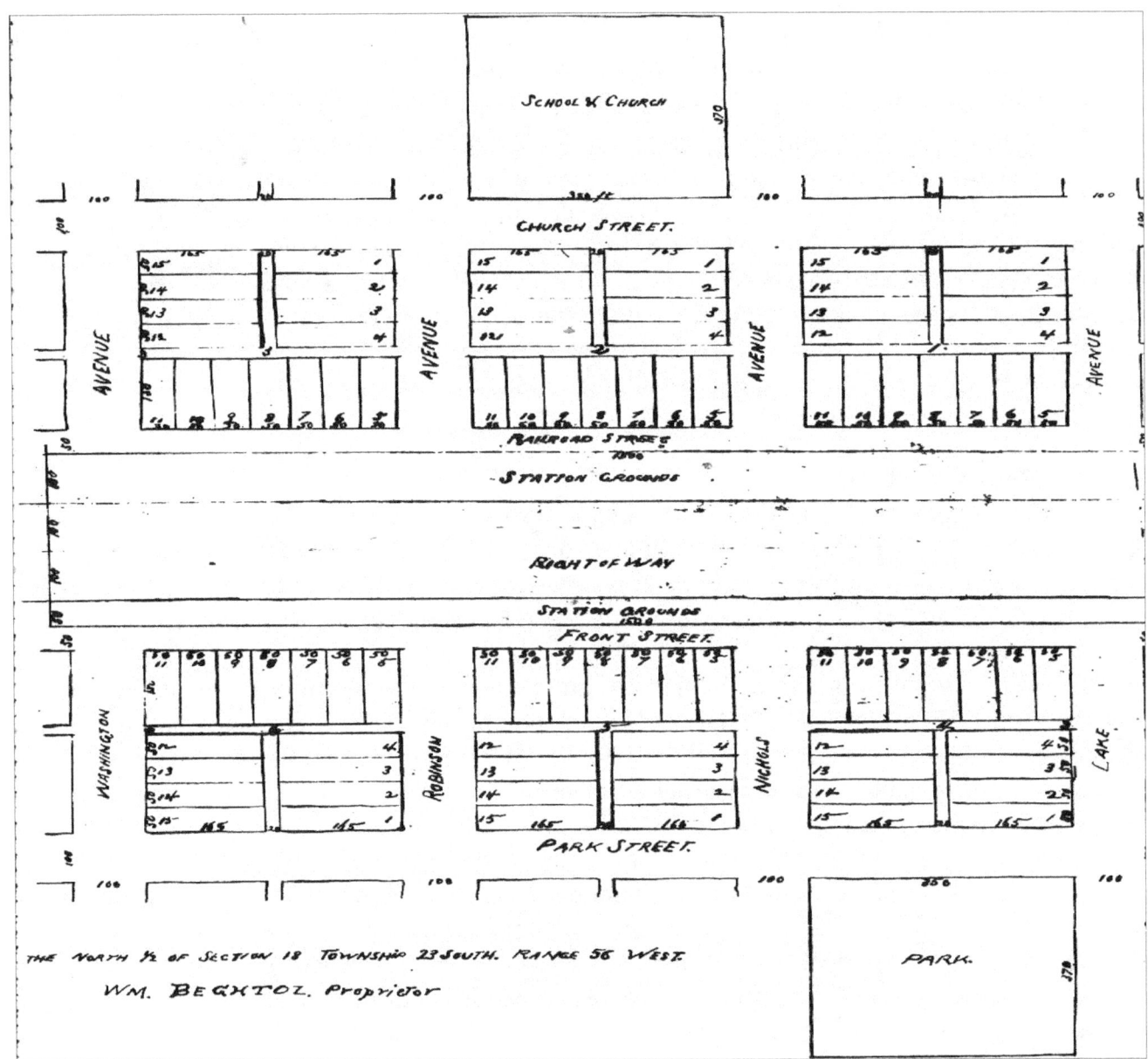

Town Site, 1876

Six-block town site of William Matthews. *From John Doll*

Washington became Ninth Str., Robinson, Main, and Nichols became Tenth Str. in the 1887 re-plat. Streets 1 thru 15 ran north and south, avenues named for trees ran east and west. Proposed additional blocks on the first plat were indicated on all borders but were not then expanded. Three large blocks were to be north and three to the south of the railroad. The future business block was to be on the 'Kit Carson Road', now Tenth Street. Kit Carson Road was on the wagon trail from Kit Carson, Colorado to destinations south. Several businesses, Swift and Nichol's frame hotel, Swink's Store, and the Swift Blacksmith shop moved there in 1876.

A Random Walk

Before The Feast   **Watermelon Day**

After The Feast

[Upper photo] Courtesy, *History Colorado, Post Card Collection, 10044481*
[Lower photo] Courtesy, *History Colorado, Post Card Collection, 10044482*

City fathers must have wondered "What hath this day wrought ?" (See also p. 238.)

65

Sen. GW Swink and the Arkansas Valley Fair

Arkansas Valley Fair, begun in 1878, is the oldest continuous fair in the State of Colorado. It is held in Rocky Ford, southeastern Colorado on U.S. Highway 50 beside the historic Santa Fe Trail. Famous for watermelon and cantaloupe, this is one of the most productive agricultural areas in the nation. A brief history of the Fair and Watermelon Day, written by the late Senator and originator of the celebration follows:

> The first Watermelon Day was in 1878. My crop for this year being very bountiful, I decided to invite all the people in the surrounding territory to partake in my crop. The country then being thinly settled the crowd was quite small, not more than 25 persons being present, and they being mostly from La Junta coming in a Santa Fe Caboose. I cut the melons on the grain door of a boxcar. Only one wagon load was required to feed the crowd and give all they wanted to carry home.
>
> Again in 1879 I gave the same invitation and the crowd was increased to about fifty, coming mostly from La Junta. They ate and carried home with them one large wagon load of melons. A grain door again served for a table, and I did all the carving. In 1880 the crowd increased to one hundred and consumed two wagon loads of melons. In 1881 there was another increase, two coach loads coming from La Junta. That year a table was built twelve feet long and the melons were increased accordingly. The same growth of attendance was noted in 1882, the pile of melons steadily growing, so that all wants were supplied. During all these years the feast was served in the old Swink Store adjoining the Santa Fe track.
>
> In 1883 there was another marked increase in the crowd, and the table for melons was transferred to the grove north of town, which incidentally was a part of my timber claim,* which had the distinction of being the first culture claim proved upon the United States. The feast of melons was accompanied by a basket picnic, a table being built separate from the melon table. On this the ladies spread a most excellent dinner for the visitors. Adjacent to the two tables was a display of plums, grapes and apples, which were given to the crowds before the day ended.
>
> In 1884 there was another increase in the crowd as well as the size of the melon pile. The free dinner also was enlarged in quantity and improved in quality. The ladies of Rocky Ford took great pride in preparing a fine dinner and deserve much credit for the valuable aid rendered. The display of horticultural products was made a feature again. In 1885 there was the usual increase in the crowd and the spread of toothsome viands. To the display of fruit was this year added the farm products. Up to and including the year I cut and served all themelons, which were eaten. In 1886 so great was the attendance that the ladies had to "put the big pot on," but they had an abundance of "grub" and as fine as could be provided anywhere. This year I was compelled to call in help to cut and serve the melons. There was the usual display of farm and orchard products, but in larger quantities than previous years.

*Sen. Swink received the first **US Timber Claim Certificate**, signed by President Grover Cleveland November 3, 1887. This Act by Congress in 1873, was a follow-up to the 1862 Homestead Act Which allowed homesteaders to get another 160 acres (0.65 km^2) of land if they planted trees on one-fourth of the land, because the land was nearly treeless.

The raising of watermelons in the Arkansas Valley was started in 1877 by the planning [sic] of about one-quarter of an acre, which produced all that could be sold in the local markets that year. The local demand increased, and from time to time the acreage was increased. Up to the year 1886 I produced all of the melons that were raised in this part of the county, and during that year I commenced to introduce them in Eastern Markets. The first two years shipping of melons was a failure financially as the proceeds were not sufficient to pay express charges.   GW Swink text from *arkvalleyfair.com*; Photo vintage postcard.

Hon. Sen. GW Swink
1836–1910

Sen. Swink and family lived at Ninth and Swink Road on the NW corner. Their house did not survive, eventually replaced by the US Post Office at 401 N Ninth Street.

For many years Swink land to the north of the post office grew alfalfa, a bucolic sight for later Rocky Ford High School students across Chestnut Avenue to the north. This field would eventually become the site of Safeway, then Wrangler Foods.   Note, see p. 302.

RFHS Photo courtesy *Rocky Ford Public Library*

Grand Opera House

On June 24, 1934 this building was destroyed by fire. Also destroyed was the **Grand Beer Tavern**, arch at right. Repairs began January 24, 1935 with re-opening May 1, 1935.

The **A&W** wooden facade at this time occupies the space at left (and below). Although then A&W, a name change to W&W came years later after a franchise change, see below.

Grand Theatre, 1949
Ten windows, upper level were retained in the remodeling shown in this photo. Bricks were stuccoed and the three-arch openings at street level 405 S Main retained. The marquee remains but without the vertical towering GRAND.

Starlite Drive-In, east on US 50, was a popular alternate theatre in summer.

Photos, courtesy *Rocky Ford Public Library*

W&W Root Beer during a Saturday matinee at the movies.

The **Grand** today

Color photo courtesy
Matt Mendenhall, Mike Budge, rockyfordcolorado.net

St. James Hotel

In 1888, Mr. Swink and other businessmen built a two-story brick hotel on the southeast corner of Walnut Avenue and Main Street. It had two ground floor store rooms with hotel apartments above. A feature of the hotel was a two-story privy on the alley with an elevated walkway between the two buildings. Hotel management changed several times until eventually Mr. Swink took over the building to satisfy the partners. The hotel had been the West, but renamed Swink's Hotel. In 1892 a Colorado Springs man leased the place, had the privy removed [1896] and made some other changes. He renamed it the St. James Hotel, a name it carried for the next 50 years.

According to the 1911 Rocky Ford Business Guide, Mrs. HG Harter was the proprietor after several changes in management. Mrs. WS (Lila M.) Eichelberger was managing and living in the hotel in 1914, along with her husband and Rocky Ford Police Chief, William S. Eichelberger, also the Fire Chief at the time.

No ground-level entry to the privy is mentioned nor a reason for the demise of the structure. A two-story facility might suggest that a ground level entrance existed. The design of like structures in other towns placed the upper facility a little farther back of the lower so that the drop was directed behind the wall of the ground bench. A ground floor entrance in some locations was abandoned during seasons of high snowfall.

The St. James was subject of the city council's agenda as late as February 18, 1948 when the police chief reported its unsanitary condition. Although the reason was not given there was concern referred to the Health Committee with no further comment. The town's citizens in general were careless with rubbish disposal and with maintenance of open cess pools on many properties. Several instances in city council minutes related to these problems. Examples relating to hotels:

> April 30, 1907. Communication from BU Dye in reference to the sanitary condition of the Longworth Hotel [410–412 S Main Street] that the cess pool in the rear was running over and asked that the city take some action to remedy same. Referred to the Health Committee. Note: Mr. Dye lived at 420 S Main Street, very near the hotel on the same side of the street.

> June 3, 1915. The cellar or basement under the Elk Hotel on South Main [311 ½ South Main], and also under the building [adjacent or nearby, referred to by lot numbers] contained a large quantity of unwholesome, offensive and filthy stagnant water giving off strong offensive odor to the passers by, making the surrounding unhealthy and creating a serious nuisance at each place and recommended that at each and all of these places the nuisance be abated and the premises be put in a sanitary condition.

Among other sanitary concerns in early Rocky Ford: a dairy at Thirteenth Street and Pine Avenue; horse corral near Fourth and Fifth Streets; corrals at 404 S Eleventh Street and 500 N Fifth Street. A dumping ground was also cited at Eleventh Street and Chestnut, used by many it was posted by sign discouraging further use. Council also recommended September 15, 1914 that all alleys be cleaned of trash, rubbish, and vegetable and animal matter, particularly in the business district.

Ornamental parapet of the St. James was removed sometime before the photos on pp. 24 and 139 c 1920–1930s.

St. James Hotel, with its two story privy at the rear.
Photos above courtesy *Rocky Ford Public Library*, *Rocky Ford Public Museum*

Rocky Ford Magazine v. 1 no. 1

The original St. James, above, year unknown, showing the hotel with its corner entrance at 300 S Main. Nine men in the large photo are not identified. *Rocky Ford Tribune* would locate here.

To the right of the hotel were Palace of Sweets, 302, Delmonte Grocery and Cantaloupe Cafe, 304, the new St. James Hotel entrance to second story rooms at 304 ½, Gem Theatre, 306, rooms above Gem, 306½, Arlington Café, 308, Holsun Grocery, 310, Ma's Place at 310 ½ offered meals and short orders. At 312 S Main confectioner Edw. B. McColm had his business. [Address changes were frequent on this block, see p. 72.]

Cantaloupe Café would appear as on page 24 and at right, above. The entrance to the hotel, indicated by the horizontal sign left of the upper windows, led to stairs and the rooms on the upper floor. Such an entry warranted the 304 ½ street number designation. A vertical sign shows the word *Rooms* appearing faintly on the right of the entrance.

Privies were common on rural properties as well as in the city limits of Rocky Ford into the 1940s. Many remained as wood or coal sheds after their original function.

> **July 7, 1934. City Council action**: Alderman Carman explained that complaints were being made that toilets are being dug and others are being used without water and are creating an unsanitary condition over the city. Moved that Health and police departments be instructed to proceed to inspect and see that all properties within the city limits are in a sanitary condition. Carried.

The building to the right of the hotel and cafe at 306 S. Main, p. 24, was the GEM Theatre, managed by A. Staples. Evangelist IG Martin was advertising a meeting "Each Evening at 7:30 Beginning October 30." The day was at hand according to the wagon sign, "To-Night." GEM Theatre was not for motion pictures but was a public meeting place for plays, readings, and other social events. Both the St. James, and GEM buildings were razed, along with the entire east side of the 300 block in 1955, *future* site of McCLain's Super, pp. 160–161. Adjacent the Gem was Stauffer's Meat Market, formerly at 917 Walnut Avenue.

Public Meeting Halls in the *Rocky Ford Directory* for 1914–1915:

Bijou Amusement Hall, 417 S Main.
City Hall, 203 S Ninth.
Elk's Home, 301 N Ninth.
Gobin Block, Elm Ave SE corner Ninth.
Godding Block, 302 N Main.
Hagen Block, 402 S Main.
Hagen-Recker Block, 207 ½ S Main.
IOOF Hall, 200 S Main.
Gem Theatre, 306 S Main.
Wolfe & Swift Block, 207 ½ S Main.
K of P Hall, 401 N Main.
Kimzey-Cover Block, 309 N Main.
Masonic Hall, 411 ½ N Main.
Maxwell Block, 957 Railroad Ave.
Moose Hall, 950 Walnut Ave.
Opera House Block, 407 S Main.
St. John Building, 401 S Main.

Hotels and Rooms:

Bolton Hotel, 908 Elm Avenue.
Central Hotel, 208 N Main Street.
Hotel Best, Mrs. CA Arnold Miller, prop., 410–412 S Main.
Hotel El Capitan, Thomas A. Davey, prop., 501 N Main.
Hotel Rockford, W. Jordan, prop. 1001 Railroad Ave.
Longworth Hotel, 410–412 S Main Street.
National House, Mrs. WL Woodward, prop., 920 Front Street.
Pacific House, 920 Front Street.
Royal Hotel, 908 Elm Ave.
St. James Hotel, Mrs. WS Eichelberger, prop., 302½ S Main, later 304½ S Main.
Elk Hotel, Mrs. Alvia Corcoran, prop., 311 ½ S Main.
Amos Flats, north-side and south-side Chestnut Ave between Main and Tenth Streets.
Hagen Block, Mrs. SL Hagen, prop, 400–402 S Main Street, rooms.
The Berkeley, Mrs Viola Farris, proprietor, 519 N Main, (boarding house).
Rector Hotel, 908 Elm Ave., ph. 196.

Businesses of 300 Block S Main

The east side of the 300 block housed 12 businesses and illustrated the competition for space for rooms to rent, hotel, eateries and groceries. Floor space for each was small and often shared.

300 S Main, Rocky Ford *Tribune*, a weekly, published by Int Stanley and Sons; the original St. James Hotel entrance.
302 S Main, Palace of Sweets, Walter G. Brown, prop; Cantaloupe Café.
304 ½ S Main, stair entrance to the St. James Hotel.
304 S Main, Delmonte Grocery, JS Denny and SA Lopez, proprietors.
306 S Main, GEM Theatre, TR Gilmore, prop., A. Staples, manager.
306 ½ S Main, Rooms to let above the GEM Theatre.
308 S Main, Arlington Café, Granville and Mary Anna Hooper, proprietors. The Hoopers also advertised Rooms Above.
310 S Main, Holsun Grocery, George R. Daring, proprietor.
310 ½ S Main, Ma's Place, Regular Meals and Short Orders, Fine Chili, Mrs. Florence Asher, proprietor.
312 S Main, Confectioner, Edward B. McColm.

There are discrepancies in the directory addresses. The GEM is shown in the photo directly adjacent the Cantaloupe Café, p. 24, rather than Delmonte Grocery as the address indicates. There is part of a Coca Cola sign visible at sidewalk level on the front of the building immediately left of the St. James Hotel entryway. Possibly the grocery was in that location. Two businesses existed at 302 S Main, one inside the other, viz., Palace of Sweets inside the Cantaloupe Café. One could also have been a later occupant.

The door to the St. James Hotel had a transom above for lighting the stairs and many buildings, as on this block, had canvas canopies above their entrances and display windows. Each was raised or lowered by a folding crank on the front of the building that operated a roller mechanism. Business names were often printed on their front edge. Many awnings fell out of use over years as the elements did their work, either by sun, wind, hail, or heavy snows.

Bricks for the town's buildings were fired at NW Terry's 1894 brick yard and kiln at the east end of Maple Avenue. The yard apparently was just beyond the Fifteenth Street intersection in part of the area known as Garden Place. The American Beet Sugar Company required 1,000,000 bricks for their new factory in 1900 and one by one the original adobe or wooden town buildings were replaced by more permanent brick.

A business opened in 1904 at the site of the electric facility on Twelfth Street south of the railroad. The Cement Stone Company at 209 S Twelfth Street began manufacturing building blocks of the larger variety circa 1906. From that time, buildings incorporated them in new construction.

City Council business, as recorded:
May 1, 1934: "Communication from State Board of Health request the city to discontinue the disposal of sewage into the river read. The city attorney was authorized to take the matter up with the State Board of Health as the Ways and Means of disposing of sewage."

Rocky Ford Police and Firemen

Many in Rocky Ford may not have heard of Jesse B. Craig, Sr., Jacob A. Kipper, or Louis Box. They might also not know of Clyde F. Summers or William M. Lueker. These men were all citizens of the town and at some time during their lives came into positions in the emergency services for the city.

Chief Marshal Jesse B. Craig, Sr. and his partner, Night Marshal Jacob A. Kipper were called to respond to a domestic dispute. The two had just returned from La Junta on the train while transporting a prisoner. They went to the Harris residence and found Bob Harris had been drinking and quarreling with his wife and his parents.

Bob Harris had been in trouble before and was known to the Marshals. When they attempted to arrest him a fight broke out and Harris' father, mother, and wife all joined in fighting the two officers. Bob Harris ran to another room and came back with a .44 revolver and shot both officers. Both staggered outside the house and collapsed in the front yard. Bob Harris ran off but was captured two days later. Marshal Craig (*photo not available*) died on the front sidewalk that day, a Tuesday, July 4, 1911. He was 59 and was beginning his second term as Chief. He left a wife and two children.

Marshal Kipper died 14 days later Tuesday, July 18, 1911 at Denver's St. Joseph Hospital. He left a wife and two sons at 701 Spruce Avenue.

Robert Harris, prisoner #8180 was convicted of murder in the first degree and sentenced to death. His sentence was later commuted to life in the Colorado State Penitentiary where he died December 30, 1926.   Photos and paraphrased text courtesy *The Officer Down Memorial page, odmp.org*

Jacob A. Kipper

Patrolman Louis Box was attempting to arrest a 26 year old army private wanted for allegedly assaulting a 15 year old girl. As Patrolman Box questioned the man, he suddenly drew a knife and cut the officer's throat. The soldier was convicted of first degree murder and sentenced to death. On October 17, 1945, President Truman commuted his sentence to life in prison.

Photos and paraphrased text courtesy *The Officer Down Memorial Page, odmp.org*

Patrolman Box had been a member of the Rocky Ford Police Department for six years. He was born March 8, 1898 in Huntington, Arkansas and died April 18, 1945. He left his wife Mathilda (Hilda) and six children at 515 N Seventh Street.

Photo courtesy *Patricia Cole (Gerlock)*

Clyde F. Summers and **William M. Lueker** were members of the Rocky Ford Fire Department, Mr. Summers as City Clerk and Fire Chief and Martel (Mart) Lueker as volunteer. Mr. Lueker was owner and operator of a Sinclair service station and was a boating enthusiast who built his own inboard motor recreational craft. He lived with his wife Ethel at 604 S Twelfth Street. Mr. Summers and wife Sylvia lived at 205 S Ninth Street.

During a flood on the prairie south of Crooked Arroyo, water gathered volume and force on its way to the Arkansas River July 1953. Both men were in a fire department rescue boat searching the area between the Santa Fe Railroad tracks and US Highway 50. As they moved along in their search for victims they came to an area where much debris had collected and blocked a trestle. As they passed near, the accumulated material suddenly gave way to water pressure and pulled the two men and their boat under the railroad and through the trestle. The date was July 12, 1953.

Text courtesy *denverfirejournal.com*, paraphrased by author

Early Firefighters
In the left wagon is driver George Frantz and first Fire Chief Fred A Karpe, along with Mark Denson, Arthur Childs and CG Mathews. In the right wagon is driver Chester L. Jennings along with AH Karp, Carl Lunquist and AP Smith. (See also pp. 131–132, 326.)   Photo May 30, 1906

The Old Republic
This Republic fire engine was in service approximately 30 years, 1919 to 1949. It was restored by Rocky Ford Fire Department volunteers in 1982–1983. The men in the photo and the date are not identified but appears to be c 1920s–1930s. The location is the present fire station at 201–203 S Ninth Street.

The Republic, now restored, is housed in the Rocky Ford Museum Carriage House.

Brochure photos courtesy *Rocky Ford Chamber of Commerce*

The Republic Motor Truck Company manufactured commercial trucks c 1913–1929 in Alma, Michigan. The basic chassis was modified to produce many types, including trucks for use by fire departments as fire-fighting units.

Rocky Ford High School

An account of the former red brick building RFHS, states that it was "built around the old building," pp. 67, 182–183.

A Carnegie architectural style was employed for both the 1908 high school and library, built in 1909. The original library, below left, is now the Rocky Ford Public Museum at 1005 Sycamore Avenue.

Original library, now museum, and high school photos courtesy *Rocky Ford Public Library*.

Modern photos courtesy *Matt Mendenhall, Mike Budge, rockyfordcolorado.net*

Rocky Ford Public Library is a new building at 400 S Tenth Street on the same grounds near the original building.

IOOF Hall

Woodside Seed Growers advertisement on north side of 200 S Main. IOOF building in 1914–1915 Rocky Ford City Directory shows that Lodge No. 87, JB Ritter, Sec. met every Tuesday. Zoar Encampment No. 8, HI Jameson, Scribe, met first and third Fridays.

Photos courtesy *Matt Mendenhall, Mike Budge*, rockyfordcolorado.net.

Entablature on parapet and facade with inset carved stone plaque: Odd Fellows Hall 1892. Barely discernable in the painted three chain links in large photo are the letters "F, L, T," for the group's motto, "Friendship, Love, Truth."

S Main at 200 housed Food Bank, left store front, 202 at right, Boys and Girls Club. Low building, far right, once housed Govreau Grocery, later, Fiesta Café at 204 S Main.

First Methodist Episcopal Church

Courtesy *Rocky Ford Public Museum*

This church was on the NE corner of Ninth and Elm, c 1914–1916. View is to the north on Ninth Street past the BPOE home out of the photo to the left. The church is actually the third one built. The first was a temporary one in 1891 with a board floor, frame walls and canvas roof on the SE corner of this intersection. The second brick one built in 1893 was replaced by the larger brick building in 1906 on the NE corner of Ninth and Elm.

This photo serves to show features of a developing town. City council made arrangements November 7, 1933 to pave US 50–Elm Avenue. There were already concrete crosswalks at the time of this photo, one visible at lower right. The aerial photo of Rocky Ford, *Frontispiece*, p. ii , shows a paved Main Street in 1936 with curbs and sidewalks in place. Other streets were paved beginning in May 1937, first with Ninth Street south from the railroad.

Early in the town's development when water became available from Rocky Ford Canal, council ordered and planted 3000 cottonwoods along streets three blocks each way from Main and the railroad. Residents greatly appreciated the shade and mature appearance to their streets but disliked the cotton in the air. Several other species were planted so that in most photos of the town there is an abundance of trees, many American Elms planted between 1903 and 1909 under RM Pollock, mayor.

Mr. Swink's timber claim to the north was also improved by more planting in his desire to remain in compliance with the government's requirements to improve timber availability. Many trees of the same age are visible in Watermelon Day photos.

Watermelon Day 1916

Rocky Ford Magazine vol. 1 no. 1, Summer 1998

A crowd gathers in 1916 near the Santa Fe Depot for the annual Watermelon Day celebration during the Arkansas Valley Fair. Many hundreds to thousands arrived by train every year for this and Fair events. Railroad Park in the background features a fountain behind a tree seen also in the photo on p. 18. The triangular sign, once a common sight at railroad crossings, warns: "Railroad Crossing, Look Out For The Trains." Some autos and carriages, taxis for the day, offered ten cent per person transportation to the fairgrounds while the band warms up at lower left. Carriage horse hoofs are clean and whitened for the day.

Rocky Ford Concert Band played at many public events and holiday celebrations. In the author's lifetime there were observances of Decoration Day at a stone bandstand at the cemetery and concerts in Library Park under the trees in the 1940s. Summer musical programs in the park have recently been revived.

Dorman Photography, 1910

A 1940s Parade

coloradoplains.com

Arkansas Valley Fair time with bunting over Main Street and on some buildings. From left, Holland Drug, Donk's Variety behind light pole, and City Drug Store at Elm Avenue and Main Street.

Military vehicles sometimes came from the Army Air Force Base at La Junta, or more likely Rocky Ford's own National Guard unit. Two heavy vehicles, possibly tanks, are in the rear.

Single traffic control light pedestal in town is visible at the intersection of Main and Elm. The former three-globe street lights are replaced by the much taller photocell operated ones.

Main Street one block south of that above after a November 1930 snow storm. Many citizens will recall that snow was not removed from streets. Pathways were opened for 2-way traffic with snow piled in the center to remain there until melted.

Small building at far left center was Frank Boraker's shop, p. 16.

Courtesy *Rocky Ford Public Museum*

City Water Works and Dump

Washington Avenue at 1000 is site of the City Water Works and settling ponds. Part of the golf course now covers a former open dump site below the Reservoir Hill road extending almost to the Catlin Canal. Nearly continual, smoky fires burned in the area. The site was southwest and starting near the present seventh green and the bridge over the Catlin Canal from Main Street.

Recognizing the need for change, the city established an open dump above the east bank of the Arkansas River May 11, 1927, past the bridge on the road to Dye Reservoir—*marker*. There, a caretaker couple lived in a small house on the property. By July 1, 1968, statutes required the area to be developed as a sanitary landfill sometime before development of Otero County Landfill south of State Highway 10. It then functioned as a tree dump.

Early in Dye Reservoir history people fished and boated there. A house on the north shore served as a country club accommodating swimming. In the 1920s a golf course was designed among the sand hills and sage brush.

Illustration by *mapquest*

The hill known as Reservoir Hill by early residents later was renamed Play Park. The former was site of a swimming pool, a new one was later built north of Washington Ave Fairway and seventh green were laid out on the hill, reclaiming the open dump that had been in use for years, lower right corner. The new RFHS school west of the golf course was built where Alta Vista Camp once was located.

Earl Zimmerman Air Field SE of the lake was dedicated in 1929. Earl Zimmerman, a WWI pilot from Rocky Ford, later died in a test plane at Colorado Springs. Many local pilots learned basic flying skills at this field before WWII.

Courtesy *rockyfordgolfcourse.com*

Smith's Café, 1929

Courtesy *Rocky Ford Public Museum*

Smith's Café, 206 S Main Street, purchased by Billy Smallwood and Woodrow Hayes January 23, 1933. Sellers, Mr. and Mrs. Bill Smith, at left above, are identified with Nora Crowel second from right. Nora B. and J. Frank Crowl (sic) in 1945–1948 directory lived at 200 N Fifth Street.

A popular drive-up, a favorite of many, was **Huri-Back Lunch** aka **Wimpy's**, located on the west curve of Elm Avenue between Second and Third Streets. Elm Avenue side is shown in the 1940s where many parked. Inside were a counter and stools for those wanting a table. The young man serving, Don Gause, is today proprietor of Don's Mens Store. (See p. 241 for another view of Huri-Back Lunch.) October 15, 2016

Postcard photo courtesy *Ruth Muth Grenard*

Huri-Back Lunch

```
FORM #2                    LIST
                Forty Basic Food Items And Meals
                    As Required by Order Of
                   Colorado District Director, OPA

  (Make out this list in TRIPLICATE. Then Copy the items and prices onto the
   FORM for posting in your establishment. Then forward all three copies of
   this list to your War Price & Rationing Board.)  " Base" 40 item corrected
              as to base period April 4 to 10, 1943
 1. T-Bone Steak with French F    65¢  21. Combination Ham & Cheese     20¢
    Short Cut Steak with French
 2. Fries                         55¢  22. Assorted canned soup         20¢
    Wimpy Steak Deluxe with cheese
 3. egg, & French Fries           45¢  23. Lettuce & Tomato Salad       15¢
    Grilled Pork Chops with French
 4. Fries                         45¢  24. Sliced Tomatoes, per order   15¢
    Wimpy Steak with french
 5. Fries                         40¢  25. Home-made chili              15¢
    Ham & Eggs-Fries- Toast                                per order
 6. Drink                         50¢  26. French Fried Potatoes        15¢
    Two eggs Fries Toast
 7. Drink                         30¢  27. Home-Made pie, per cut       10¢
 8. Buttered Toast                10¢  28. Tea-per pot                  10¢
 9. Toasted Extra                  5¢  29. Hot chocolate                10¢
10. Wimpy                         10¢  30. Assorted Cold Drinks          5¢
                                            potato salad
11. Cheese                        10¢  31. Toasted Ham Sandiwhc         25¢
                                            Toasted Ham Salad Sandwich
12. Cheeseburger                  15¢  32. French Fries                 25¢
13. Cold Ham                      15¢  33. Fresh Oyster Stew            40¢
14. Fried Ham - Shoestring        25¢  34. Home made soups              10¢
                                                               Dessert
15. Toasted Tuna-fish             15¢  35. All side dishes of Veg &     10¢
16. Bacon & Tomato                20¢  36.
17. Lettuce & Tomato              15¢  37.
18. Ham & Egg                     20¢  38.
19. Bacon & Egg                   20¢  39.
20. Egg                           15¢  40.
                                         FOR USE OF PRICE PANEL ONLY
    ESTABLISHMENT  Huri-Back Lunch             APPROVED
    ADDRESS  Rocky Ford, Colorado         Same as base period prices
                                              April 4th to 10th, 43
    NAME OF OWNER _____              Filed with
    DATE _____              War Price & Rationing Board #
                                         Signed _____
```

Courtesy of *Jerre Gonzales*

The menu reflects scarcity of coffee during WWII. Wimpy menu items 3, 5, and 10 are named from the 1930s character, J. Wellington Wimpy, portly epicure always on the alert for food, who frequently implored, " I 'd gladly pay you Tuesday for a hamburger today." We remember Wimpy from *Popeye* cartoons by EC Segar. Huri-Back Lunch received the popular Wimpy's *alter idem aka* during several years' popular patronage of this trolley car lunchroom on a foundation.

Rocky Ford Obelisks

A narrow two-lane concrete highway—US 50 coming into town from the east— joined an unpaved road. This was the main entrance to town on east Railroad Avenue where stood the obelisks. Sometimes this structure was called 'the arch' which suggested a curved centerpiece, but two pillars were joined by a straight horizontal connecting member above the road. Both the pillars and the horizontal member served to advertise major industries in Rocky Ford economy. Early resident Rex Sprinkle described his first sight of them August 1928 for the *Rocky Ford Centennial, Daily Gazette*, April 10, 1987: "There was a white Leghorn hen at the top ... and a white Leghorn rooster ... ."

The hen was at left and rooster to the right of a large melon and sugar beet, also displayed. Bright morning light all but blended with the fowl silhouettes, p. 330. Visible at each end of the large melon are the feet and combs, hen at left, rooster at right.

A horizontal cross-member spanned the distance between the two pillars later supporting a large, wooden, green-striped watermelon. The beet was gone. Vertically painted on one pillar was the word WELCOME; ROCKY FORD was painted on the other. The large block letters were faded c 1941 when I first saw them but were distinct enough to read. This early structure had already been modified before its later appearance, p. 149. Published date of construction was during 1928–1929, a project of Mayor William B. Gobin with contributions from the community.

Poultry rearing was prominent in Rocky Ford and at several locations in the Arkansas Valley for many years, both chicken and turkey farms. Melons were always an abundant crop and provided employment for many in the growing, marketing, and shipping. OC Frantz, a prominent poultry-raiser and contributor to the construction of the arch provided the likenesses of the white Leghorn rooster and hen seen on the cross-structure.

In time, the Leghorns disappeared, followed later by the wooden melon and beet. January 30, 1987 the obelisks were separated, one placed at Huri-Back Park on the west and one farther east near the US 50 west-bound divide, marking the major entrances and exits of the town.

Leghorns in the illustration below are similar in profile to those representations Mr. Sprinkle saw in 1928. A melon of the striped variety was the shape and appearance of the wooden one.

zazzle.com   bellybytes.com

Swink and Russell 1871 Store

Courtesy *Rocky Ford Public Museum*

This photo may be one of few in existence of one of the first buildings at **Old Rocky Ford** on the Arkansas River. A rudimentary stockade was built in 1870, soon replaced by this adobe store. The Asa Russell and George Amos families and WS Hendricks built houses near this Swink and Russell store in 1871. All moved in 1875 to file claims near the railroad and new Rocky Ford.

The first store and homes of these pioneers were cottonwood logs set in the ground, with a roof of poles covered by dirt. The adobe structure of Swink and Russell was an improved one most likely benefitting from the work of a Mexican family living a little east of the store in two hillside dugouts. Jesus Creo, his wife, and brother-in-law likely shared knowledge of adobe construction.

Adobe was beginning to crumble. The outer layer had fallen left of the door and the place appeared empty. Soil of the adobe was reclaimed by the river in 1921 when the Arkansas took many structures along its length, also several lives. Rocky Ford's first house of business was gone.

The Ford

Courtesy *Rocky Ford Public Museum*

A photo of the *'rocky ford'* for which the city was named. Quality of this photo and that of the 1871 store appear to be the work of the same photographer.

The crossing is typical of many areas along the banks but its stones are not visible, existing under water. One can walk across at some places in shallow water although at places it is deep and swift. Water quality is much different today bearing heavy sediments. Quicksand was and is a danger for those unaware of it along the river.

There are accounts of other fords on the Arkansas, one between Rocky Ford and Swink, another east of La Junta. The first was known to the Spanish and Mexican herders and farmers preceding the arrival of settlers from the east. Locals knew it as *Valle Inpredodo*, meaning Rock Valley and described it as 'a slab of stone.'

Another crossing was at King's Ferry, used by travelers on the Santa Fe Trail. Location was downriver a few hundred feet from the mouth of King Arroyo just east of La Junta.

Little else is known of these crossings. The river channel has changed many times since and only general descriptions can be given for their locations.

Earliest Rocky Ford Businesses

Railroad Avenue was the original Main Street at the time these businesses were arrayed along the railroad tracks, facing south. Right of the small tree is the Shoe Shop with the proprietor standing in the doorway. The taller store front next right is Swink's Rocky Ford Feed Store. The next building is that of BU Dye & Son, advertising Agricultural Implements, Walter A. Wood Binders, Mowers, and Self Rakes.

The lower line above the BU Dye window advertises Mitchell Wagons, Glidden Barb Wire and Twine. A Livery Stable is right of the Dye store advertising Feed & Scale and Stable. A Blacksmith & Repair Shop is far right. Enlargement of this photo shows that a man is weighing the horse and flat-bed wagon on a Fairbanks scale at forefront far right.

Buildings below, left to right, are De Seeley Hotel, Shoe Shop, Rocky Ford Feed Store, BU Dye & Son, Livery Stable, Blacksmith & Repair Shop.

Photo appears in several printings dated 1881, 1884, and 1886.

Courtesy *Rocky Ford Public Library*

The large De Seeley Hotel occupies the former location of Andy Nichol's frame hotel on the west corner of the block cater-cornered from the 1876 adobe Swink Store. This description indicates the corner of Tenth and Railroad where Roy's Conoco would be later, with these businesses arrayed east along Railroad Avenue. Elm Avenue would eventually develop to the rear, north of this building block, and be contiguous with the future US Highway 50.

The 1887 re-platted town site would place the business district on the new Main Street a block west and parallel to Kit Carson Road, oriented north and south. The old main street above would be maintained along the railroad with several changes of businesses but without downtown improvements. At publication, Railroad Avenue from the east entrance to Rocky Ford thru to Tenth Street has never been paved.

Mr. Doll wrote of a tree planted by Santa Fe officials that was appreciated by travelers for shade in a campground at the Eleventh Street and Railroad Avenue intersection. It matured as a large cottonwood just to the east of the above buildings. The campground location was convenient to the Swink store where many travelers apparently re-supplied their needs on their way west.

GW Swink's 1876 Adobe Store

The *Frontispiece* bears this image of GW Swink's 1876 store but because of the acute angle and altitude the photo was taken such a building is hard to define. There is in the area described by Mr. Doll a building with both roof description and size. This section of the *Frontispiece* appears to show such a building with "pitched shingle roof... north of the tracks and west of the crossing." For reference, the Wig-Wag signal on the Tenth Street crossing is enclosed in the small box and the lower border of the photo is near the line of the Santa Fe siding tracks. The siding, just a few feet from the south side of Swink's Store, provided ease of loading and unloading. (See p. 92 for a view of the store front.)

The store was built on railroad property, at the completion of the railroad in 1876, north of the tracks and west of the crossing that later became Tenth Street. The building was 20 x 40 feet, had a board floor and flat roof. The building was later board-sided with a pitched shingle roof addition, the first building at the town site and last to be torn down.

Photo enlarged from *Frontispiece*

The flat-roofed building at center under smoke is the carpentry shop of George O. Teats, later to be site of John Deere agency. Adjacent building near photo bottom is the board-sided adobe store of GW Swink, now with a pitched shingled roof. Site of Roy Taylor's Conoco is far right center. Swink's store was reported razed by Denver Post April 21, 1946.

BU Dye built his feed and implement store and a blacksmith shop next to Will Dye's barn. The Cal Seeley family came to Rocky Ford about 1880. They bought and operated Andy Nichol's frame hotel for a few years before replacing it with a new two-story adobe building. The new hotel building had 10 bedrooms, a dining room, and kitchen. It was plastered inside and out and featured a veranda across the front of each floor.

Facing wall above the veranda appears un-plastered, pp. 88, 100, and reveals what may have been a refinement in adobe block production, addition of emulsified asphalt.*

Fine aggregate added to asphalt globules in water suspension, assisted by an emulsifying agent such as soap. This mixture resists water and erosion when used in making adobe.

Water, Artesian Style

One of the five artesian wells completed by Charles McVay and his crew for investors within the period 1895–1897.

pubs.usgs.gov/pp/0052/report.pdf

Men in the photo are not identified nor is the well in the drilling sequence. The sight of such clean, flowing water was a happy experience for townspeople who had been using raw water* from the Rocky Ford Canal or the river. This photo appeared in the government report, also citing Mr. Gilbert who recommended Charles McVay for his well-drilling experience.

> G. K. Gilbert, 1896, *Geology and Underground Water of the Arkansas Valley in Eastern Colorado.* U.S. Geol. Survey 17th Ann. Rept. pl. 2, p. 551–601, 13 pls., 5 figs.

Mr. Gilbert's report, for sale by the Government Printing Office, likewise is cited in:

> *Water in the Dakota and Purgatoire Formations in Otero County and the Southern Part of Crowley County, Colorado, 1963.*

* Raw water could be cleared by filtering through layers of sand and charcoal. Others boiled it as recommended, many did neither. Some directed raw water from ditches near their homes directly into cisterns where sediment was eventually removed after gravity had done its work. Such water was clear and esthetically acceptable, but not safe. Mattie (Swink) Lamon described a method of clarification by adding crushed prickly pear cactus to barrels of water. Particulate was adsorbed to the pulp and removed after settling. Water was clear for use after a second settling though likely would benefit from boiling to destroy microbial activity.
    Paraphrased from Mattie Lamon interview, *Rocky Ford Daily Gazette,* January 26, 1981.

Part 4: Selected Rocky Ford History

A Walk Through Old Town Site

Swink's 1876 Store & Post Office	92	Tom Welch Repair	96
Enlarged photo of front, exposed adobe	92	City Council business, 1926	96
The New and Old Mix	93	The New Town Site	97
Steward Sheet Metal Works	93	Information from Pioneers and Early Settlers	98
Steward Sheet Metal Works storage	94	Author's Observations	99
Van Dyk Insurance Agency	94	Architectural Details of First Buildings	100
Rocky Ford Feed Store	94	De Seeley Hotel cornice	100
De Seeley Hand Pump	94	Shoe Shop facade	100
De Seeley Hotel	95	Rocky Ford Feed Store facade	101
Rocky Ford Obelisks	95	Dye Livery front	101
Santa Fe Railroad	95	B. U. Dye & Son store front	101
A Cottonwood	95	Dye Blacksmith and Repair Shop front	102
Re-platting in 1887	95	Fairbanks Scale	102
Cement Stone Co.	95	City Council note, 1892	102
Johnny Doll Pine Avenue Garage	96		

People see different things looking at old photographs, have different memories and emotions depending upon their familiarity with the subject.

Photographs among the following pages are presented much as received, except for cropping and fitting size to space on a page. Many are scanned from newsprint or faded copies of copies. Some businesses shown in them are without accurate addresses and few were dated. We are fortunate to have some of them at all because of the present state of their condition. Some were found without authorship and have long been in the public domain.

Many photographs in this collection have been provided by amateur photographers, preserving their memories and personal moments in their town's history.

Worth noting is that an amateur loves whatever has been chosen to do and does it often without professional training.   *Author*

Photo courtesy *Rocky Ford Public Museum*

Swink's 1876 Store and Post Office

Santa Fe Railroad end-of-line in Colorado was named Granada in 1873. Rails were extended to Rocky Ford by 1875–1876 with service beginning March 1876 to Las Animas, La Junta, Rocky Ford and Pueblo. George W. Swink was appointed first agent for the railroad since his foresight moving from his partnership with Asa Russell and their 1871 river-side store placed his new store near the tracks.

The time of this photo was well after the adobe structure was board-sided and covered with a pitched, shingled roof. Deconstruction might have been underway, indicated by the missing right side of the roof overhang.

Part of the siding is also missing from this east front view, revealing the adobe behind the studded frame that held lap siding. The structure had a wooden floor and large access doors to the siding track, not visible in the shaded south side. It must have appeared an unappealing structure with its original flat roof.

Kit Carson Road, front of the store, crossing the main and siding track is now Tenth Street, renamed in 1887 when the town was re-platted.

Use of this building since it served as the Swink Store, Santa Fe Railroad as depot, and Rocky Ford as Post Office is not known after 1910 when GW Swink died. The *Denver Post* reported the building razed April 21, 1946.

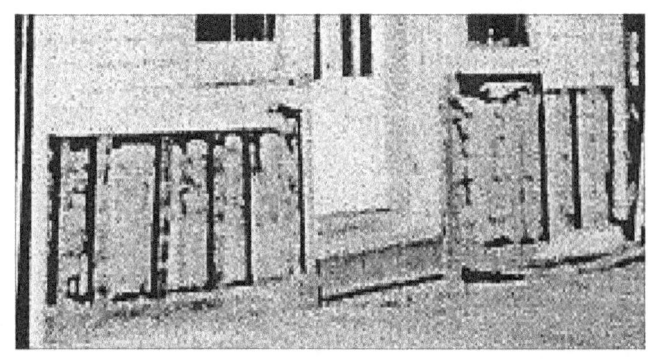

Enlargement reveals weathered adobe wall at store front.

The New and Old Mix

Locating and dating buildings existing before the statute city of Rocky Ford emerged has been a challenge. Not always are locations specific. For instance, George Swink's first homestead in Colorado ..."was above the ford near the river and about 100 acres of the land became an island when the river was high," from John Doll. First structures at Old Rocky Ford were on Mr. Swink's homestead.

A monument, p.296, stands on the east side of SH 71 a short distance south of the river bridge that notes the Old Rocky Ford site about one-half mile east and north on the south bank of the river. Another account with a hand-drawn map shows the original ford about 100 yards to the east and because of changes in the river's course, now is covered by the lower end of a corn field. All trace of the natural materials first rustic buildings were made from having been recycled into the land by the 1921 flood.

First buildings at Old Rocky Ford were similar to wattle and daub with latticed roofs covered with brush and earth. Materials at the site, stones, sticks, and logs were mortared with earth mixed with grass to make adobe. The family structures of Asa Russell, George Amos, and WS Hendricks appeared near the first business building, the Swink and Russell Store, the only one of adobe construction.

Materials for adobe are, grass, plant stems, straw or animal hair used as a binder. These are mixed with soil, preferably with some clay, and water, then formed in wooden frames. When frames are lifted wet mud is baked by the sun to make a hard brick. The knowledge for production and use of adobe was probably supplied by Jose Creo, his wife, and brother-in-law living a little east of the ford in dugouts on the crest of a small hill. Lay of land favors the north river bank for dugouts.

Location of a building by Landmarks and reference points. Neighboring buildings, as in the background of the top left photo p. 48, shows a building extant today, once George O. Teat's General Contractor, Carpenter Shop, Cabinet Millwork, and Electric Floor Surfacing business. The building later housed the John Deere agency. Its roof is visible in the enlargement of a section of the *Frontispiece,* photo p. 89. Its significance; being near site of Swink's 1876 adobe store.

Diagonally northeast across Tenth Street from Swink's Store on the corner of the intersection with Railroad Avenue was Andy Nichol's wood frame hotel, eventually the site of De Seeley Hotel. The same aspect of the De Seeley is present in the photo of Roy Taylor's Conoco. The buildings east of the De Seeley lay in the same direction that later businesses did east of Roy's Conoco in 1929. One of Mr. Taylor's neighbors was **Steward Sheet Metal Works**, fronting on 1004 Elm Avenue.

Facade on Railroad Avenue appears, left, perhaps fronting a former saloon. Steward's Railroad Avenue entrance at center joins the Kitch Pontiac bldg at right.
Courtesy *Rocky Ford Public Library*

Steward Sheet Metal Works storage, below, shows the type of high facade that many first buildings had at the town's beginnings, but this was of cement block. Building façade is partially shown bottom p. 93.

Van Dyk Insurance Agency is the Elm Avenue front of the building at left. The agency at 1006 Elm Avenue, eventually moved to 1601 Elm.

The facade of the **Rocky Ford Feed Store** shows the same type of cornice capping what appears to be milled lumber. The number of courses and type of material is different yet both show a symmetry seen in early buildings.

Hotel De Seeley hand pump, below. Water table was 12 feet. Photos enlarged from p. 88, courtesy *Rocky Ford Public Library*

De Seeley Hotel guests enjoyed access to water from the hand pump at the right front of the building, pp. 88, 94. An enlargement of photo p. 88 shows the apparatus standing over a wooden barrel half. The well location on the NE corner of Tenth Street and Railroad Avenue, if its casing remains, might yet be discovered. *Provenance.* To wit, the discovery of the well casing within the crumbled walls of Bent's Old Fort years after the fort's destruction was a major factor locating inner walls and rooms when the fort was reconstructed. When the Seeley's bought the hotel from Andy Nichols, it was known as **Hotel Welcome Home** as printed in the *Las Animas Leader* January 22, 1878. They renamed it and operated it for a while before building a new structure. Eventual buyers renamed it Rockford, short for Rocky Ford Hotel. The hotel was later razed and the site was eventually replaced by Roy's Conoco, p. 48.

Rocky Ford Obelisks,*on Railroad Avenue, in their original conjoined form stood nearest the intersection with Sixteenth Street, had that street been extended north across the tracks. This site was over Railroad Avenue nearest Curve Liquor (building extant) as we knew it in the 1950s. It is significant town planners designed an approach from the east leading into the first business block between the current Tenth and Eleventh Streets. Railroad Avenue, originally Main Street, was not paved westward of Kit Carson Road for many years.

Santa Fe Railroad, after all, was the reason to move Old Rocky Ford to its new site. Settlers were arriving frequently from the east on their way west to homestead or prospect. West from the obelisks a short distance on Railroad Avenue, but before the appearance of the obelisks, was a wagon camp near the intersection with Eleventh Street. This area was designated by the Santa Fe, on its land, for a place for tired travelers, their horses and mules to overnight and resupply. A **cottonwood** was planted by the railroad that developed into a large shade tree over the years. Its location was pointed out by GW Swink descendant Jerre Swink years ago to Rocky Ford historian John Doll. The tree, then alive but year not recorded by Mr. Doll, unfortunately is not shown in the 1936 *Frontispiece* although several young trees are.

Re-platting in 1887 absorbed the original 1876 plat of William Matthews. That first plat had not adhered to legal limits and boundary measurements. In the process, the new business district was moved one block west and turned right angle to the railroad. Planners likely saw in the original plat a half street developing with businesses on one side and the railroad on the other all the way through town. Since the railroad did not run true east and west, the new Main Street and its business block, now at right angle to the railroad, oriented approximately five degrees east of north. After all, it was easier to move the town.

Cement Stone Company was established 1904 at 209 S Twelfth Street. An alternative to brick and an advantage in faster construction of large buildings became available when the first cement blocks were produced there September 11, 1906. Within a few years the electric generator building, town hall at Eleventh and Front Streets, first high school in 1909, Carnegie Library in 1908, Libby Canning Factory, a warehouse at Tenth Street and Swink Avenue, and the Herring & Griffin and Santa Fe Trail Garages were built using the new product.

---

* An obelisk is a slender, four-sided column tapered to a pyramidal top, as viewed now at the east and the west portals to Rocky Ford. The appearance of the original structure from which the obelisks were separated is shown on p. 330, c early 1900s. This original structure shows the obelisks were modified to support a horizontal member called an entablature or architrave. The architrave in this case supported the large wooden melon and a sugar beet.

Photo courtesy CJ Muth

Facade of **Johnny Doll Pine Avenue Garage** resembles that of the Rocky Ford Feed Store, (pp. 88, 94) but without the cornice.

Rocky Ford Centennial Recollection of the *Daily Gazette* published **Tom Welch Repair** for the April 10, 1987 edition. Then, Tom Welch Repair had been in business more than 50 years at 400 S Twelfth Street. The building appears as in the 1950s. Pine Avenue Garage was photographed in June 2013 some time after exterior painting. The building facade and general appearance has changed little over the years.

Facades, once universally part of building fronts, were disappearing from many Rocky Ford businesses. Few examples remain, such as at left. Often, they were a pretentious 'false front' that presented a building as substantial or imposing, sometimes with large, ornate cornices over false windows. The vertical area provided by the facade was its redeeming feature. The business name was there along with the goods advertised for sale inside.

Many early buildings were unpainted but if the owner afforded the covering, it would be white or more likely gray. The latter seems to have been almost a universal choice, such as the well-known *barn red* of later years. Perhaps technology hadn't progressed in paint formulation. Most likely the gray price was right.

Mr. Welch was known for his welding. His portable generator near his Pontiac was towed many times to farm sites and other places where an arc weld was required. No doubt he also accommodated, as did Mr. Doll, many neighborhood kids whose bicycle tires were casualties of the *goat heads* or *wood tacks** that grew abundantly in neighborhoods, often in the sidewalk joints and cracks.   **Puncture vine*

Both businesses faced to the south, especially convenient in winter when doors were open many days for customers with large vehicles or machinery.

City Council business
Recorded June 4, 1926: Matter of allowing merchants to sell Fire crackers for the 4th of July. Moved they be allowed to sell same the first 3 days of July until midnight July 3, 1926 no fire cracker to be over 5" long.

A Walk Through Old Town Site

The New Town Site grew with development of the historic first business houses described by pioneers. Though this book is about Rocky Ford business in the early part of the twentieth century, some recollections of the last of the nineteenth century are included. Excerpts follow from Rocky Ford businessman and historian John Doll's book and those of pioneers and early settlers' published recollections in local newspapers.

From *The Story of Early Rocky Ford:*
> In 1876 when the railroad was completed through the valley, George W. Swink built an adobe store where the Kit Carson Road (p. 302) crossed the railroad. The Santa Fe Railroad then built a small depot only a few yards from the store and named the station Rocky Ford.

A few years later Mr. Swink built an ice house just west of his store along the tracks to store ice harvested from Swink Lake. The lake area much later would become the Stauffer pens for livestock adjacent their abattoir near the end of Maple Avenue where Nineteenth Street is joined.

> May, 1876 William Beghtol ... hired William Matthews to lay out a six-block town site. There were three large blocks each side of the railroad and one of those blocks lay east of the Kit Carson road. This became the future business block. Swift and Nichols moved their business to the railroad that spring. Andy Nichols built a frame hotel on the west corner of the block cater-cornered across from Swink's store. Swift built a blacksmith shop in the middle of the block.

> In the spring of 1887, the Santa Fe Town Company laid out a new town site which included the early plat of 1876. The town company moved the main business street one block west at right angles to the railroad and laid the new town with the streets running cater-cornered to the old one. This left small triangular tracts where a street was reconciled to the surrounding homestead and township lines.

William B. Gobin came to Rocky Ford April 12, 1887 for the Town Company lot sale. He observed the town then consisted of Swink's store, Swift's blacksmith shop, Seeley's hotel, Dye's livery barn, the station [Santa Fe Depot], school house [Little White School built in July 1877], and homes of GW Swink, John Swift, and Levi Beghtol. These were built in the years between the railroad survey in 1876 and the date of the photograph on p. 88.

John Doll wrote of Will and BU Dye's "... two-story adobe livery barn on the east corner of the old business block built after they arrived in 1877." This location indicates Railroad Avenue and Eleventh Street, but not the first construction on Railroad Avenue. Archives of Colorado State University Library show both 1884 and 1886 as the dates of the photograph on p. 88. The same photo is also identified from 1881 by a resident. Construction of the buildings along Railroad Avenue then would be in the period 1876–1886 including variances.

Apparent differences among pioneers' and early residents' statements about occupants or owners of early businesses was sometimes influenced by their time of arrival in Rocky Ford or change of business location or ownership as the town grew.

In 1894, so many people had moved to Rocky Ford that the Town Commissioners determined to re-plat the town. At that time it was laid out to its present limits [without additions]. The streets were laid out running north and south and numbered beginning at the west side of town. The east west roads were called avenues and named after trees. The houses and places of business also received numbers* at that time.

*The *Enterprise* in 1895 informed residents the town clerk supplied their street and lot numbers.

South of the railroad and east of 14th Street, Garden Place was made up of 2–5 acre tracts, which were laid out a few years before. Blocks in the new plat were 300 feet square, contrasting with the 350 feet of the older plat. Before the land was taken into the town, the houses were built in accordance with the homestead lines. Now they would sit 'cater-cornered' to the streets. Most were later aligned with the town. The little triangular areas, formed where the streets of the town met the county roads, were pushed to the edge of the town in this plat, and many later became parks.   John Doll, *The Story of Early Rocky Ford*, 1987.

Information from Pioneers and Early Settlers

The only house [see p. 303, houses and first structures] at that time [at the arrival of the Santa Fe Railroad in 1876] at the town site was a small adobe residence which had been erected a little while before by George W. Nichols.... Mr. Swink built a large store room and engaged in general merchandising. A large hotel was built by Andy Nichols where the Seeley house now stands, and John Swift built a blacksmith shop a little way to the east. These were the first buildings on the spot where now flourishes the beautiful and prosperous town of Rocky Ford.   Mattie (Swink) Lamon letter, *Rocky Ford Enterprise* December, 1892.

Main Street of Rocky Ford ran east and west, from Will Dye's barn at the east end to the De Seeley Hotel and Swift's blacksmith shop on the west end. Swink's store was an adobe building on the railroad right-of-way.
Mattie (Swink) Lamon letter, *Rocky Ford Daily Gazette* c September, 1967.

Mrs. Lamon's interview is an accurate description of the first businesses in the relocated Rocky Ford. Main Street was actually Railroad Avenue on the north side of the tracks. Will Dye's barn at the east end was at the intersection with Eleventh Street. De Seeley Hotel and Swift's blacksmith shop on the west end, the intersection with Kit Carson Road, later Tenth Street.

North of the railroad, on the northeast corner of Railroad Avenue and Tenth Street was Hotel De Seeley ... East of the Seeley Hotel was a blacksmith shop owned by Frank Hauck ... Also on railroad property facing west was the grain, feed, and implement business of BU Dye and Son.   LeRoy Elser letter, *Rocky Ford Daily Gazette* Aug. 26, 1955.

Swink's store was built on railroad property north of the tracks and west of the crossing that later became Tenth Street. Andy Nichols built a frame hotel on the west corner of the block cater-cornered across from Swink's store.   John Doll, *The Story of Early Rocky Ford*, 1987.

> About 1880, the Cal Seeley family (note, page 303) came to Rocky Ford. They bought Andy Nichol's [single-story wooden] frame hotel and operated it a few years before replacing it with a new two-story adobe building. That building had 10 bedrooms, a dining room, and kitchen. The hotel was plastered inside and out and a veranda was built across the front of each floor.
>
> John Doll, *The Story of Early Rocky Ford*, 1987.

Adobe was covered by plaster stucco visible on the hotel side and lower level front, leaving only the upper front blocks and bricks visible. Plaster was a mixture of lime or gypsum in water or possibly a grout of sand, lime and water.

The new hotel shows both small brick and large block construction, visible at the front (p. 100). Construction masonry is clearly visible in the enlargement but Rocky Ford Cement Brick and Tile Company didn't produce the first large cement blocks until September 11, 1906 at 209 S Twelfth Street. NW Terry's brick yard began production October, 1894. Prior that year *Enterprise* told of a brick yard in the west of town producing brick in 1888. Production of such sophisticated-appearing blocks may have been possible at these yards but none of the three brick yards could have been producing materials timely for construction of the 1881–1886 hotel.

It is possible that bricks came from production sites not in Rocky Ford.* A clay mine at Thatcher, Colorado was known to have provided clay for early La Junta and Trinidad brickyards. The Thatcher Clay Mine was about halfway between the two cities on the Santa Fe Trail road later to be US 350 and the Santa Fe railroad. Possibly some of the material was used in Rocky Ford.

The re-designed plat of 1887 shows an approximate five degree east-of-north aspect because the railroad is not lying true east-west. Therefore, streets at right angle to the railroad lay north by northeast to south by southwest and avenues north by northwest to south by southeast. Mr. Elser's observation that BU Dye and Son '*facing west*' [on Railroad Avenue] agrees with the aspect of all of the businesses on that block. They were facing approximately five degrees west of south. Reference to the city map on p. 61 will help to clarify.

* Brick kilns in Garden City, Kansas, La Junta, Pueblo, and Trinidad, Colorado were operating in the 1880s.

Author's observations

Many photos of the business buildings of Rocky Ford were searched for this history. In the early days of town it is clear that the pioneers did not think of buildings as historic or worthy of preservation. Logs, facades, and adobe, after all, were expedient, but temporary. People thought in terms of usefulness and whether their buildings would eventually need to be changed to accommodate growth. Thinking so, it didn't take long for all those first buildings to disappear. In the middle years of the twentieth century the beauty of design of many brick buildings began to disappear before the modern, less detailed generic fronts that for many buildings appear beneath the distinguished. For some blocks of the city, buildings have been cycled completely to deconstruction. There may be others in the future.

Although this narrative primarily considers businesses on Main Street, Elm and Swink Avenues, much more could be written about other attributes of Rocky Ford. I hope such interest will stir some author in the future to write about them.

Architectural Details of First Buildings

The Shoe Shop facade, below left and center, appears to be of rough-milled thin lumber. Buildings of the early nineteenth century were painted if their use required it and the purse of the owner afforded it. More likely, window frames, doors and their frames received paint and interiors decorated with plaster or wall paper.

Top left cornice of **De Seeley Hotel** reveals ornately-layered brick, capping large block All are coursed with light-colored mortar. Sides of the building and the front above the ground-level veranda are plastered, top left, covering the adobe spoken of by pioneers.

Plaster (lime or gypsum) or a grout of sand, lime and water may have been the material used to cover walls and lower front of the hotel.

Shoe Shop next to the De Seeley is built of chinked logs, center right, with a board roof and a low, shallow-depth wooden facade.

Cottonwood trees were planted soon after town incorporation in 1887. Three thousand were provided by the first town council to be placed on each street three blocks each way from Main Street and the railroad. Many American Elms were also planted between 1903 and 1909 under a later council.

Young trees had to be protected by fine to prevent visitors to town from using them to tether their horses. Horses were eating the limbs while their owners went about their business.

Photos enlarged from p. 88.

Facade of GW Swink's **Rocky Ford Feed Store** at right is of quality milled lumber fronting what appears to be a shingled roof, barely visible. The facade appears painted, as was a well-lettered sign.

Dye Livery, below, is of brick with what may be stone or concrete lintels over doors, windows. Coping or capstone tops the brick. Bricks and blocks in these first buildings precede brick production in the 1888, 1894, or 1904–1906 kilns when brick yards in town apparently began production.

Agricultural Implement Store of **BU Dye & Son** above is of wood with painted sign. The vertical slats apparently act as cover for a window or large opening such as at the right side of this building. Perhaps the lack of shade trees at this time required this innovation.

Photos enlarged from p. 88.

BU Dye Blacksmith and Repair Shop next to Dye Livery is also of brick. It has a shingled roof and wooden facade of vertical lumber supporting a framed, painted sign. The cupola likely serves as ventilator for the whole building while the chimney vents a hood over the forge, the heart of this kind of business.

A man tends the **Fairbanks Scale** as he weighs the team, driver, and his flat-bed wagon. After this weight is known and subtracted from the gross weight which includes the load the driver is after, the net weight will be known for fair pricing.

Photos enlarged from p. 88

First business buildings developed in the new Rocky Ford along Railroad Avenue eastward from Kit Carson Road. The block grew toward what would become Eleventh Street from the former wooden frame hotel on the NE corner of Kit Carson Road and Railroad Avenue. That building of Andy Nichols was sold to Mr. and Mrs. Mrs. JS Seeley who eventually tore it down and built their more substantial hotel.

Main Street in 1887 developed from the original Robinson Avenue, Ninth Street from Washington Avenue, and Tenth Street from Nichols Avenue, known as Kit Carson Road, p. 64. Construction methods were becoming sophisticated, as well as expertise of the contractors and constructors.

Many business buildings and residences date from local brick production in 1888–1894; El Capitan, American Beet Sugar Company, and Hagen building at 400 S Main Street are among several 1900 examples. Large blocks were manufactured by the Cement Stone Company beginning 1906, after opening in 1904, at 209 S Twelfth Street.

City Council note, 1892: The year 1890 was the real beginning of the Fair. There was a healthy spirit of competition developing which led to the organization of the Arkansas Valley Fair in 1892. In 1894 the English Lumber Company agreed to build a grandstand at the racetrack.

Part 5: A Photo History

A Walk Past Local Businesses

Fairground Walls; Post Card	105
Horse Stall, WW II POW Cells	106
Exposition Building	106
Main & Swink Avenue, K of P Hall	107
K of P Hall, Lewis Bros. & Johnson	108
Mural, Mint Saloon	108
Braden's Rexall Drug; Coffee Shop	109
N Main 200 Block, even	109
Dawley Hdw, Furn. & Embalming	110
Masonic Hall	110
Lewis Bros. & Johnson, N Main 300 Block	111
HP Talhelm Bakery & Grocery	112
Cartwright Building	112
J. Wood Peery Cash Grocery	112
Golden Rule Dept. Store, Maxwell Bldg.	113
Block 100 S Main Street	114
RW English Lumber Co.	114
Rocky Ford Trading Co.	115
Arkansas Valley Fair Parade, 1900	116
City Council business, 1902	116
Christmas Decorations	117
Rocky Ford Ice & Mercantile Co.	118
Rocky Ford Bakery & Lunch	119
Hagen-Recker Block	119
Garwood & Butterfield Furn. & Hardware	120
HF Hagen Bldg & Modern Rooms	120
Hotel Best	120
McKenzie Furniture	121
BU Dye House & BU Dye portrait	121
Watermelon Day, 1900	122
Gibson Lumber Co. Photo	122
Grand Opera House c 1913	123
Southern Colorado Power (SoCoPoCo)	124
The Land Office	125
Cheek Block	126
City Drug Store, Ichi Ban Restaurant	127
City Sprinkler, 1919 Truck	128
B&M Implement Co.	128
Rocky Ford National Bank	129
AT&SF RR Depot	130
St. James Hotel, Fire Wagon	131
Recker's Hall	132
Hale Building	133
Gobin Block	134
Gobin Block Businesses	135
WR Bish Hdware & Furn. Co.	136
Lyons & Burmood; First Prize Food	136
A & W Root Beer; W & W Root Beer	137
Weid Building	138
David Stanbridge Post No. 8	138
Hancock's	139
SoCoPoCo	140
Don's For Lad & Dad, Western Auto	141
Gandara Mercantile	142
Pilgrim Holiness Ch.; Pleasure Time	142
Beverage Co.; Plews Motor Co.	142
Cartwright Building	143
The Oasis, Henry's Cleaners, Cut & Style	144
Bender's Clock & Lock	144
Harry Barnes & Traffic Light Pedestal	145
HF Hagen Building; Cad's Cleaners	146
Central Shoe Repair	147
Yoder-Casterline, Inc.	148
McDougal Farm Equipment	148
Rocky Ford Obelisks	149
Arkansas Valley Seeds, Inc.	149
Law Motor Lines; O-Boy Market	150
Rocky Ford Auto Parts	150
Arkansas Valley Broom Factory	150
Berry's Truck Stop; Curve Liquor Store	151
Polly's Café; The Chuck Wagon	152
Huri-Back Lunch	152
Brandt Blacksmith Shop	153
Wilkin's Laundromat; Model Cleaners	153
Hoyt's Tire Shop	154
Rocky Ford Co-op Creamery	154
Spot Café; Shorty's Tavern	155
Otero Co. Health Dept.; City Hall	156
Bish Bros. Lumber Warehouse	156
First Natl Bank; Maxwell Bldg	157
Green & Babcock Lumber	158
Polar Ice Lockers	158
Swink Barn	159
Rhoades Food Center; McClain's Super	160
Ustick Funeral Home	162
Western Motel	162
Lincoln School	163
School Administration Office	163
Washington School	164
Little White School	166
Pollock Hospital; Mexican Cemetery	168
Cherry Corner	169
Grimsley & Keck	170
Jim Montgomery Auto Sales	170
St. John Building; Baker's Jewelry	171
EDCO Metal Works	172
Melon City Royal Service	172
Rocky Ford Food Market; Valley Supers	173
Food Stamps	173
Douglas Mkts; O-Boy Grocery & Cabins	174
Lamplight Lounge; Tobacco Ultd	175
Park Avenue Barber Shop	175
Garry Moore Texaco Service	176
Clark's Food Market, 2nd St side	176
SoCoPoCo, Rocky Ford Station	177
Clark's Food Market, Elm Av. side	177
Bill & Bob's Service; Enco Station	178
Silver's West Side Food Market	179
Chase Auto Repair	179
Borden Plumbing & Heating	180
Evan's Jewelers	180
Rocky Ford High School	181–183
Baseball Team, 1912	182
Businesses of West Elm Ave	184
Coca Cola Bottling Co.; Smith's Corner	184
Johnson's Superior Station	184

Nikkel's Superior Station	184	
Safeway Stores	185	
Park Avenue Barber Shop	186	
Freddie's Corner	186	
Fenlason Realty; Carousel	187	
Rice Seed Co.; Model Cleaners	188	
Unique Cleaners; Henry's Cleaners	189	
Brown Studio	190	
Johnson-Ebert Photography	190	
Chevron Service; Nava Cafe	191	
Dutch & Dutchess Motel	192	
Fenlason Agency; Valley Supply	193	
Wright Motor Lines	194	
Rocky Ford Daily Gazette	194	
Fenlason Agency; Telephone Off.	195	
Mart Lueker Service Station	196	
Jackson Transfer & Storage	196	
Help UR Self Laundry	197	
Bender's Clock & Lock	197	
Gen. Chevrolet; June Chevrolet	198	
Daring Real Est & Insurance	199–200	
Dr. E.L. Morgan Clinic	200	
Roy Smith Model Shoe Repair	201	
Cad's Cleaners; The Music Rm	201	
Ark Valley Fairgrounds Grandstand	202	
First M.E. Church	203	
Wallace Oil Co.; Casa Luz	203	
Rocky Ford Floral Co.	204	
Freeman's Fine Pastries	205	
Beman Building	205	
Presbyterian Church	206	
American Beet Sugar Co.	207	
US Post Office	208	
Rocky Ford Fire Truck No. 1	208	
City Hall; New City Admin. Bldg.	209	
Hancock Real Estate Insurance	210	
Braden's Rexall Drug	210	
Cox's Daylight Donuts	211	
Pete Stout's Skelly Service	211	
Curtis-Erikson Carpet	212	
Claude's Shoe Shine Shop	212	
First Industrial Bank	213	
Dub's Superior Service	214	
High Chaparral Inn	215	
Loaf 'N jug; The Pop Shoppe	215	
Smith's Department Store	216	
JC Penney Co.	216	
Western Motel Cabins	217	
State Bank of Rocky Ford	218	
St. Peter's Ev. Lutheran Church	218	
CS Williams Co.;		
JC Robinson Seed Co.	219	
McKenzie, Used Furn., Appl.	220	
Chamber of Commerce	220	
Harada Farms Daily Fresh Mkt	220	
PJ's Emporium	221	
West Side Farmer's Market	221	
Rusler Implement Co.	221	
Bender's Clock & Lock	222	
Christian Ch., Disciples of Christ	222	
Catholic Church, St. Peter Parish	223	
Mission Deli	224	
William B. Gobin Bldg; Royal Hotel	224	
Farmers Insurance Group	224	
Rocky Ford Federal Savings	224	
Jimbo's Drive-In Restaurant	225	
Valley Ambulance Service	225	
Joe's Service	225	
Don's Bar	226	
Gobin Building; Quality Market	226	
Halle's Dress Shop; Royal Hotel	226	
Diamond Mine Jewelers;		
Hiway Liquor	226	
Easy Wash;		
Melon City Royal Service	227	
George Nelson's Conoco, Elm Av.	228	
George Nelson's Conoco, 9th St	228	
Bish lumber & Feed Store	229	
Grimsley & Keck	230	
Railway Express Agency	230	
Model Cleaners; Oberling Motors	231	
Western Wool Processors, Inc.	231	
Bish Bros. Co.	232–233	
Sunny Side Pharmacy	233	
McKenzie Furniture Co.	234	
Central Shoe Repair	234	
Hotel El Capitan	235	
Kaplan's Clothing; Hardt Hdw	236	
Gambles	236	
Liberty School	237	
Watermelon Day, After The Feast	238	
Road Crew, 1895	239	
Young's Soft Water Service	240	
Bender's Clock & Lock	240	
Huri-Back Lunch and Wimpy	241	
St. Paul's Ev. Lutheran Church	242	
Christine's	242	
Kitch Pontiac	243	
Tastee-Freez	243	
First Christian Science Church	244	
Immanuel Congregational Ch.	244	
McClelland Motor Parts	245	
B&M Implement Co.	245	
Physician's Hosp.; Bauer Home	246	
OK Used Cars, June Chevrolet	247	
Middleton Standard Station	247	
Municipal Swimming pool	248	
Kimsey-Cover Fire	249	
Grand Opera House, 1912	250	
Ticket Booth	250	
Grand Opera House, 1913	251	
Neil O'Brien Minstrel Show	251	
A & M Auto Repair; Auto Clinic	252	
Curve Motel	252	
Watermelon Day, 1901	253	
Colorado Gov. William E. Sweet	253	
Watermelon Day c 1915–1918	254	
Watermelon Day 1893	254	
Watermelon Day c 1900	255	
Watermelon Day 1911	255	
Watermelon Day c 1910–1920	256	
Souvenirs	256	
Watermelon Day (undated)	257	
Watermelon Day c 1920s	257	
Watermelon Day 1894	258	
Watermelon Day (recent years)	258	
Rocky Ford Garage	259	
Dog House; St. John Building	259	
American Crystal Sugar Co.	260	
Encore	260	
North American Dehydrate Co.	260	
Blackford & Baughman Garage	261	
Ada & Robert M. Adams House	261	
Roy Taylor & Star Automobile	261	
Land Office	262	
St. James Hotel	262	
Cantaloupe Café; Fiesta Café	262	
Reynolds Metals Building	263	
Discount Tire; Wright Motor	263	
Rocky Ford Fed. Savings & Loan	264	
Peggy's Café	264	
EDCO Metal Works	264	
Johnson & Govreau Coal	265	
People's Transfer & Coal	265	
Donk's Variety Store	266	
Braden's Drug Store	266	
Southern Colorado Power Co.	266	
JC Penney, Co; Evalynn's	266	
Fraser Dry Goods	267	
Don's for Lad and Dad	267	
Love's Shoe Store	267	
The Oasis; Lee's Barber Shop	267	
N Side Cut-Rate & Package Liquor	268	
Hesteds Store; Kaplan Merc.	268	
Kaplan's Clothing	268	
Beman Building	269	
Hardt Hardware; Gambles	269	
St. James Hotel; Army Navy Store	269	
Cantaloupe Café	270	
Stauffer Food Co.	270	
P & M Café; Karl's Café & Liquor	270	
Trail Café	271	
June Chevrolet	271	
June Chevrolet Used Cars	271	
Standard Credit Co.	272	
Clute Manufacturing Co.	272	
Nikkel's Superior Service	272	
Johnson's Superior Servicer	272	
Motor (Supply) Co.	272	
Rocky Ford Pump House	273	
Hawley Store	274	
Airplane Inn	274	
Southeast Colorado Exposition	275	
Baker Jewelry; Holland Drug	276	
Todd Airfield	276	
People at the Fair	277	
Rench Grocery	278	
Rumsey Grocery & Bakery	278	
Hale Building;		
N Main 400 Block, odd	279	
Rocky Ford Garage	280	
Rocky Ford Auto Co.	280	
Children of School District No. 4	281	
Everson Tabernacle	282	

A Walk Past Local Businesses

Fairground walls evoke memories for generations of fair-goers. *Daily Gazette* July 12, 1990

Dukes and Sever post card, 200 South Main, Maxwell Building at right.

Horse stalls built of adobe in 1938 by Works Progress Administration (WPA) during the Franklin Roosevelt presidency.

Courtesy, *Ruth Muth Grenard*

POW Cells during WWII

These stalls on the eastern bounds of fairgrounds have been repaired and preserved as part of local history. Stalls on the west bounds were torn down and replaced by wire fencing. During WWII they briefly housed German POWs arriving by train.

Open windows with vertical iron bars are opposite these doors and faced a perimeter road around the fairgrounds. Guards easily patrolled the stalls and because they formed a straight line, could stand at one end and observe any activity about them. Roofs sloped toward the rear wall with the only window. Solid interior walls separated each unit.

With the only resources their uniforms and clothes they carried, no attempt to escape was ever reported. Knowledge that they were deep inside central US, totally dependant on government for their care and unable to speak English apparently was enough to discourage escape.   See p. 303, *Notes on Text*.

Units were being used at the Arkansas Valley Fair well into the 1990s. They were designated an endangered landmark by *Colorado Preservation* whose grant in 2007 enabled local volunteers and others from neighboring states to make over 800 adobe bricks in May of that year for repairs.   Courtesy *AVF 2009*

Across the fairgrounds from the adobe stalls this large building stands at 705 N Ninth Street to house events of many kinds during the Arkansas Valley Fair. At other times of the year school district events are held in its large interior.   Courtesy *facebook.com/Rocky Ford*

A Walk Past Local Businesses

Main Street at **Swink Avenue,** view south c 1913. In 1914 the indicated **Kimzey-Cover** building would be destroyed by fire. Rocky Ford National Bank clock at 201 N Main is visible at distant center. Ornate building of **Funk's** and **Economy Variety Store** is at right.

N Main 401, **K of P Hall**, left, chartered September 10, 1896, opened November 6, 1902. **Masonic Hall**, right, was dedicated in 1902. Block occupants were **Fenton Drug Co, Palace Drug Store,** and **Burrell Seed Growers Co**.

A watermelon topped the spire over signs *Seeds*, and *DV Burrell*.

Photos courtesy *Rocky Ford Public Library*.

Knights of Pythias Hall
N Main Street at 401 c 1913. **US Post Office** was once in a corner room c 1902, eventually moved to the present location at 401 N Ninth Street March 13, 1936. Swink Av. at 917, behind the man and tree, was entrance to **Thompson-Claypool Undertakers,** see their ad, p. 329.

Photos courtesy *Rocky Ford Public Library*

Lewis Brothers & Johnson Mercantile Co. opened August 29, 1905 in the **Godding Block** after purchasing **Dawley-Wilson Hardware & Furniture Co.** August 16, 1905.

The latter dealt in hardware and furniture, now adding implements to their stock. Photo above of 300 N Main is from 1910. Beman, Inc. Studebaker, eventually occupied this site.

Mural, left, is on the Elm Avenue side of the former Mint Saloon and Kaplan Mercantile, 208 N Main. A colorful scene faces the Beman Building.

Courtesy *Rocky Ford Daily Gazette.*

A Walk Past Local Businesses

The Coffea Shop, right, eventually occupied the corner at 209 N Main that was **JC Braden's Rexall Drug Store,** above, from 1914 to 1933. The drug store then was moved to 921 Elm. **Dr. JA Lawson** held the second floor at 209½ from 1911–1915 with second address 924 Elm for stairway entrance to second floor. He later moved to 913 Elm and remained there until his death March 22, 1932.

Directly across Main Street stood the Mint Saloon at 208. The building was future site of Kaplan Mercantile with Central Hotel rooms on upper floor interim years.

Photos courtesy *Rocky Ford Public Library*

Photo courtesy *Rocky Ford Public Museum*

September 8, 1898 the entire 200 block of N Main Street east side, above, burned. It started in **Fenton Drug Store,** spread to **Price & Lance Dry Goods** at 200 N Main, to **Kearby's Pharmacy,** then **Gerbing Meat Market** in the brick building, and Colonel Robb's **Mint Saloon** at 208 N Main. Buildings were replaced with brick by 1900 and the saloon again occupied 208 N Main, far left.

109

Dawley Hardware, Furniture, Undertaking & Embalming in 1899 was in business at 300–302 N Main. **Beman, Inc.** located here later with the Studebaker agency.

Photos courtesy *Rocky Ford Public Library*

Knights of Pythias Hall, S Main at 401, and **Masonic Hall** at 411.

Facing page, bottom right, shows 301–315 N Main beginning with the Hale Building, replaced by the First National Bank Building in 1922. Eventually, Empire State Bank occupied. Harry C. Morse purchased HW O'Bryant's Jewelry and opened for business in the post office building 402 S Main June 17, 1895. In 1903 he moved three times on N Main, last to 204 N Main remaining there until his retirement c 1940. In this photo his business was located in the space at 301 N Main, near the first lamp post. The Bernard-Cover Building at 307–309—pointer—replaced the Kimzey-Cover Building destroyed by fire March 4, 1914.

BPOE Lodge, sign at right center, met on the upper floor of the Masonic Hall after chartering in 1909. Elks facility at 301 N Ninth Street was built in 1913–1914.

Lewis Brothers Hardware & Furniture Co. in 1899, formerly HA Dawley Hardware, Furniture, Undertaking & Embalming, 300–302 N Main Street. Business was also former Wilson Hardware and Furniture Store February 1902. Later, known as Dawley-Wilson Hardware & Furniture Company, sold to WD and GW Lewis and AS Johnson. **Lewis Brothers & Johnson**, above, opened Tuesday, August 29, 1905, then changed c 1919–1925 to Johnson Hardware & Furniture Store. February 4, 1928 business was auctioned.

Photos courtesy *Rocky Ford Public Library*

N Main at 419–423, **HP Talhelm Bakery & Grocery** at 419. **Cartwright Building** was site of auto agency for Reo dealership, later Buick dealership. Eventually The Roxy Theatre was succeeded by the Rex at 421 N Main. **J. Wood Peery Cash Grocery** was at 423 uniquely set on the corner between the Main Street entrance of the garage and its Chestnut Avenue entrance across the street from the Pollock hospital behind the El Capitan Hotel.

Courtesy *Rocky Ford Public Library*

Pollock's Hospital, built in 1907, was largely the effort of Dr. RM Pollock who organized the Rocky Ford Hospital Association. The building is extant to the rear of El Capitan facing Chestnut Avenue at 915, across the street from the garage entrance at far right.

Note: July 2, 1924 city council refunded a $5 portion of license tax to Mrs. HP Talhelm whose husband was murdered on the highway (SH 71) to Orday [sic]. H. Talhelm once worked in Stauffer's market.

A Walk Past Local Businesses

N Main Street at 201–209 during a holiday before 1922.* The all-flag decoration suggests July 4 or possibly Fair time. **Golden Rule Department Store** is at 203, **Rocky Ford Grocery** at 205, **Fleak Clothing Company** at 207 and **Braden's Rexall Drug Store** at 209.

Photos courtesy *Rocky Ford Public Library*

This 1909 photo was likely taken from the rooftop of 110 N main, the Jackson and Lawson business. Maxwell Building, 200 N Main with angled front corner entrance is lower right.

Installation of concrete sidewalks, curbs and gutters began 1919 with Main Street paving in 1921 requiring removal of many trees. Trees along the west side of Main Street in the lower photo had been removed before the time of the top photo.

Buildings at 207 and 209 in the 1909 photo were draped with bunting from rooftops to awnings possibly suggesting store or building openings. City Drug Store had moved from 202 N Main Street across to 209, and later back across Main to 200 in 1928. City Drug Store had been in a frame building on the block that burned in 1898.

Other businesses burned then were Price & Lance Dry Goods, Kearby's Pharmacy, and Gerbing Meat Market. New brick buildings were built in 1899 and first occupant of 208 was the Mint Saloon.

*Hale building, top photo center background was replaced by the First National Bank building in 1922.

Block 100 S Main Street, 1920 from near the railroad tracks. The small white building corner at far left behind the wagon and below is the future site of Bish Brothers. In this photo it is the location of **RW English Lumber Company** at 104 S Main.

South Main at 200—building with **Smirl's Shoe & Garment** sign—is the **IOOF Hall**. **First National Bank** opened across the street in the **Hagen-Recker Building**, 201 S Main January 25, 1905. The tall parapet—*pointer*—in the distance is the front of **St. James Hotel** at 300 S Main Street at Maple Avenue. (See pp. 70, 139, for views of the building with and without a parapet.) Horse and auto traffic are now mixed.

Photos Courtesy *Rocky Ford Public Museum*

Reduced photo of that at right when first published in the *Enterprise*.

Both are placed here for sign and resolution comparisons.

Rocky Ford Trading Company

Photos Courtesy *Rocky Ford Public Library*

N Main 100–108 circa 1916. Photo was taken from across Main Street near the afternoon shadow of the triangle railroad crossing sign visible in lower part of this photo and virtually in the photo p. 80.

The building was 50 years old, owned by JW Tracey, recently purchased from WR Bish. Right portion burned May 21, 1949 sparing two buildings left of the arched entryway, protected by the narrow passage under the arch. See also photos bottom p. 136. Fire occurred on a Saturday at the rear of the building at right and above.

Rocky Ford during the Fair. Main Street looking south from Railroad Avenue. Gibson Lumber Company is at right center.

Rocky Ford, 1900 Main St. looking so. west from Railroad Ave. Gibson Lumber Yd. in left foreground.

Arkansas Valley Fair Parade, 1900 *Courtesy Rocky Ford Public Museum*

Horsepower is everywhere on Main Street near the **AT&SF Railway Depot**. Several trains and their passengers from surrounding communities arrived each year for the annual festival.

Railroad Park south of the tracks is undeveloped. Many trees planted beyond the area since 1888 are showing maturity but north and south parks would not have trees and grass until **Gibson Lumber**, later Newton Lumber Company, was moved across Ninth Street in 1906. The depot at this time was a wooden structure built in 1887—top left photo p. 130.

This photo appears to have been taken from the roof of the Maxwell Building, 200 N Main, across Railroad Avenue from **Jackson & Lawson Transfer Co.**, lower left. The wood-sided 1887 depot would be replaced in 1907 by the present brick building. **Pacific House** hotel sign is visible left of center on **Hagen-Recker Hall** Front Street side.

City Council business, as recorded: The origin of **Reservoir Hill**

```
July 29, 1902 -- That a deed be recieved from the parties owning the hill
                 known as the Cullings Hill" and which the City Reservoirs
                 are located deeding said site and right of way thereto
                 from the High Line Canal to the City and fully are exist-
                 ing against the city in regard to said reservoir and
                 right of way. Also the city attorney procure an abstract
                 to title to said site and approve same before closing
                 said deed. Further that he be authorized to pay the sum
                 of $500.00 in full of above.
```

A Walk Past Local Businesses

Christmas Decorations Courtesy *Rocky Ford Public Library*
Chamber of Commerce on December 7, 1937 asked the city council for donation for the first ever Christmas decorations in the city. The year of this photo is unknown. Council minutes indicate a later approval of $50 for street decorations December 2, 1941. Future chief **Clyde Summers** is holding the ladder, other men are not identified. Background left is the **Rocky Ford National Bank** at 201 N Main. **Rocky Ford Trading Company** is at right at 100–108 N Main.

Courtesy *Rocky Ford Public Library*

Rocky Ford Ice & Mercantile Company business began 1905. A previous venture December 27, 1897 began with a group and an ice storage building south of the railroad at 100 S Tenth Street. Rocky Ford Ice and Mercantile bought the building and operated two years before selling to **WR Bish** in 1907. This 1910 photo shows workmen in attendance and at least two carts and two delivery wagons waiting to be loaded.

    Mr. Bish renamed the business **Polar Ice & Storage Company** and began a delivery service. July 1919 the building burned but with little damage to the ice-making equipment. A brick building was built around the machinery while it was still able to produce ice. Mr. RT Walker bought the business in the fall of 1919 and began to offer cold storage lockers until home refrigeration decreased his business. Before development of electrical refrigeration, ice was supplied from **Swink Lake,** located on the future site of Stauffer's livestock pens east of town near the end of Maple Avenue. "Mr GW Swink of Rocky Ford, Las Animas county* has just completed one of the finest artificial lakes in the State. It covers an area of 20 acres, and has an average depth of ten feet." [See pp. 298–299, comments about Swink Lake].   *Rocky Mountain News*, 11 Jan. 1882.

* Rocky Ford was in the new Otero County in 1889 when Bent and Las Animas Counties were restructured.

A Walk Past Local Businesses

Rocky Ford Bakery and Lunch — Courtesy *Rocky Ford Public Library*

Photo is from 1907 at 914 Front Street in the **Hagen-Recker building**. Karl Weid owned and operated this business for many years.

Hagen-Recker Block — Courtesy *Rocky Ford Public Library*

Undated photo of block beginning SW corner of S Main and Front Street. This 1897 building housed Shaw Clothing Store at 203 S Main, **Briscoe Staples & Fancy Groceries** at 201 S Main, and **Pacific House** [hotel] around the corner on Front Street—large sign right of center.

Garwood & Butterfield Furniture & Hardware Store, 400 S Main Street, in the **HF Hagen Building,** c 1913. Construction began July 1900 and Farmers Department Store occupied in 1903. Dobbs & Lyons Furniture & Undertaking c 1910–1913 were followed by Garwood & Butterfield, left, and in 1917–1919, Butterfield's Hardware and Furniture.

Courtesy *Rocky Ford Public Library*

Carl, Sr. and Millicent Ustick bought the Dobbs and Lyons undertaking business in 1913. At the death of HF Hagen c 1903, Mrs. Susan L. Hagen owned, operated, and lived in the **Hagen Modern Rooms** at 402 at right above.

View of the east side of the 400 block of S Main at right shows the **Hagen Modern Rooms** sign just below center. Scene was photographed some time before the appearance of the three-globe street lights appearing above.

Hotel Best with its distinctive balcony over 410–412 S Main remained until its deconstruction in recent years.

Courtesy *Rocky Ford Public Museum*

A Walk Past Local Businesses

Courtesy *Rocky Ford Public Library*

McKenzie Furniture, 400 S Main c 1950s–1960s, occupies **HF Hagen Building**. The 400 block of South Main, both sides of the street, end with family residences at Sycamore Avenue, the **BU Dye** house at 420, far right and below. The **Ada** and **Robert M. Adams** house, p. 261 at 423 S Main, is directly across from the Dye house, both exist today. Buildings between the Hagen Building and the Dye house at 420 S Main have been removed.

Across Sycamore Avenue and the Rocky Ford Canal residences face Main Street toward the south and Washington Avenue.

Photos from *Rocky Ford Tribune* January 3, 1903

Bloomfield Usher Dye moved to Colorado from Ionia, Michigan in 1878 seeking to improve his health.

121

Courtesy, *Denver Public Library, Sub-Folio collection, 20004956*

Watermelon Day September 7, 1900. Enlargement reveals on closest banner, *Welcome*; second, *Dry Goods, Carpets, Furnishings [illegible]*, *Walter's Famous [illegible]*; [*Walter's* might have been Walter's Lager Beer brewed in Pueblo], the third banner, *Rocky Ford [illegible]*.

GR Daring Transfer & Coal Company, and People's Transfer & Coal businesses were at right. Jackson & Lawson at the SE corner of Main and Railroad Avenue were local distributors for the latter but because of poor quality of coal the business soon failed.

At right center were businesses selling Buggies and Wagons. Across Main to the west, **Gibson Lumber Company** occupied the future site of north railroad park—large painted sign. The long, lumber storage building is also visible right center of photo p. 116.

The lumber yard had several managers and names, at one time was Newton Lumber Company. When the existing brick depot was built in 1906 Mayor RM Pollock convinced the railroad managers to move the lumber business across Ninth Street south of the railroad. The park was expanded and planted with trees and grass.

A Walk Past Local Businesses

Grand Opera House c 1913 Courtesy *Rocky Ford Public Library*

This block at 401–406 S Main Street housed **AP St. John Vacuum Cleaning** and **ML St. John Repairs** on the corner, right, at 401. **Charles L. Lawrence Signs**, **Wallpaper and Paints** at 403. **Lena Huguein,** dress maker, **Joel W. Todd,** attorney and notary, Mrs. MJ McMorris, and CA Perry occupied 405–405 ½. Rocky Ford Gazette moved into 407—left archway—from 954 Elm January 9, 1906 when JB Lacy was editor. Grand Opera House originally occupied 405–407. Theatre remodeling was completed August 2, 1930 and after a 30-year occupation from 1902 building burned June 22, 1934.

A&W Root Beer would one day occupy the space at 409 between the theatre and a veterinary and physician's office next building south at 411.

Over the years 401 was site of Van Antwerp Sanitarium and Chiropractors; a confectioner, Henry C. Sherman; Langford Used Furniture at 403; Beauty Nook and Freeman's Fine Pastries at 415; WJ Cleveland, veterinary surgeon and physician and surgeon HE Lovejoy at 411; Ebbert Seed Company, Van Buskirk Seed Company, and DV Burrell Seed Growers Company at 419–421.

Scribner's School of Dancing was at 415½, and the Bijou Amusement Hall at 417. At 423, extant on the south corner with Sycamore, was the residence of Ada B. and Robert M. Adams and Mrs. M. Elizabeth McDermid.

St. John building at 401 and the neighboring building at 403 above have been razed.

Southern Colorado Power Company
N Main Street at 301.
The front of 301, in shadow, faces Main Street, and the side in the sun is along Elm Avenue. The building front is visible in the 1918 photo below.

Courtesy *Rocky Ford Public Library*

North Main Street has changed much from the photo below. Globe lamps have been replaced as well as removal of street intersection markers. Southern Colorado Power Company opened offices here October 26, 1929 on the site of the original Hale block. Second floor held the offices of Rocky Ford School District R-2 after Lincoln School was remodeled. In the future, Family Worship Center would locate here at 921 Elm, then 504 S Tenth Street. Main Street was paved beginning 1921 but had a hard gravel surface until then.

Courtesy *Rocky Ford Public Library*

A Walk Past Local Businesses

Land Office

Courtesy *Rocky Ford Public Library*

Elements of door and window design on front of the 1890s **Land Office** are yet visible in the white building below existing today between **Doc and Bonnie's Café** at 309 and **Rocky Ford Drug Store** at 301 S Main.

A boardwalk is visible and a newly-planted cottonwood tree, one of the 3000 planted after the incorporation of the town in 1887. Trees were planted three blocks each way from Main Street and the railroad.

On April 30, 1896 council minutes indicate the opening of South Main Street with walnut trees planted along its route. The Land Office building housed **Aubert Eye Clinic** in the lower photo. **Archie's Diagnostic Center** sign is left of dormer above Doc and Bonnie's awning.

Photo Courtesy *Rocky Ford Public Library*

Courtesy *Rocky Ford Public Library*

Rocky Ford Garage, Banta-Smith Auto Co. Cheek Building, 419–421 S Main, c 1902.

Building housed the **Scribner's School of Dancing** on the upper floor at 415 ½ with social dancing instruction and dances each Tuesday and Saturday evenings.

Door and window configuration of the current building is as above. The major change has been the removal of the balcony. **Central Shoe Service** moved next door to 415 from 209 S Main and a series of seed growers occupied the lower floor of Walter Cheek's Building, the last being Burrell Seed Growers Company.

Photo courtesy *Matt Mendenhall and Mike Budge rockyfordcolorado.net*

A Walk Past Local Businesses

City Drug Store and Ichi Ban Restaurant

Courtesy *Rocky Ford Public Library*

City Drug Store at left, N Main at 202. **Sam Nishimura's Ichi Ban** [Number One] **Restaurant** at right. Boardwalks in the 1890s were not all replaced yet by sidewalks, fifteen miles would be completed by 1925. The restaurant would move to 310 N Main and City Drug to 209 N Main probably to move into new brick buildings that replaced some framed wood buildings and adobe construction. City Drug would move again to 200 N Main in 1928.

City directory placed the restaurant also at 202 N Main Street, apparently because the same large building houses both businesses in this photo.

Young ladies in this photo apparently were visitors among staff of **Book Stationery Store** somewhere on Eighth Street in the 1900s.

Courtesy *Rocky Ford Public Museum*

Courtesy *Rocky Ford Public Library*

Dodge Brothers Garage
A city sprinkler truck, 1919 vintage, is at work near 406 and 400 N Main Street—behind the truck. Bruse's Variety Store is at 312 N Main, right, across Swink Avenue.

N Main at 404 was undeveloped and the Dodge Brothers Garage at 406 was at one time occupied by **Rocky Ford Garage**, James K. Lumbar, prop., who also once occupied 419–421 S Main Street.

B & M Implement Co., 400 N Main in 1949. Walter Breitenfeld and John Muth occupied the building and dealt in *Case* farm implements and service. The franchise was bought by Paul Kitch whose business at 1014 Elm Avenue, p. 243, was destroyed by fire March 20, 1965. *Sam*, the iconic cast iron Case eagle shown on the corner, escaped damage and was reclaimed by JI Case Co.

Courtesy *Rocky Ford Public Library*

A Walk Past Local Businesses

Courtesy *Rocky Ford Public Library*

Rocky Ford National Bank
Building formerly housed Rocky Ford State Bank. Bank above opened business April 27, 1908. The iconic outdoor clock was removed years ago and currently is housed in the Rocky Ford Public Museum Carriage House. Pedestal lights are at all Main Street intersections.

Rocky Ford National Bank employees stand front of doors flanked by bank signs, seen above. Golden Rule Department store at 203 N Main is

adjacent the bank under awning in the JH Igo building, built originally for Hendricks Brothers.

Courtesy *facebook.com/Rocky-Ford-Colorado*

Rocky Ford State Bank, below, a forerunner of Rocky Ford National Bank in 1900 before addition of the large clock and removal of trees.

Rocky Ford *Centennial Recollections* April 10, 1987

AT& SF RR Depot

Courtesy, *History Colorado, Fred Mazulla Collection 10024501*

"1887—A new combination passenger/freight house [above] was constructed in 1887, being a frame building size 24' x 109' on the site of the present depot.

1906— This depot was moved westward across 9th Str. and remodeled into a new freight house and offices for Agent FG Curran and his seven man crew [below]. Brick sidewalks had been installed on east and north sides."

Note: Santa Fe officials built a small sand-colored station between the tracks a few yards west of Swink's 1876 Store. Ties were placed between tracks and the space filled with cinders for a walkway. No photo has been found of this first station.

1907—The present depot [above] was constructed by JB Betts, probably using brick from Fred Cheek's Brick kilns, commencing December 2, 1906, and occupied March 26, 1907. Also in 1907, the Wells Fargo Company (later known as the Railway Express Company-REA) built the red brick building just west of the depot facing west on to 9th Street.

1936—Retired cashier Norman Clifford advises prior to 1936, the freight crew on 9th Street was moved into the brick depot, resulting in paper work being done at the depot and freight unloaded, stored, and delivered from the old freight house.

1939—A separate implement dock was built west of the depot between the old freight house and the main line. The dock was originally 20 feet wide by 120 feet long, and in the late 1960s was shortened due to deterioration. This was built to replace the dock that was removed with the freight house in 1941.

1941—A freight room and dock (including a scale and foreman's office) was added to the depot in 1941, and several other improvements were made, ... With all functions now being handled at the brick depot, the old freight house on 9th Street was demolished."

Photos and text from DK Spencer, *The History of the Rocky Ford, Colorado Depot*, August 19, 1987.

A Walk Past Local Businesses

St. James Hotel c 1906

Courtesy *Rocky Ford Public Library*

This 1888 building was owned or leased by several individuals during its existence, first by GW Swink and partners who called it the **West Hotel**. There were several changes in management to assuage the partners' concerns over their investment. Mr. Swink then took possession to assure investors of a sound venture. Called **Swink's Hotel**, it was leased to a Colorado Springs businessman who made some changes and renamed the hotel St. James. The name lasted to the razing of the building in 1955 for the construction of Rhoades Food Center.

The fire wagon represents a major improvement over the earlier equipment in the 1906 photo p. 75. Display above and before one of the largest buildings in town at the time, p. 132, was apparently to show the capability of the new fire department.

The first Hose Company organized April 13, 1894. June 5, 1901 Rocky Ford Fire Company elected officers. August 4, 1902 City Council Ordinance 94 created the Rocky Ford Fire Department. January 4, 1906 the city took possession of a new fire wagon, displayed above and on p. 132. Display of the Fire Wagon must have assured many in town after several fires destroyed some frame business buildings. Men in photo were not identified.

Recker's Hall c 1906

Courtesy Rocky Ford Public Library

HF Hagen Building, left, corner of Main and Walnut joins the **Charles Recker Building**. The *Enterprise* stated, the partnership built the "... finest in Rocky Ford and would be a credit to a town much larger."

This 1897 block faced Main Street, Walnut Avenue to the south, Ninth Street to the west, and Front Street to the north. Among the businesses located there were Opera House Pharmacy at Main and Walnut, Craig Meat Market on Walnut, Stark Furniture Store, Daniel's Bicycle Shop, **Wilson's Hardware & Stoves**, Johnson's Undertaker & Embalmer, Rocky Ford Grocery Store No. 2, **The Shaw**, men's clothiers, Gibson and Fenlason Realty Co., Opera House Pharmacy, JT Hill Sewing Machines & Organs, Stark Furniture, and Dr. Seay Moore Kellogg, O. Path., second floor.

The presence of firemen and new Rocky Ford fire wagon appears to have been to display ability to protect lives and property in the tallest building in town. The pressure needed from hand pumps on board would have required much effort of operators but six fire hydrants were also in place as of 1891 to protect the business district. February 21, 1907 the city successfully tested a new pumping station for fire hoses. Center and right parts of this block were fire-damaged in 1952, razed and the area is now site of City Administration Building, 203 S Main Street. Men are standing on the surviving **HF Hagen Building**, Main and Walnut, pp. 146–147.

Hale Building

Courtesy *Rocky Ford Public Library*

North Main Street at 301 to 315, beginning with the 1895 **Hale Building.** This photo predates that of this same block page 111, duplicated below. Hale building was replaced in 1922 by First National Bank building, in turn later occupied by Empire State Bank at 301.

Kimzey-Cover Building—pointer—above photo, was destroyed by fire March 4, 1914. Its **Bernard-Cover** replacement at right exists today on this block.

Visible refinements on Main Street are sidewalks and electric lighting from tri-globe lamps.

Courtesy Rocky Ford Public Library

Gobin Block Courtesy *Rocky Ford Public Library*

Gobin building begins at intersection of Elm Avenue and Ninth Street and continues east on Elm to an alley. Although many changes have occurred in businesses since its construction in 1907, the upper floor has remained hotel space; the **Bolton** at this time and Royal Hotel later.

Near corner site beginning 900 Elm Avenue was once the location in 1891 of the temporary First ME Church, eventually to build north across Elm. Successive church buildings were on the NE corner of this intersection in 1893 and 1906.

Ark Valley Memorials, 701 Elm Avenue. This site was formerly occupied by Hoyt's Tire Shop. Ark Valley then relocated to 304 N Tenth Street and further to 1001 Elm Avenue.

Courtesy *Rocky Ford Public Library*

A Walk Past Local Businesses

Winsor Agency in the Gobin Building, at 900 Elm Avenue, formerly at 916 Elm.

Courtesy *Rocky Ford Public Library*

Millinery Shop of Mrs. Nellie Conquest, right, at 924 Elm in 1910. The proprietor stands third from left. Gobin Building at times housed the **Rocky Ford Army Store, Royal Hotel** and a theater early in history of the building.

Postal card photo courtesy *Doris Baublits*

Preparation at left was to accommodate the *Rocky Ford Daily Gazette* at 912 Elm Avenue.

Courtesy *Rocky Ford Public Library.*

Street level store fronts appear empty on either side of a loan company, right. The Sinclair station of Martel Lueker across Ninth Street appears in the distance, far right.

Courtesy *Rocky Ford Public Library*

135

WR Bish Hardware & Furniture Company at 108 N Main. This building, now with a different front, survived the fire that destroyed part of the original Rocky Ford Trading Company.

South side of the Bish building, left, shows the same three high windows and basement covers as on the Lyons-Burmood site below. N Main at 200, Maxwell Building, is at left in both middle and lower photos.

Yoder-Casterline, Inc. later occupied the corner building at right at 110 N Main where Jackson & Lawson were early occupants dealing in coal, grain, hay, and feed. **Lyons-Burmood** 108 N Main later occupied the building as once did **Big A Auto Parts**, below.

First Prize Foods, left, and **Yoder-Peterson, Inc.,** above, occupied the former 110 address of a Transfer, Coal, Storage, and Feed business on the corner.

Photos courtesy *Rocky Ford Public Library*

A Walk Past Local Businesses

A & W Root Beer

Not A & W

Courtesy *Donna Abert, CD Remember Rocky Ford*

W&W Root Beer, far left in this photo, came into being apparently because of change in the A&W franchise, not from lack of popularity. Few remember there once was an A & W located east of Rocky Ford on US 50, noted in printed history, location lost to memory.

The *Kettles in the Ozarks* and *Lord of the Jungle* were the Saturday Kiddies matinee.

Weid Building (WEID above arch) housed Moose Hall at 950 Front Street. Though active in early years meeting every Thursday, Lodge No. 306 did not endure. The **American Legion** established the **David Stanbridge Post No. 8**, chartered June 19, 1918, and occupied this building.

Aragon's Tavern eventually located here and Post No. 8 moved to its new location at 966 Walnut Avenue. The right side of this building held the painted American Legion logo visible from Main Street, p. 139.

Photo courtesy Rocky Ford Public Library

Memorial Bridge Rededication Veteran's Day November 11, 2015

Photo courtesy *DAR and Susan Brown Holsclaw*

Citizens of Rocky Ford will recognize this bridge over the Rocky Ford Canal on Maple Avenue dedicated first on November 21, 1920 to honor local men who fought in WWI, 1917–1918.

Rocky Ford Woman's Club, active then, sponsored fund drives to build this bridge and another on Walnut Avenue in conjunction with the Presbyterian Church. Daughters of the American Revolution (DAR) and members of the military were there for the ceremony.

A small box (time capsule) with a 1917–1918 servicemen's honor roll was placed in the north wall and bronze plaques placed on both north and south walls. On the south: "A tribute to those who served their country in the World War"; on the north, above: a quotation from Horace:* "I have erected a monument more lasting than bronze and higher than the royal site of the Pyramids." DAR participants in the November 2015 event were from left, Suzie Mathewson; Claralee Stafford, Secretary; Susan Holsclaw, Regent; and Darla Youngblood, Registrar.

*Quintus Horatius Flaccus, 65-8 BC; Roman poet known for his odes.

A Walk Past Local Businesses

Hancock's, 300 S Main Street was housed in the original St. James Hotel building. Structural elements remained through the years, especially of the upper story. White brick was distinctive among Main Street buildings. Street level fronts were sites of several businesses over the years.

Cantaloupe Café once occupied the white store front at right. The St. James parapet, long absent here, is seen pp. 70, 114. Weid building, narrowly visible far left, houses the American Legion with its logo over the 7-Up sign.

Serv UR Self Laundry on Railroad Avenue north of G & K building. The laundry was west and part of the building housing Jackson Transfer and Storage at 201 N Ninth Street.

Photos courtesy *Rocky Ford Public Library*

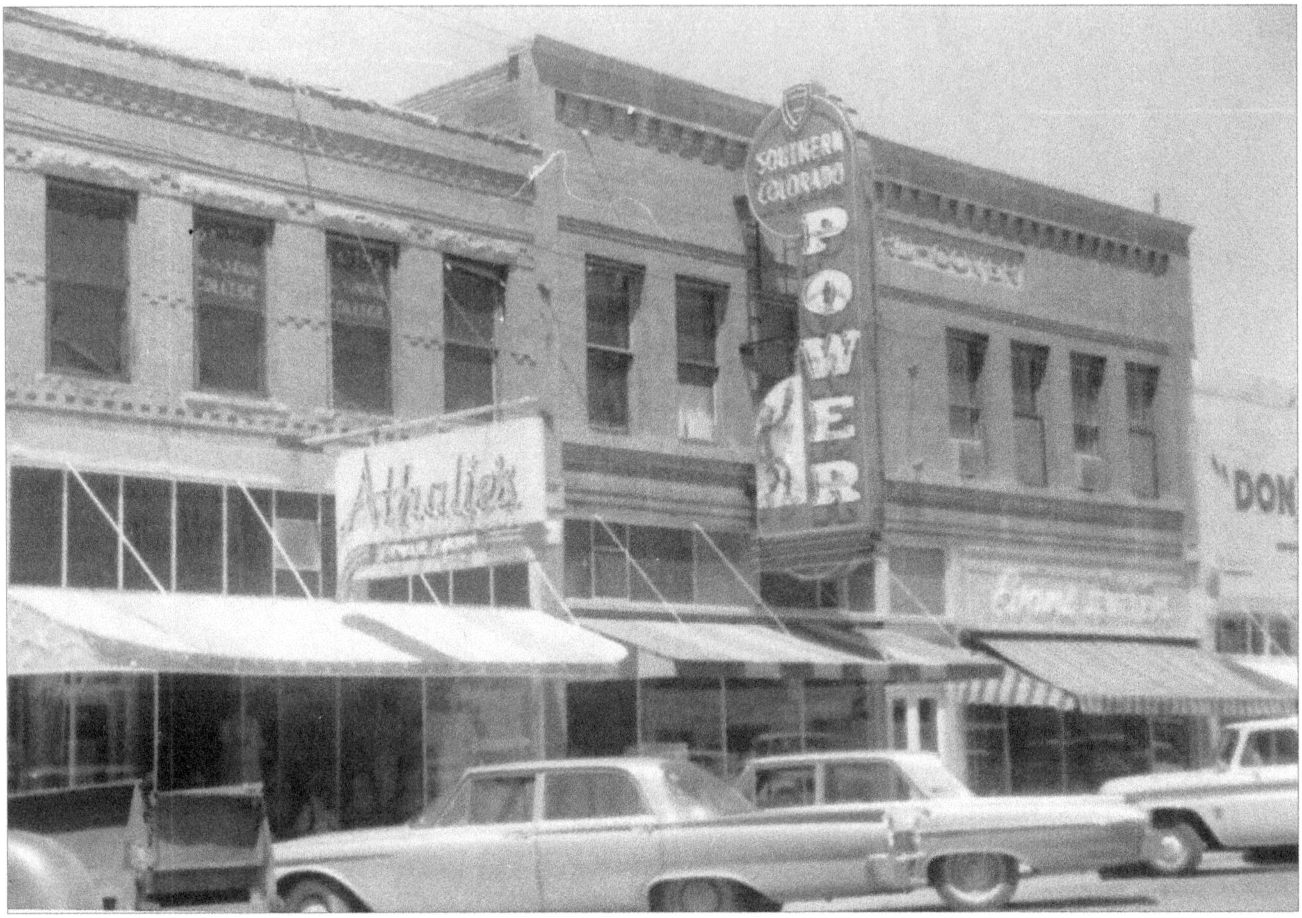

Athalie's, Southern Colorado Power Co., Evan's Jewelers, and **Don's Mens Store** from 305 to 311 N Main Street.

Athalie's occupies former site of JC Penney Co. at 305, Southern Colorado Power Company 307, Evan's Jewelers, former site of Fraser Dry Goods 309, Don's Men's Store 311, formerly The Economy Store. Taller building above and at right is the **Bernard-Cover Building,** successor to the Kimzey-Cover Building destroyed by fire 1914.

Photo, right, shows the **Bernard-Cover** building with **Evalynn's at** 307 and **Fraser Dry Goods Co.** at 309 N Main Street c 1950s.

Photos courtesy *Rocky Ford Public Library*

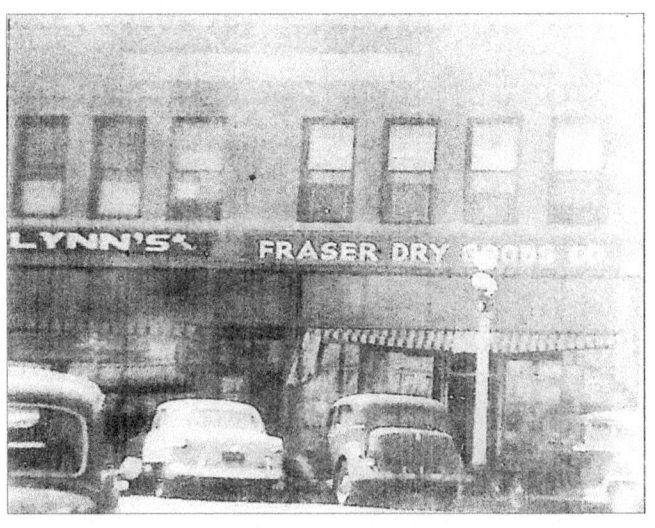

A Walk Past Local Businesses

Evans Jewelers 309, **Don's** at 311, and **Love's** at 313 N Main Street.

Vacancy at 305, former JC Penney Co. is being prepared for Athalie's. *Future* site of JC Mercantile. **Western Auto** is at 307, formerly of 205 N Main, and **Evans Jewelers** is at 309.

Evans Jewelers, far right, would relocate to 400 N Main. Harris Pharmacy would eventually occupy 307–309.

Photos courtesy *Rocky Ford Public Library*

Gandara Mercantile, Alta Vista Camp
1916–1955

At closing of Alta Vista, right, by the American Crystal Sugar Co. all buildings were demolished to make room for the new high school. Community buildings were all of adobe.

Frank R. Gandara moved his stock to this location at 517 N Main and continued his business in general merchandise. At right in this and photo below is **The Berkeley**, now razed, a boarding house at 519 N Main.

North Main Street at 517 was once the Pilgrim Holiness Church, later housing the **Farm Bureau** with Pleasure Time Beverage Company next door at 515.

Pleasure Time Beverage Company at left advertised many flavored beverages for 6 cents a bottle. Plews Ford Motor Co., earlier occupied 511-513-515 N Main, next to the Pilgrim Holiness Church.

Photos courtesy *Rocky Ford Public Library*

A Walk Past Local Businesses

Courtesy *Rocky Ford Public Library*

Cartwright Building
April 1982 photo reveals damaged structure sometime after a heavy snow load on the roof. Cost of reconstruction and safety concerns were considerations in the decision to raze the building.
    Rex Theatre once was located here. J. Wood Perry Cash Grocery, which stood at right, was razed earlier. It had been the site of North Side Cut-Rate Package, Liquor Store and Pool Hall.

City Council business, as recorded:

Address numbers were first assigned businesses in 1894. The number of new citizens and houses then were requiring attention also for location.

```
Feb. 1, 1901 --   Moved that the city attorney be instructed todraw
                  up a house numbering ordinance.  Carried.
```

The Oasis in the **Cartwright Building** at 421 N Main. The history of this building is summarized on pp. 9 and 112 while the building housed other occupants. At the time of the Oasis photo the city's youth enjoyed their own club before a snow storm destroyed the roof, and ultimately contributed to the razing of the building.

South from The Oasis, right to left, **Henry's Cleaners** at 419, **Cut & Style** at 417, and **Bender's Clock & Lock** at 413. The Masons met at 411½ in the **Masonic Hall** building at far left.

Cut & Style building at 417 is seen on p. 278 with its original business occupant.

Photos courtesy *Rocky Ford Public Library*

A Walk Past Local Businesses

City Engineer, Harry Barnes, oversees removal of the town's only traffic control light that functioned since November 17, 1933 in the intersection of Main Street and Elm Avenue. The **Beman Building** at 300 N Main is in the background. Suspended traffic lights were in place and working when the base was lifted onto a city truck.

City Council business, as recorded: July 7, 1950; Moved that 2,000,000 cigarette stamps be purchased. Carried.

Actual stamp size smaller.

Traffic Pedestal in service was signed all four surfaces NO U-TURN painted in large letters. Photos courtesy *Rocky Ford Public Library*

HF Hagen Building 207–209 S Main corners on Walnut Avenue. The site was once the address of Opera House Pharmacy. **Central Shoe Service** at 207 S Main at right once located at 415 S Main, the former site of Freeman's Fine Pastries adjacent the Walter Cheek building, p. 126.

To the far right this building joined Recker's Hall on Main and Front Streets which continued west to Ninth Street. The buildings were joint venture of HF Hagen and Charles Recker. The corner Hagen and Recker portions were destroyed by fire, witnessed by the author on the way to school one morning in 1952. It was razed for construction of the City Administration Building.

Walnut Avenue, south side of the Hagen building looking toward Main, shows the canopy on the front corner of the building visible in both photos. **Cad's Cleaners**, white building, during the life of the business once located at 305 S Main and here at 917 Walnut Avenue. **The Music Room**, p. 201, is nearest the power pole.

Photos courtesy *Rocky Ford Public Library*

A Walk Past Local Businesses

HF Hagen building 207 S Main Street

Central Shoe Repair in the north store front at 209 S Main has a new sign and retains 'Service' in the name on the front window just above the car hood. Business would eventually move to 415 S Main Street.

New city Administration Building was built on this block in the 1960s requiring the deconstruction of the remaining HF Hagen Building.

Former office of Dr. Seay Moore Kellogg, Osteopathic Physician, occupied the suite directly above Central Shoe Repair c 1911. See his signed second-story window in photo p. 132.

Architectural artwork is apparent in construction of many early Rocky Ford brick buildings. The Front Street view of the Recker building, p. 119, was not as ornate as its front on Main Street.

Photos courtesy *Rocky Ford Public Library*

Yoder-Casterline, Inc., 110 N Main Street. The SE corner of Railroad Avenue and Main Street, above, was site of Yoder-Casterline, Inc, next door to **Lyons-Burmood** at 108.

Building, right, was **Yoder-Peterson**, formerly the site of McDougal Farm Equipment Service, bottom photo. Elevator in the distance along Railroad Avenue belonged to Heil Bean at this time with offices later located at 110 N Main.

An addition to the left side of the building near the railroad tracks is on or near the site of Swink's 1876 store, reported demolished by the *Denver Post* April 21, 1946 edition.

Photos courtesy *Rocky Ford Public Library*

McDougal Farm Equipment
109 N Tenth Street.

In the 1920s this building was the carpentry shop of George O. Teats millwork and cabinetry business—background of photo top left p. 48.

A Walk Past Local Businesses

Rocky Ford Obelisks

Gateway obelisks on Railroad Avenue were early used for advertising at the east entrance to Rocky Ford.

Joe Yoder, Hazel Stevens, and Bob Appleman stand at right with one of their trucks in 1948. Their business, **Arkansas Valley Seeds, Inc.** is located at 100 S Twelfth Street.

Obelisks were separated and moved January 30, 1967, one to the west curve at Huri-Back Park and the other to the east entrance of town, both near US 50. (See p. 330 for appearance of the original structure c 1920s.)

Photos courtesy *Rocky Ford Public Library*

Law Motor Lines, 1315 Elm Avenue   Photos courtesy *Rocky Ford Public Library*
Sinclair products and a popular café were parts of this business. **Rocky Ford Auto Parts**, below, 1009 Elm Avenue, extended east from the original **Arkansas Valley Broom Factory** at 1007 Elm Avenue, left below, to include the former **O-Boy Market** site at 1021 Elm.

Family of Betty Gobin Winsor stand in front of the Broom Factory, left.

O-Boy Market, right, before removal.

A Walk Past Local Businesses

Berry's Super Service, US 50 curve, Fifteenth and Elm Avenue offered multiple services for both autos and trucks.

Across US 50 from Berry's was **Curve Liquor Store** near the obelisks once standing over Railroad Avenue rear of the building. This photo was taken in January 1967 as the obelisks were being removed. One remains at left to be loaded and moved.

Text for p. 150 bottom three photos:

Rocky Ford Auto Parts business, center p. 150, represents several additions over years that extend east along Elm from the former Arkansas Valley Broom Factory to include O-Boy Grocery and Cabins site. Rocky Ford Auto Parts site was later occupied by NAPA. Broom factory was the enterprise of Paul I. Gobin and George R. Cameron. RD Lewis Fruit Company occupied the building later. He was known by some as *'Banana Lewis'* for the large bright illustration of same on his delivery trucks. Across Elm–US 50 to the south was the Luetcke Pontiac Company, and later the Kitch Pontiac Agency at 1014 Elm Avenue.

Polly's Café, 1701 Elm Avenue on east curve US 50, is closed. Chuck Wagon, formerly at 601 Elm Avenue, center, and the **Huri-Back Lunch Room** at 210 Elm, below, have been razed.

Tank 'N' Tummy eventually occupied 601 Elm Avenue. Current business offers *Fresh Pop Corn* and *Pop Corn Balls*.

Photos courtesy *Rocky Ford Public Library*

Good Food once served here is now a memory.

A Walk Past Local Businesses

Wilkin's Laundromat

Brandt Blacksmith Shop building on Swink Avenue near the intersection with Second Street for many years was owned and operated by the grandfather of Don Wilkins. It became the business site of Wilkin's Laundromat, right.

Photos above are of 312 S Main

Don Wilkins also once owned and operated **Model Cleaners**, the business of Bob and Esther Nagel at 900 Walnut Ave, below.

Although the store front is changed, brickwork and window outline above the awning and around the sign appear the same. Model Cleaners building was razed in 1985.

Robertson Dairy was behind the location above at 963 Maple Avenue facing McKenzie Furniture.

Photos courtesy *Rocky Ford Public Library*

Hoyt's Tire Shop, 701 Elm Avenue. *Future* site of Ark Valley Memorials.

Photos courtesy *Rocky Ford Public Library*

Rocky Ford Co-operative Creamery, Seventh and Elm. Milk and cream separated on farms were brought here. Farmers were paid per pound weight of butterfat content. Rocky Ford's first creamery was owned by LW Babcock at 1300 Elm Avenue in 1897. Building above was built in 1915, closed in 1982 due to lack of milk production on farms.

A Walk Past Local Businesses

Spot Café at 912 Swink Avenue was at one time the bus stop for Continental Trailways Bus Lines, a function also shared with City Drug Store and El Capitan over the years. The *viga* or log roof/ceiling beam appears here and at the rooflines of Rocky Ford National Bank building and the Maxwell building site of Walker's Men's Store at 200 N Main.

Construction plans of the WPA for the Post Office in 1935–1936 include a review of the immediate neighborhood that indicated the Spot Café is of adobe construction and that a "filling station" was across Swink Avenue at 901, the *future* Cherry Corner.

Shorty's Tavern, white-front with 'Beer' sign at 411 S Main, was owned by a quiet couple who lived in the upper apartment. Their generosity toward *Gazette-Topic* carriers, daily assembled rear of their place and the *Gazette* office at 415, was to give each who asked a candy bar from their freezer.

Gazette office, 415 S Main, would eventually become site of Freeman's Fine Pastries. Office and clinic of Dr. CR Schuth at 413 S Main Street was left of Shorty's Tavern.

Photos courtesy *Rocky Ford Public Library*

Otero County Health Department building at 207 next to the fire chief's house at 205 S Ninth Street.

City Hall at 203 and the **Fire Department** at 201 S Ninth Street.

Bish Brothers Lumber Warehouse near the railroad looking south on Ninth Street toward the Fire Department, City Hall, and County Health Department. HA Dawley Hardware originally occupied both lumber and hardware buildings with curved facades.

Photos courtesy *Rocky Ford Public Library*

Rocky Ford National Bank at 201 and **Holland Drug** at 203 N Main Street in 1949.

Fashion Center and future Walker's Men's Wear site, 200 N Main. Building in 1949 was stuccoed brick, as was the bank above and Grand Theatre. Site was the **Maxwell Building,** a favorite spot for a roof-top vantage point for photographing Arkansas Valley Fair and other Main Street events. Note the use of roof *viga* here and on pp. 155, 175.

Photos courtesy *Rocky Ford Public Library*

Courtesy *Rocky Ford Public Library*

Green and Babcock Lumber, 102 N Tenth Street. Small signs at left on the facing of the lumber barn advertise brand products offered by the business. Future site of Brewer Construction Co.

Courtesy *Rocky Ford Public Library*

Polar Ice Lockers at 100 S Tenth Street, across tracks south of Green and Babcock, was also site of **Rhoades Meat Processing Department**. Ice production or cold storage-related businesses have operated here since 1897 with Rocky Ford Ice and Mercantile Company. Many rural families stored their frozen foods here before rural electrification in the 1940s.

A Walk Past Local Businesses

Swink Barn

Courtesy *Rocky Ford Public Library*

This large barn, familiar sight to many, seemed little-used for years.

A March 22, 1977 council note published; "Fire destroyed the hugh old historical (sic) barn at south city limits. Barn was built of lumber which George W. Swink purchased at the St. Louis World's Fair in 1904."

The barn was just south of the conjunction of Cottonwood Lane with Lincoln Street.

Courtesy *Rocky Ford Daily Gazette* issue March 22, 1977

Rhoades Food Center

**Shopping Center
Hancock's** and **Rhoades**

**McClain's Super
& Model Cleaners** at far right.

Photos courtesy *Rocky Ford Public Library*

A Walk Past Local Businesses

"Rocky Ford History Coming Down" was the headline May 2, 1985 when the announcement was made that the McClain's Super Foods building would soon be razed for a new parking lot to be built on the south side of a new building.

The building site over many years had been location of a bakery, a theater, Citizens Utilities, and the first business at 300 S Main, the St. James Hotel. The hotel was new in 1888 and lasted until 1955 when it was taken down and replaced by **Rhoades Food Center.**

The three photos of p. 160 show some of the changes that happened on this block over the years along with the building occupants in business there. Two photos on p. 24 show the block as it appeared in the 1920s, more than thirty years after construction in 1888.

New McClain's Super, view from the south.

OB and Ben Stauffer opened their meat-cutting shop on this site in 1905. They had been operating since 1902 at 917 Walnut. As their business grew, it was expanded into adjacent spaces on the block. A major remodeling was finished in 1955 for Rhoades Food Center and Stauffers moved business to their packing plant on the east side of town.

McClain's Super Foods in the photo at bottom of p. 160 received its all-metal front in 1961 and new entrance on the north side to make customer access easy from the parking area. The news article told of retail groceries in business in this location for at least 80 years. Two of the earliest ones were the Public Grocery and Market in 1897 and Delmonte Grocery sometime later. Dairy Bake Shop located on this block in later years and the theater referred to above was the Gem Theatre, a meeting place for public social events such as plays, and readings.

Far right of bottom photo on the foregoing page was Model Cleaners at 312 S Main. That building, also shown at center p. 153, would be demolished to make room for a parking area on the south of the new McClain's Super.

Photos courtesy *Rocky Ford Public Library*

Ustick Funeral Home at 305 N Eighth Street. The family of CM and Millicent Ustick lived to the north, right, at 307. The business, once known as Ustick Undertaking Company, was formerly located at 918 Elm Avenue in the Gobin Building. Successions of this business were Ustick, Donelson, Johnson and Ford Ustick.

Western Motel, 515 Elm Avenue. Cabin views rear of the office, pp. 192, 217.

Photos courtesy *Rocky Ford Public Library*

Lincoln School at 601 S Eighth Street would eventually become the **School District Administration Building**. The transition from the 1915–1916 original structure's red brick to stucco and paint is below left, now in the area known as Lincoln Park. The flag at half-mast is for an unidentified event. A favorite place for students, some in photo below right, to visit at lunch time was Leroy's Grocery just south of the school at 723 S Eighth Street.

Photos left and above courtesy *Rocky Ford Public Library*

Lincoln School students pose for a class picture c 1943.

Photo courtesy *Sam Hernandez*, center

Washington School first opened for classes fall of 1889 when Rocky Ford was part of Bent County. County commissioners decided the school be built south of town near Washington Road where were few houses in the area. Photo from author's personal collection

The author's boyhood home dates from 1885, extant on Thirteenth Street east of the school. Many students walked to Beek's Grocery, 1100 Pine Ave, during lunch hour to spend their pennies. Author stands right of the Elm tree on school grounds, winter 1942–1943.
  When the first half of the school was built in 1889, top photo p. 165 "... the town folks pitched in and built a board sidewalk to the school." Pioneer William C. Steele, *Rocky Ford Tribune*, 1917.
  Streets were roads, many unpaved almost through the 1940s. City Council authorized the paving of US 50–Elm Avenue in 1933 but only Main Street had been paved by 1936. Other streets were paved beginning 1937 and for several years after.
  Student enrollment in 1896 was 440 in Rocky Ford schools requiring additional classrooms. Space was used in the original frame and adobe Recker building at Front and Main Streets. Other classes were held in one of the store rooms of the St. James Hotel. The school board issued bonds to raise money for a new school [Liberty] to be built on the block where the Little White School was on Tenth Street between Swink and Chestnut Avenues. Washington School was also enlarged for more classrooms and offices, the final construction in 1902.
  Photos this page and bottom p. 165 show the building after it was enlarged with additions of steel upper floor fire escapes. City Council notes that a fire destroyed the school's outbuilding, the nature of building not given. The school appeared in the 1920s as in the bottom photo page 165 after white paint covered the brick. Painted exterior remained into 1954 when the school was razed and became site of Pioneer Memorial Hospital in the 1960s. That building was later to become part of Pioneer Nursing Home, 900 S Twelfth Street.

A Walk Past Local Businesses

Washington School, c 1889

Photo courtesy *Rocky Ford Public Library*

Washington School c 1920s
Photos courtesy *Rocky Ford Public Museum*

Washington fourth or fifth grade class of 1904, no doubt some of the city's future leaders.

Pueblo Chieftan February 25, 1988
David Vickers photo

Little White School

The first school building in Rocky Ford stood two blocks north of GW Swink's timber claim, now part of the fairgrounds. Site was between the timber claim and original six-block town site of William Matthews. Size of the original adobe school was 15 feet square with seats and desks for 20 students in four rows of five.

School was near Swink Avenue intersection with Tenth Street and a cemetery with graves of two people struck by lightning July 1877 while the school was being built. Originally adobe in 1877, the school was covered with wood siding and painted white after being moved to the future Liberty School site. [Apparently, adobe was removed prior final move to 407 N Twelfth Street]. The name 'Little White School' became common after the painting. Additions in 1896 made it possible to house 60 students.

"Rocky Ford has 356 pupils in the schools, and more are added each week. The Old School ... has been enlarged by adding a room and now accommodates 60 small pupils."

Enterprise November 9, 1896

The need for classroom space grew as the number of students increased. Citizens, anticipated the growth and had approved the construction of the first part of Washington School in 1889 at the southern edge of town. Need for the Little White School decreased

Construction of Liberty School began in 1899 requiring the relocation of the Little White School. School and burial remains were moved, the burials re-interred at the current cemetery and the school moved to 407 N Twelfth Street.

"Mr. Marble has purchased the Little White School from superintendent Hendricks. It will be moved to a lot he bought of Senator Swink, where it will be rebuilt for a rental property."

Enterprise October 1, 1897

In 1922 Roxaena Altheide, daughter of GW Swink, bought the school and remodeled it for a home which she rented. Between 1922 and 1976 the building had several owners, the last being La Clinica at 405 N Twelfth Street next door. The building, at its new location, is preserved as an Otero County Historical Building.

A Walk Past Local Businesses

Rules for Teachers 1872
1. Teachers each day will fill lamps, clean chimneys.
2. Each teacher will bring a bucket of water and a scuttle of coal for the day's session.
3. Make your pens carefully. You may whittle nibs to the individual tastes of the pupils.
4. Men teachers may take one evening each week for courting purposes, or two evenings a week if they go to church regularly.
5. After ten hours in school, the teacher may spend the remaining time reading the Bible or other good books.
6. Women teachers who marry or engage in unseemly conduct will be dismissed.
7. Every teacher should lay aside each day a goodly sum of his earnings for his benefit during his declining years so he will not become a burden on society.
8. Any teacher who smokes, uses liquor in any form, frequents pool or public halls, or gets shaved
   in a barber shop will give good reason to suspect his worth, intention, integrity and honesty.
9. The teacher who performs his labor faithfully and without fault for five years will be given an increase of twenty-five cents per week in his pay, providing the Board of Education approves.

Country School Legacy found in http://platteriver.unk.edu/SchoolRoom.htm.

Rules for Students 1872
1. Respect your schoolmaster. Obey him and accept his punishments.
2. Do not call your classmates names or fight with them. Love and help each other.
3. Never make noises or disturb your neighbor as they work. Be silent during classes.
4. Do not talk unless it's absolutely necessary.
5. Bring firewood into the classroom for the stove whenever the teacher tells you to.
6. If the master calls your name after class, straighten the benches and tables, sweep the room, dust and leave everything tidy.

Rules for Teachers 1915
1. You will not marry during the term of your contract.
2. You are not to keep company with men.
3. You must be home between 8:00PM and 6:00AM unless attending a school function.
4. You may not loiter downtown in ice-cream stores.
5. You may not travel beyond the city limits unless you have permission of the Chairman of the Board.
6. You may not ride a carriage or automobile with any man unless he is your father or brother.
7. You may not smoke cigarettes.
8. You may not dress in bright colors.
9. You may under no circumstances dye your hair.
10. You must wear at least two petticoats.
11. Your dresses must not be any shorter than two inches above the ankle.
12. To keep the schoolroom neat and clean you must: Sweep the floor at least once daily; Scrub the floor at least once a week with hot soapy water ; Clean the black board at least once a day; Start the fire at 7:00 AM so the room will be warm by 8:00 AM

Principles of Teaching found in http://teacherworld.com/potrules.html

The above rules have been either attributed to various sources or claimed by as many others over the years. All are suspected fraudulent by some authorities who are unable to verify origins.

Pollock Hospital, established 1907

Dr. RM Pollock worked in one of the town's pharmacies for a while, received his medical degree in 1895 and practiced medicine while serving as mayor three consecutive terms, 1903, 1905, and 1907. One of his passions was to develop city parks. He supported the building of the road on Reservoir Hill, planting grass and trees in Railroad Park, installation of curbs and gutters, street parking and the building of the library. He provided for the development and installation of a sewer system and city water supply while he promoted building a new depot.

Photo enlarged from 1935-1940 vintage postcard, p. 8.
Courtesy *Rocky Ford Public Library*

Photo below is thought to be a section of the cemetery designated **Mexican Cemetery**. Other parts of the cemetery were similarly made up of family areas, some reflecting an ethnic design in markers and artwork on headstones. The area pictured is believed to be owned by Otero County.

Photo courtesy *Rocky Ford Public Library*

A Walk Past Local Businesses

Goeringer Realty, center, and later Hancock Real Estate occupied this site. The service station this location was identified in WPA construction plans for the post office, p. 155 and below. Corner of the post office is visible at below left behind the realty sign.

Cherry Corner. This drive-up building was once a service station. The concrete service island and pump base remain in front. Located at 901 Swink Avenue, Cherry Corner was popular with RFHS students a block north at 801 Chestnut Avenue.

This 1935 photo by US Department of the Interior, National Park Service shows a view to the east over excavations for the current post office. The service station, placed at an angle on the corner of Ninth and Swink, is visible upper left. Cherry Corner is the remnant of that building.

The rear of the Knights of Pythias building at 401 N Main Street appears behind the station.

Photo courtesy US Department of the Interior, National Park Service, *National Register of Historic Places.*

Grimsley & Keck Company 101 N Ninth Street, home of **Allis-Chalmers** farm equipment.

Jim Montgomery Auto Sales occupied G & K building later. Photos courtesy *Rocky Ford Public Library*.

A Walk Past Local Businesses

St. John Building at 401 S Main with **US Department of Agriculture, Office of Employment** in the corner office. *Future* site Helmut Kienitz Bible Book Store. Building has been razed.

Baker's Jewelry, Gobin Building at 920 Elm Avenue, at one time at 205 N Main Street. This was the first site of Gobin, Inc., later Crosswhite Realty. Earl's Barber Shop is far left, barely visible.

Photos courtesy *Rocky Ford Public Library*

Edco Metal Works at 1315 Elm Avenue. The glazed block of the original Law Motor Lines building is under a coat of paint.

Melon City Royal Service at Twelfth Street and Swink Avenue. The large building at right is La Clinica del Valle at 405 N Twelfth Street. This station was across the street west of the Catholic Church at 1209 Swink Avenue.

Photos courtesy *Rocky Ford Public Library*

A Walk Past Local Businesses

Valley Supers occupied our building from 1957 to 1980. Originally built as a bowling alley it was converted into a grocery store that faced on Elm Avenue in about 1954. In 1981 when Shannon Torgler purchased the store he completely remodeled it and moved the main entrance to Swink Avenue on the north side.

In 1985 Dick and Debbie Jones purchased the store from Torgler. In 1986 we became a member of Affiliated Foods and we recently began giving Blue Stamps.

Rocky Ford Food Market

Dick and Debbie Jones described the former **Valley Supers** and their Rocky Ford Food Market business for the 1987 Centennial Celebration in Rocky Ford. Photos and their words were printed in *Recollections* of the *Daily Gazette* April 24. Building now is occupied by Family Dollar, 1275 Elm.

Bowling alley referred to on p. 170 and above was Ra-Nels Bowling Lanes, a shortened version of the names of the two owners, **Ray**mond and **Nels**on.

Courtesy *Rocky Ford Daily Gazette*

A pair of credits for future purchases in the Food Stamp Program offered by Valley Supers.

173

Douglas Markets at 500 S Twelfth Street is an example of a *Mom & Pop store*. Rocky Ford Canal was at left near this store and living quarters. Property, formerly Wolfmeyer Grocery, was operated by Fannie and Emmet A. Wolfmeyer proprietors c 1950s.

O-Boy Grocery and Cabins at 1021 Elm Avenue. This building was razed for construction of Rocky Ford Auto Parts at 1009 Elm Avenue. This market may have been a Mom and Pop at an earlier time. Bailey's Grocery, 604 Chestnut was another two blocks west of the high school.

A Walk Past Local Businesses

Lamplight Lounge and **Tobacco Unlimited**, businesses on Swink Avenue side of 400 N Main Street. Building is future site of the Old Star Bar in the Lamplight Lounge.

Park Avenue Barber Shop on Railroad Avenue in the sunlit distance, sign above trunk of car. Benches at center mark the place of long-time resident shop owner Frank H. Boraker, p. 16.

Photos page 174–175 courtesy *Rocky Ford Public Library*

Courtesy *Rocky Ford Public Library*

Garry Moore Texaco Service at 1001 Swink Avenue, later to be Midtown Texaco.

Clark's Food Market at 208 N Second Street was among the first buildings motorists encountered when entering Rocky Ford at the west curve. Cabin rental, right rear, was part of this business. Courtesy *Rocky Ford Public Library*

Clark's Grocery and **Camp**
Another view from Elm Avenue is on facing p. 177. Building was razed for construction of **Matthews & Sons Electric**, below, at 210 Elm Avenue. Courtesy *facebook.com/Rocky.Ford*

A Walk Past Local Businesses

Southern Colorado Power Company, the new power plant on the 200 block of S Eleventh Street near Front Street. April 3, 1950 was ground-breaking for the station which functioned well for several years until an internal explosion eventually resulted in razing of the building.

Leo and Bill **Clark's Food Market** faced Elm Avenue but addressed at 208 N Second Street, (see facing p. 176).

Photos courtesy *Rocky Ford Public Library*

Bill and Bob's Service 902 Walnut Avenue between Main and Ninth Streets. This location was their second. First location was at 208 S Main Street, below. The 1920s location of Smith's Café was 206 S Main—Pepsi Cola sign below. Toggery, Men's Clothing & Furnishing located there later.

Enco Station building, was previously owned by Champlin Oil, Howard Reynolds, and finally Ira and Rex Ellis. Building was moved to US 50 east to Mameda property and now houses Colorado Produce. Across Main from this future Bill and Bob's, known as the *Smith Brothers*, was the earlier Red Cross Pharmacy at 209 S Main Street, GA Blakely, proprietor and jeweler, and William Grossarth, later circa 1911–1915.

Photos courtesy *Rocky Ford Public Library*

A Walk Past Local Businesses

Silvers West Side Food Market, Third Street at Elm Avenue. Site once housed Curtis-Erickson Carpet and Wards. Mars Nite Club was on Elm Avenue, eventually to be R&R Nite Club, BB Nite Club and B&B Liquor at 220 Elm Avenue across US 50–Elm Avenue.
Chase Auto Repair, below, 1410 Elm Avenue. The property also offered rental cabins, right in the trees, bordering on Railroad Avenue to the south. Fourteenth Street is to the right foreground.

Top and bottom photos courtesy *Rocky Ford Public Library*
Nite Club photo courtesy *https://www.facebook.com/rocky.ford*

Evan's Jewelers is here located at 400 N Main Street across the street from **JC Penney, Co.** at 401 N Main. A former JC Penney location was 305 N Main, lower photo p. 141.

Borden's Plumbing and Heating 404 S Main. Borden's is also visible in the block photo page 121. **Chamber of Commerce** is next door at left, one of the many locations the chamber has occupied over the years. The Borden address in 1914–1915 was that of Mehlin & Sons, Records and Musical Merchandise, still later shoemaker Anderson E. Morris would locate there.

Photos courtesy *Rocky Ford Public Library*

A Walk Past Local Businesses

Rocky Ford High School opened June 20, 1908 at 801 Chestnut Avenue when boardwalks were common in much of town. Chestnut Avenue was not yet paved.

Courtesy *Rocky Ford Public Museum*

Trees were maturing; the building appeared as on p. 182 in 1918 before the remodeling into its configuration on p. 183. That building stood until a new RFHS was built at 100 Washington Avenue, west of Play Park Hill.

Photo courtesy *Rocky Ford Public Library*

Rocky Ford High School photo c 1918

Courtesy *Rocky Ford Public Museum*

RFHS Baseball Team
Champions of the 1912 Southern Colorado-Northern New Mexico League. Team photo, p. 31, was pro or semi-pro, based in Denver. This RFHS team predated the *Meloneer* name and dominated their league in 1912. Their pitcher struck out 18 opposing players. Their school, built in 1908, was four years old when they won the championship.

Courtesy *Rocky Ford Public Library*

A Walk Past Local Businesses

Courtesy *Rocky Ford Public Library*

Rocky Ford High School as generations of students remember it. The blue spruce at center, if the same, has grown from the younger tree on p. 182, overshadowed by its deciduous neighbors.

The new Rocky Ford High School at 100 Washington Avenue was built in 1963.

Courtesy *Home Page rockyford.k12.co.us*

Businesses of West Elm Avenue

Coca Cola Bottling Company plant at 114 Elm Avenue, above, in the 1950s.

Johnson's Superior Station in the 1950s, above. Now painted, the original appearance was an earthen hue, glazed block construction.

Smith's Corner, a produce market and antique business established 1987 now occupies this site. Building fronts on Elm Ave–US 50 entering Rocky Ford. The left face is to the west on First Street or 300 Market St where much produce is sold in season.

Smith's Corner photo courtesy rockyfordcolorado.net

Nikkel's Superior Service Station was previous business located here. Later, a drive-thru car wash was added at the Second Street entrance, right in the two photos above.

Remaining photos courtesy *Rocky Ford Public Library*

A Walk Past Local Businesses

Safeway Stores at 800 Chestnut, future Wrangler Foods; Rocky Ford Food Market, across the street from the former Rocky Ford High School. The site of Safeway in the 1940s was 310–312 N Main with a parking area at 312 N Main Street. Courtesy *Rocky Ford Public Library*

This building is adjacent and east of the Methodist Church at 901 Elm, used for Sunday School classes. Former site of the USDA and Kenneth Lofgren, Onion Growers Co-Op. The clinic of Dr. Larson, and later, of Dr. EL Morgan at 913 Elm is far right. Courtesy *Rocky Ford Public Library*

Park View Barber Shop, 911 Railroad Avenue, moved from 903. Original front before stucco application.

Freddie's Corner occupies Railroad Avenue at Ninth Street next to **Tiny Juarez Café** as they appeared April 1970.

Photos courtesy *Rocky Ford Public Library*

A Walk Past Local Businesses

Fenlason Realty, 911 ½ Railroad Avenue, adjacent Park View Barber Shop. The barber shop facade is barely visible at top left of this photo, more so in top photo, p. 186. Fenlasen Agency also housed the office of the **High Line Canal Company**.

Carousel, 300 block N Main Street, future Duckwalls, Global Treasurez. **First Industrial Bank,** 300 N Main, far right, was formerly on Railroad Avenue, p. 213.
Photos courtesy *Rocky Ford Public Library*

The Rice Seed Company, 607 Elm Avenue was across the street from Veatch Market at 610. Vine and zinnia seed were advertised by faded letters on the west end of this building. **Church Furniture by Woodcraft**, advertised on the roof, illustrates another use the over years.

Model Cleaners at 900 Walnut Avenue. An earlier laundry was that of Gee Ging* who opened a hand laundry c 1892 in the back of a barber shop on Walnut Avenue.

JD Wolf opened a steam laundry in 1901 on the corner of Tenth Street and Walnut Avenue. This competition took Mr. Ging's business: "John, the Chinaman who has served his customers the past 10 years or so, could not compete with Mr. Wolf's Modern Steam Laundry, so is going home to China."

Rocky Ford Enterprise, 1901

* Spelling by *Doll*. Other spelling reported in *Keck* was Gee Ginn. Phrase describing him in the news considered derogatory.

Photos courtesy *Rocky Ford Public Library*

A Walk Past Local Businesses

Unique Cleaners, 975 Railroad Avenue, neighboring **Wilson Plumbing.**

Henry's Cleaners, formerly Horton's Market; Pizza A-Go-Go. Henry's was once located at 419 N Main Street. This location is on the south side of Elm Avenue between Thirteenth and Fourteenth Streets.

Photos courtesy *Rocky Ford Public Library*

Johnson-Ebert Photography, Macklin Photography, and Brown Studio at different times have occupied this location at 915 Elm Avenue.

Brown Studio at 915 and **Whittaker Agency** dealing in real estate at 917 ½ Elm. This building is next the alley separating Dr. Elmer Lee Morgan's office at left.

Photos courtesy *Rocky Ford Public Library*

A Walk Past Local Businesses

Chevron Service at 1200 Elm Avenue. Across Twelfth Street at center is the **S&H Green Stamp Store,** formerly Pete Stout's Skelly Service. Chevron Service site is now Cork Brothers Liquor.

A hotel and discount shoe store are far left, front of 400 N Main. **Nava Café, & Liquor Store**, and a barber shop are also occupants of this building. Nava Café once known as Star Bar or Star Cafe.

Photos courtesy *Rocky Ford Public Library*

Dutch and Dutchess Motel is painted on the side of this building adjacent and east of the Western Motel. The gable of the Western is visible above the Dutch and Dutchess in this photo.

The above building from its west side at right was once a 1940s grocery.

Photos courtesy *Rocky Ford Public Library*

A Walk Past Local Businesses

Freddie's Corner, Park View Barber Shop at 903 Ninth Street, above hood of the car, and a bar that would become Tiny Juarez Cafe, the **Pickwick** at 909, **Central Liquor** at 911, and the **Fenlason Agency** at 911 ½ and 917 Railroad Avenue.

KAVI Radio promotion at **Valley Supply, Inc.**, 400 N Main. Radio personality Lloyd Rider is in a booth above Main Street, see ladder.

Photos courtesy *Rocky Ford Public Library*

Wright Motor Lines, Inc. George Wright took over and operated Law Motor Lines at 1315 Elm Avenue. Building above is 1601 Elm, *future* site Reynolds Machine Shop. Discount Tire moved from 402 Elm, occupying and expanded north in this building. Photo from 1958.

Army Store in the Gobin building at 912 Elm Avenue. The empty space above was once a millinery shop, café, and market.

Army Store site, left, and empty space was occupied by ***Rocky Ford Daily Gazette***.

Photos courtesy *Rocky Ford Public Library*

A Walk Past Local Businesses

Telephone Offices, 923 Elm Avenue, directly east of the Beman building at 300 N Main Street.

Fenlason Agency 923 Elm Avenue in space once occupied by the Telephone offices above. Building presents a new face with doors brought forward to an even surface across the front. Among other addresses of this business were 911½, 913, and 917 Railroad Avenue.

Photos courtesy *Rocky Ford Public Library*

Mart Lueker Service Station
Martel Lueker owned and operated this service station across the street from the BPOE Lodge. Photo is of the east or Ninth Street side of his building opening front on Elm Avenue. Photo enlarged from bottom right photo, p. 135. Service station has been razed.

Citizen Utilities and **Jackson Transfer and Storage** occupy the two store rooms at Railroad and Ninth Street. The Jackson business was also agent for Weicker Transfer and Storage. Directly east across Ninth Street was Freddie's Corner and Tiny Juarez Cafe.

Photos courtesy *Rocky Ford Public Library*

Double A Heating & Air Conditioning now occupy this 201 N Ninth Street site.

A Walk Past Local Businesses

Help-UR-Self Laundry, future Model Cleaners at the SE corner of Walnut and Ninth Streets near a skating rink at left. **Presbyterian Church** is across the street at 303 S Ninth Street.

Photo courtesy *Rocky Ford Public Library*

Bender's Clock & Lock, 959 Walnut Avenue once located at 413 N Main Street. This building and 961 behind tree at right were razed for construction of McClain's Super. Walnut at 959 was *future* site of Beauty Nook.

Rocky Ford Historical Museum once was temporarily housed in these buildings.

Photos courtesy *Rocky Ford Public Library*

Taller building far right is 400 N Main. Through the years this site at 404 was the home of Mrs. Effie Hall who rented rooms to five individuals. McClelland Motor Parts would locate there later, followed by Donk's Furniture. The building at 406 nearest the street light was, in turn, site of the Dodge Brothers Garage, c 1914, and later, the Rocky Ford Garage of James K. Lumbar, proprietor.

Mr. Lumbar at one time did business in the Walter Cheek building, 419–421 S Main. Empty space at 408—left in photo—now the IDEA Center, once was a home, then later Templeton-Bush McCormick-Deering Implements and Donk's Furniture. Nelson-June Chevrolet operated at this site 1936–1939 when the business became June Chevrolet at 966 Elm Avenue.

General Chevolet in 1931 at 404–406 N Main.

Photos courtesy *Rocky Ford Public Library*

June Chevrolet used cars occupied 101 N Tenth Street, formerly Plews Ford Motor Company, and later, Arkansas Valley Memorial Co. Circus was in town whose arrival was studiously attended by at least one spectator, below.

A Walk Past Local Businesses

Daring Real Estate and Insurance in the 900 block of Elm Avenue with Methodist Church at 901 Elm, far left. **Braden's Rexall Drug Store**, once at 209 N Main moved to location at right, below.

Enlarged section of top photo shows future location of **Love's Café** at 915 Elm—pointer. **Daring Real Estate and Insurance** is at 919 Elm.

Photo courtesy *Rocky Ford Public Library*

Dr. E L Morgan office and clinic 913 Elm Avenue. An alley separates this building from that below. and those in the photos p. 199. Building currently houses Sanders Accounting.

Whittaker Real Estate & Insurance, left, **Daring Real Estate & Insurance**, center, on 900 block Elm Avenue.

Photos courtesy *Rocky Ford Public Library*

A Walk Past Local Businesses

Roy Smith Model Shoe Repair and **Cad's Cleaners** on Walnut Avenue.

Model Shoe Repair has been replaced by **The Music Room**. Both **Cad's Cleaners** at right and The Music Room were owned by Bob Cadwallader.

Photos courtesy *Rocky Ford Public Library*

Arkansas Valley Fairgrounds Grandstand back wall offered space for many business sponsors. Among them were: L. Findlay BAY Station, CO-OP, Swede's Conoco, Radio Station KAVI, Hotel Best, Valley Motor, Freeman's Fine Pastries, Don's for Lad and Dad, Gambles, Hancock's Men's Clothiers, Western Auto, Rocky Ford Drug Store, Cad's Cleaners, Daring Insurance Agency, and Howard and Betty Winsor.

This building was destroyed by fire May 1968. Ground was broken for a new grandstand on site January 26, 1970 and the new structure was ready for the 1970 fair. Some history of this and other grandstands on the fairgrounds is on p. 32, accompanied by a post card photo. This building is identified in the post card by the roof extension, partially visible here at far left.

Extension was added to better shade spectators from afternoon sun on west end seats.

Several large cottonwood trees once stood behind the grandstand. Many other trees remaining on the grounds are the remnants of George W. Swink's timber claim yet offering shade to the vendors, concessionaires, and many visitors at Fair time.

Photo, right, is front of the grandstand at an earlier time, (see p. 281).

Photos courtesy *Rocky Ford Public Library*, top, *Public Museum*, right.

A Walk Past Local Businesses

First Methodist Episcopal Church at Ninth and Elm. (See p. 79 for early photo c 1914–1916.)

Photos courtesy *Rocky Ford Public Library*

Casa Luz, 1211 Elm Avenue, west of the former Valley Super building on Elm Avenue at 1275 Elm, far right near pickup.

Dave and Hazel Schooley once lived upstairs over their curio shop. Selective Service office and a credit union occupied at other times before Casa Luz.

Wallace Oil Company, now Tank 'N' Tummy Convenience Store, 1305 Swink Avenue. Casa Luz Mexican Food Restaurant, top right photo, at 1211 Elm was to the right of Wallace Oil.

Rocky Ford Floral Company 1415 Pine Avenue, Anton Nelson, proprietor. Staff c 1951–1954 included Alberta Hale, Elizabeth (Betty) Eichler, Martha Irvin, Corrinne (Posey) Parr, Kazuko (Kaz) Harada, Virgil Hammond, Kathleen Ryan, Robert W. Weigand, and David J. Muth.

Courtesy *Rocky Ford Public Library*

This business, under succeeding ownership eventually closed and while the building was vacant was destroyed by fire along with a neighboring barn at 1405 Pine. Photo courtesy *C J Muth*

A Walk Past Local Businesses

Freeman's Fine Pastries at 415 S Main. Cheek Block is at left, 419–421. Site once occupied by *Rocky Ford Daily Gazette*; Central Shoe Service.

Lewis Brothers and Johnson building in 1899. Change in upper, front windows with new brick is evident on that area of the Beman Building, below.

Department of Employment, now **Daylight Donuts,** is just visible at right on Elm Avenue in the **Beman Building.** Built at 300–302 N Main by TE Godding for HA Dawley in 1899.

Photos courtesy *Rocky Ford Public Library*

Presbyterian Church, 303 S Ninth Street
The first church was built in 1881.

Church before 1925. Church sign had not yet been added to this 1907 building, nor its landscaping. Entrances are on Ninth Street, at left, and on Walnut Avenue, at right.

A basement was added in the 1960s by Lester Burchett. Bridges over the canal were added in 1896 and the canal was eventually covered by paved street.

Photos courtesy *Rocky ford Public Library*

A Walk Past Local Businesses

American Beet Sugar Co., (ABSC) factory, c 1902, produced sugar the first campaign October 1900 thru 1934. Then, American Crystal Sugar Company, (ACSC), continued to the last campaign in 1979.

ABSC retained the name until 1934 when the company was renamed American Crystal Sugar Co. and Denver headquarters moved to Moorhead, Minnesota.

Campaign activity c 1920s–1930s.

Photos courtesy *Rocky Ford Public Museum*

Factory control panel c 1910s.

Close of business, ACSC last campaign, 1979.

Officers and volunteers gather around **Rocky Ford Fire truck No. 1** c 1930s. Building remains as the fire and police stations while city administration moved to 203 S Main Street.

Photos courtesy *Rocky Ford Public Library*

US Post Office, Rocky Ford, 81067, 401 N Ninth Street. This 1936 building was constructed by the Works Progress Administration (WPA) during the Franklin D. Roosevelt administration. Built on former home site of George W. Swink family, marked by historical monument, lower right.

Drive-thru mail deposit was added to the north side of the building, at right, above. Excavation for building footings in 1935 revealed the water table at 18 inches, requiring a 'raft foundation' for support against settling.

A Walk Past Local Businesses

City Hall at 203 S Ninth Street was bordered by the fire chief's home at 205, left, and the fire station at 201 N Ninth Street, which remain. Fire and police now occupy this c 1919 building after the move of City Hall to its new location, below.

Photo courtesy *Rocky Ford Public Library*

Recker's Hall is shown p. 132 as it stood on Main Street with its north side facing Front Street. The exposed north side of the surviving HF Hagen Building is visible p. 234, bottom, then used as advertising space.

Photo courtesy Matt Mendenhall, Mike Budge, *rockyfordcolorado.net*

City Administration Building is located at 203 S Main Street, former sites of Recker's Hall, destroyed by fire in 1952, and the H.F. Hagen building.

Hancock Real Estate and **Insurance** business. Clinic of Dr. BB Blotz was on the upper floor entered at door to stairway beyond drug sign, far right.

Hanging bunting at the Elm Street entrance during fair time. Two ladies are unidentified.

Edwards Rexall Drugs currently, Braden's Rexall Drugs, Gobin, Inc., and eventually, Family Worship Center occupied 921 Elm. The latter eventually moved to 504 S Tenth Street.

Photos courtesy *Rocky Ford Public Library*

A Walk Past Local Businesses

Cox's Daylight Donuts on the south side of Elm, at one time Karl's Café at 958 Elm Avenue. On Main Street to the right this building fronted at 208, the site of Kaplan Mercantile. The Central Hotel rooms occupied the upper floor in 1911–1915.

Stout's Skelly Service, Elm Avenue at Twelfth Street. The absence of gas pumps and sign over the bay doors indicate a closing. Future S&H Green Stamp Store opened at this location.

Photos courtesy *Rocky Ford Public Library*

Curtis-Erickson Carpet, once located 206 N Main Street; Hardt's former location. **Wards** was also part of this business now located in the former Silvers West Side Market at Third Street and Elm Avenue. Site was once a former consignment store, a restaurant, now a second hand store.

Claude's Shoe Shine Shop, 315, left door, **Chamberlain Realty,** 313, right door in the white front on S Main Street. Christian Science Reading Room once occupied 313. These businesses were neighbor to the arched entrance at 311 ½ of the **Elk Hotel** rooms on the upper floor.

Photos courtesy *Rocky Ford Public Library*

A Walk Past Local Businesses

First Industrial Bank site on Railroad Avenue.

First Industrial Bank in the Beman Building. 300 N Main Street.

Beman Building

Photos courtesy *Rocky Ford Public Library*

Dub's Superior Service, Elm Avenue. The large building at left has been removed and the remaining structure rebuilt as Easy Wash, right and below. Photo below shows new construction.

Dub Morris was proprietor of this business.

Photos courtesy *Rocky Ford Public Library*

A Walk Past Local Businesses

High Chaparral Inn and **Restaurant** at 1319–1321 Elm Avenue. The restaurant was once enlarged to house Polly's Café, nearest vehicles. Building was enlarged again and became Peggy's Café when Polly Seeley moved to 1701 Elm Avenue. Peggy Bates operated the restaurant before moving to 1701 Elm after Polly's Café closed. Restaurant at 1701 Elm was then renamed Peggy's Cafe.

High Chaparral Inn 1321 Elm Avenue

Photos courtesy *Rocky Ford Public Library*

Loaf 'N Jug at 305 N Tenth Street. **The Pop Shoppe** at this time occupied a part of the same building. Gasoline service islands are behind the photographer.

Smith's Department Store, 309 N Main. An early occupant was Price Dry Goods Co. Other occupants have been Fraser Dry Goods and Evans Jewelers. Western Auto, 307 and Fraser Dry Goods, 309 were later site of Harris Pharmacy. Photos courtesy *Rocky Ford Public Library*

JC Penney Company at 401 N Main in the Knights of Pythias building. This location was once occupied by the Post Office and Aldis Food Market. *Future* location of Lewis Furniture; Carmax.

A Walk Past Local Businesses

Western Motel Cabins, front and rear views. The rear of the Western Motel office is at right. The front faces Elm Avenue.

Photos courtesy *Rocky Ford Public Library*

State Bank of Rocky Ford drive-thru, 901 Elm. The rear of the Spot Café on Swink Avenue is visible at the left drive-thru lane.

St. Peter's Evangelical Lutheran Church at 604 and parsonage at 602 Elm Avenue. Church was stuccoed adobe after a 1925 remodeled frame house was removed. Congregation organized in 1906 with about 60 adult members under the Kansas District Mission Board and dedication was held July 11, 1937.

Photos courtesy *Rocky Ford Public Library*

A Walk Past Local Businesses

CS Williams Company, Twelfth Street and Elm Avenue.

JC Robinson Seed Company at left, **CS Williams Feed and Agricultural Chemicals** right at Twelfth and Railroad Avenue. *Future* site of Simplot, Highbe Popper, Sawyer- Meade Co. Later, Meade operated by Jerry and Barbara Macklin.

Photos courtesy *Rocky Ford Public Library*

George McKenzie Music and Furniture Company at 400 S Main, left, with hotel entrance, formerly the Hagen Modern Rooms, **McKenzie Used Furniture** the **Maytag Store**, and **Chamber of Commerce** at 402, next door to Borden's Plumbing and Heating at 404.

    Chamber of Commerce was once located in the Gobin Building and at Tenth Street and Chestnut near first site of the Little White School. *Courtesy Rocky Ford Public Library*

Harada Farms Daily Fresh Market in the 1960s.

The Haradas from left, Jean, Joyce, Gale, Margie, Ugi-manager and wife Mollie, Joane, and Rayna Hamm holding the melon.

    This business operated on the west side of Rocky Ford near US 50.

Courtesy *facebook.com/rocky.ford*

A Walk Past Local Businesses

Valley Farm Market, below, during the off season.

PJ's Emporium, above, facing Swink Avenue in building fronting 400 N Main. First use of this building was as a livery in 1900 when it was built, described by John Doll as a "large brick livery barn." The B&M Implement Company occupants in the late 1940s used the cavernous workspace with no supporting columns inside to house a showroom and equipment. Large iron rods from the roof attached to laminated beams which supported hoists for machinery.

Walt Butler operated Pizza A-Go-Go, later selling his café and a favorite pizza recipe to Mr. Scammon and partner Bill Thomas.

Proctor family operated a fruit market here at another time. View at left from Elm Avenue-US 50 near First Street or Market Street just west of the Coca Cola Bottling Company plant. Buildings were eventually razed and site taken by Rusler Implement Co.

Photos courtesy *Rocky Ford Public Library*

Dub Morris owned **West Side Farmer's Market**, once known as Valley Farm Market. Bill Will built this west-side fruit stand where Aki Ushiama operated Oriental Café.

Bender's Clock and Lock. Main at Walnut, here vacant, was 208 S Main, site of Bill & Bob's Service Station. Bender's was just east of the station on Walnut Avenue.

Christian Church, Disciples of Christ 500 S Ninth Street with Sycamore Avenue in the foreground. Improvements were underway, including removal of some trees.

Photos courtesy *Rocky Ford Public Library*

Catholic Church, St. Peter Parish, 1209 Swink Avenue. Father WS Neenan is below prior 1915. The rectory at right is extant while the original church below was replaced, above, by a former La Junta Air Base Chapel in 1949.
Photo courtesy *Rocky Ford Public Library*

Photo courtesy *Ruth Ellen Morrison* in John Doll

Former service station at Fourteenth Street and Swink Avenue became the future Tastee Freeze site facing Swink Avenue.

Mission Deli later operated in the above location facing at 401 N Fourteenth Street.

Photos courtesy *Rocky Ford Public Library*

William B. Gobin Building, Ninth Street at Elm Avenue. **Royal Hotel** remains on the second floor. **Farmers Insurance Group** is near hotel entrance, a loan company to its right. **Rocky Ford Federal Savings** occupies the former Winsor Insurance Agency, the corner at 900 Elm Avenue.

A Walk Past Local Businesses

Jimbo's Drive-In Restaurant, 1503 Elm Avenue. Former site of Bill Will's 1950s Fruit Stand. Other times, Shaeffers, Tank 'N' Tummy, and currently M & O Pawn & Antiques.

Valley Ambulance Service
Lois Sturges, Ann Hamilton, and Larry Hamilton operated this business in Rocky Ford.

Courtesy *facebook.com/Rocky-Ford-Colorado*

Joe's Service, 402 Elm Avenue. Once the location of Discount Tire, now at 1601 Elm. The building was razed and the site occupied by an ambulance service.

Photos courtesy *Rocky Ford Public Library*

Don's Bar at 958, adjacent another bar and barber shop on the Elm Avenue side of the building at 208 N Main. **June Chevrolet** is just visible at 966 Elm, far left.

Mint Saloon at 208 N Main Street. Side of the building with small, high windows is also visible in the photo at left of the same block.
Courtesy *Jeff Obermiller*

A truck, distant right center, lost part of its cargo on the 900 block of Elm Avenue. At left in the **Gobin Building** is **Quality Market** at 912 and **Halle's Dress Shop, Diamond Mine Jewelers**, and **Hiway Liquor** at 900 Elm. **Royal Hotel** occupies the second story. **Bill & Bob's Service** is distant center at 810 Elm, white building between Eighth and Ninth Streets.

Upper left and lower photo courtesy *Rocky Ford Public Library*

A Walk Past Local Businesses

Easy Wash in the previous Dub's Superior Service site. The angular vertical facade and soffit below it are prominent in this and photo p. 214.

Melon City Royal Service once located here, p. 172, at Twelfth and Swink Avenue, foreground.

Photos courtesy *Rocky Ford Public Library*

George Nelson's Conoco in a corner lot with neighbor **June Chevolet** on both sides at 966 Elm. View of the station from Elm Avenue at top and from Tenth Street, below. Building was razed.
Photos courtesy *Rocky Ford Public Library*

A Walk Past Local Businesses

Bish Lumber and Feed Store, 100 block S Main facing **Central Park** and the missile monument. These buildings were destroyed by fire.

Sharp Image Styling Salon now occupies this site facing Main Street. Location traditionally has been used by lumber, feed, grain, coal, transfer and storage businesses. The presence of the Santa Fe wig-wag traffic signal on Main Street indicates a time prior 1980 when it was removed.

Photos courtesy *Rocky Ford Public Library*

Grimsley and Keck site at rear of the business, left, on Ninth Street. At far right is the **Railway Express Agency** on the west side of the Santa Fe Depot. Photo appears to be c 1980.

This general area bordering Ninth Street near the tracks at right had been the location of the Santa Fe combination passenger and Freight Depot until 1941 when it was razed. The area also had been site of a substantial loading dock for heavy traffic freight, eventually taken down as need decreased. G & K, owned by 'Fly' Grimsley and CF 'Bus' Keck, sold Allis Chalmers farm equipment.

Photo courtesy *Rocky Ford Public Library*

A Walk Past Local Businesses

Oberling Motors, sign above Rocky Ford Onion Growers at left-was in business in the lower part of this building, also future site of Model Cleaners and Help-UR-Self Laundry. The laundry once operated at 809 Railroad Avenue.

Model Cleaners, below at 900 Walnut Avenue. Early photographer JE Orr located his studio at the Ninth and Walnut site.

Rocky Ford Onion Growers Association, above, eventually moved to 101 S Tenth Street.

Over the years physicians and clinics, those of Dr. Ted E. Martin, Dr. RT Shima, and Dr. Roy McKittrick occupied the two-story part of the building above. Bill and Bobs Service also later occupied.

Western Wool Processors, Inc.

Western Wool Processors, on Twelfth Street at Railroad Avenue, opened July 24, 1960.

Arkansas Valley Seeds, their brand *Rabbit Ears*, and Libby, McNeil, & Libby Canning Factory were earlier occupants of this site.

Photos courtesy *Rocky Ford Public Library*

Bish Brothers Company building on the 100 block S Main in the process of renewal for the Sunny Side Pharmacy. A small white building once at right has been demolished to make room for pharmacy parking. It had long ago been part of the RW English Lumber Company, at 104 S Main Street. The large building at left in the bottom photo, part of the Bish enterprise, was also razed.

Photos courtesy *Rocky Ford Public Library*

A Walk Past Local Businesses

Sunny Side Pharmacy, 106 S Main, now Sharp Image Styling Salon. Photo January 1985.

Bish Brothers Co., future site of Sunny Side Pharmacy. **IOOF Building** at 200 S Main is visible far right. Small white building, right, is original site of RW English Lumber Co., p. 114.

Photos courtesy *Rocky Ford Public Library*

McKenzie Furniture in the 1900 HF Hagen Building, 400 S Main Street.

This is the Maple Avenue north side facing Model Dry Cleaners 312 S Main Street. HF Hagen partnered with Charles Recker and invested in construction of other buildings on Main and Front Streets, neighboring edifices. Recker's Hall sided on Front Street.

Photos courtesy *Rocky Ford Public Library*

Recker's Hall, destroyed by fire, once on this site adjacent **Central Shoe Repair** in surviving HF Hagen building, 209 S Main. New City Administration Building was built here in the 1960s, now addressing 203 S Main Street. Building fire was observed by the author on the way to school one morning in 1952. Across Main Street one felt the heat but no damage occurred to proprietor Cecil Zavala's shoe business. Fire also attracted attention of east-bound train passengers that morning.

Hotel El Capitan

"The office of Wm. B. Gobin was the scene of the promotion of a new $20,000 hotel the other day. Plans were presented and a committee appointed to solicit subscriptions for building stock. FJ Capitan, HI Maxwell, FY Hauck and Dr. Fenton are appointed to this committee. The hotel will be built on the corner of Chestnut and Main. The hotel will be known as El Capitan. Mr. Gobin will have charge of construction and it will be built of local brick from Cheek's kiln."

Enterprise, October 5, 1900

Fred Cheek was manager of NW Terry's brick yard on the east end of Maple Avenue. October 2, 1894 the *Enterprise* stated: "The first load of fired brick have been removed from Terry's kiln in the east part of town." One million were eventually ordered for the construction of the sugar factory, built and ready for the first campaign October 1900. Many buildings in Rocky Ford, including El Capitan, were built with Terry's bricks. At completion of the factory, Mr. Terry sold the business to Fred Cheek and sons who placed Jake Harms as new manager.

This photo was taken prior the completion of sidewalks and pavement 25 years later. Dr. Pollock's hospital would be built in 1907 at the rear of the hotel facing Chestnut Avenue at 915 where it is today replacing the shed in this photo.

Photo courtesy *Rocky Ford Public Library*

Photo courtesy *Rocky Ford Public Library*

Kaplan's Clothing at 208, **Hardt Hardware**, 206, and **Gambles** at 204 N Main Street. Kaplan's once was the Mint Saloon. City Drug was at 202 and Sam Nishimura's Ichi Ban Restaurant at 200, right of Gambles in early history of this block.

The wooden frame building, site of the Mint Saloon at 208 owned by Colonel Robb, burned in 1898 along with the entire block. The block was rebuilt with brick and the Mint Saloon was first occupant at 208 on the corner in 1899, later, Kaplan's for many years.

A Walk Past Local Businesses

Liberty School construction began in 1899 at 401 N Tenth Street. A later view, below, shows a lower gable over the protruding front entrance to continue the roof line. The original construction contract was let to Perry Robards, W. Lawton, and George Daring for $6,600.50. The contract called for pressed red brick with Manitou sandstone trim.

Nava Manor, 965 Swink Avenue now occupies this site.

Photos courtesy *Rocky Ford Public Library*

Watermelon Day, After the Feast. Many melons had been distributed and eaten. Negotiating an exit from among remains would have kept celebrants alert. (See *Observations on Watermelon* Day, p. 284 for discussion of removal methods.)

Photo courtesy *Denver Public Library, Harry H. Buckwalter Collection, Ph00057, 10028835*

Courtesy *facebook.com/Rocky-Ford-Colorado*

Campers

City Council often accommodated travelers, sometimes on the Arkansas Valley Fairgrounds. One request, received from Native Americans for use of Washington School grounds, was denied with no explanation recorded.

Early pioneers in covered wagons were provided a campground along Railroad Avenue east of Eleventh Street with some shade there on Santa Fe property. Campers at left (demonstrative for the times) are identified as being near Rocky Mountain Lake Park in the Berkeley neighborhood of Denver, Colorado.

Photo, c 1918–1920 identified by *Western History Department of Denver Public Library*

Photo courtesy *Rocky Ford Public Library*

Road Crew in 1895 charged with maintaining county roads. A six-mule-team powered grader, just visible behind the team, required two men to operate, one to drive the team, the other to control the grader.

Chuck wagon, complete with stove, was a later version of its counterpart used on cattle drives. Rocky Ford resident Herb Royal, brother of Frank Royal, stands in the doorway. Others are not identified, but interested. As in most vintage photographs, all human faces are turned toward the photographer with advice to not move, lest they appear as a blur.

Young's Soft Water Service & Auto Supply at 610 Elm Avenue also had a used car business at left. The building was the former Veatch Market. An alley is along the right side of the building separating the market and St. Peter's Lutheran Church at 604 Elm.

Priscilla Stitch & Gift Shop, *future* site. Bender's Clock and Lock at 959 Walnut Avenue was left of this building. Both 959 and 961 were razed for construction of the new McClain's Super.

Photos courtesy *Rocky ford Public Library*

A Walk Past Local Businesses

'Wimpy' in his favorite surroundings at 210 Elm, among good friends at **Huri-Back Lunch**. The photo p. 83 shows the Huri-Back Lunch from another view. Vera Downing, wife of owner Carl D. (Pug) Downing, stands at left.

In the distant background is **St. Paul's Evangelical Lutheran Church** at 209 N Second Street, now in another role as the popular restaurant, Christine's, p. 242. At center left is the rear corner of Enlo Henry's Huri-Back Service Station at 210 Elm Avenue. Time appears to be 1940s.

Photo courtesy *Rocky Ford Public Library*

Photo from author's collection

St. Paul's Evangelical Lutheran Church and parsonage at 207–209 N Second Street. Church was built in 1910. Services were held to 1972 when its congregation could no longer sustain membership. The author's mother and father were married in the church February 15, 1934.

Christine's
The former parsonage remains and the church building, with modifications, has been an antique shop, funeral home, and currently is the popular restaurant, Christine's.

Courtesy *Mike and Christine Laurent*, website photo
christinesfinedining@gmail.com

Kitch Pontiac, 1014 Elm Avenue, was neighbor to Steward Sheet Metal Works to the right, their rear entrances on Railroad Avenue and front entrances on Elm Avenue. Left of the Kitch building was the former site of the two-story adobe livery barn owned by Will and BU Dye in 1877.

The two-story livery barn was bordered by roads that would become Eleventh Street, Elm, and Railroad Avenues. A blacksmith and repair shop, p. 88, of BU Dye in 1888 was later that year owned by Ellington and Hauck. Mr. VA Moore became third owner in 1899. Site of the livery is now Rocky Ford Family Health Center.

Tastee Freeze, Swink Avenue at Fourteenth Street. This view from Swink shows Chase Auto Repair left background. Mission Deli currently occupies this site, now at 401 N Fourteenth Street.

Photos courtesy *Rocky Ford Public Library*

First Christian Science Church, Eleventh Street and Maple Avenue, dedicated December 17, 1916, currently a private residence.   *Photos top and below right courtesy Rocky Ford Public Library*

Photo courtesy of *Doris Baublits*.
Church built 1907, disbanded October 21, 1979.

Immanuel Congregational Church 503 and parsonage at 501 S Fourth Street.

A Walk Past Local Businesses

McClelland Motor Parts, 404 N Main. This business was in the location once occupied by General Chevrolet, later by Donk's Furniture. The building to the right is 400 N Main, a site that several businesses have occupied since 1900.

B & M Implement Company, 400 N Main. Building is in transition, right, originally a large brick livery barn built by George Higgins. Gas pump was removed, corner and windows added.

Photos courtesy *Rocky Ford Public Library*

Physician's Hospital, 803 Maple. Dr. BF Blotz and his brother Dr. BB Blotz built their hospital in 1915. The first hospital built in 1907, Pollock's Hospital at 915 Chestnut was built seven years after the El Capitan and was in use until the Physicians Hospital was completed. Pollock's Hospital building remains just west of El Capitan Hotel serving as an annex to the hotel.

Bauer Home, a nursing home, once Physician's Hospital. Another view of the building after transition.

Photos courtesy *Rocky Ford Public Library*

OK used car sign of **June Chevrolet** stood over this former Elm Avenue Standard station in 1984.

Middleton Super Standard Service shown in 1949, owned by Dick Middleton after WWII. White lettering over the center portion of tile roof appears to be *Standard Oil Performance* (marker). The building was razed for the construction of Loaf 'N Jug Food Store c 1987.

Photo courtesy *Rocky Ford Public Library*

Rocky Ford Municipal Swimming Pool on Reservoir Hill was designed by city engineer Harry Barnes who also supervised its construction in 1939 by Works Progress Administration labor.

Summer fun began, for many school kids, when the pool opened Memorial Day weekend. A wading pool for the smallest children was out of the picture to the right in the center photos.

Photo courtesy *Rocky Ford Public Library*

Post card photo 1949

Popularity of the facility continued many years until this new pool was built at 104 West Washington Avenue.

Photo courtesy *facebook.com/RFPool*

Kimsey-Cover Fire March 4, 1914 involved the 300 block of N Main Street from 305 at far left to 315 at far right. **Funk's**, formerly at 307 behind the woman at left, and 312 across the street, moved again to 315 and appears undamaged. Illustration is a composite of two photos taken

from same location on Main Street. Fire line is visible as a fine cord from Funk's and the corner of the business at 307 behind the woman. Evalynn's Dress Shop, Athalie's, JC Penney, Fraser Dry Goods, Western Auto, Evans Jewelers, and Southern Colorado Power Company would one day occupy this block. The Kimsey-Cover burn site was at this time 309 N Main, The Economy Store, future site of Don's for Lad and Dad is at 311. Funk's and The Economy Store, the latter showing damage, are visible in the photo below.

N Main Street to the south from Swink Avenue in 1913. Marked building, Kimsey-Cover, was destroyed in the fire.

Photos courtesy *Rocky Ford Public Library*

Grand Opera House Block, 1912. Veterinary surgeon's office 411, left, vacant lot at 409, Grand Theatre at 407–405, Charles S. Lawrence furniture, wallpaper and paints 403, and St. John Building, 401 South Main Street under the corner canopy. *Courtesy Rocky Ford Public Library*

The triangular railroad crossing sign at the tracks is visible at lower right behind the horse-drawn delivery wagon. Wide concrete sidewalks are in place front of the Opera House and St. John building at the corner. A narrow walk continues south from front of the surgeon's office at left.

Grand Opera House Ticket Booth lost in fire, 1934, p. 68.

The Big House, 1930, with Wallace Beery, Chester Morris, and Robert Montgomery was showing.

Courtesy facebook.com/rocky.ford

A Walk Past Local Businesses

Grand Opera House in this 1913 photo was preparing for the appearance of **Neil O'Brien's Minstrel Show**, advertised above left. The space at 409 S Main Street that would become A&W Root Beer in the future was used as billboard advertising for show events coming to town.

Photo courtesy *Rocky Ford Public library*

Minstrel shows, popular into the 1920s, were decreasingly so yielding to vaudeville where many minstrel stars were finding new opportunities. By summer 1928 some minstrel shows were disbanding. The show advertised here had been in Hot Springs, Arkansas September, 1913 and in Florence, Arkansas February, 1920, according to newspapers there. Live stage performances, accompanied by the group's own band at left in the photo below, featured comedy, jokes, music, dance and singing. Rocky Ford show dates on the advertisement above are not legible.

Neil O'Brien c 1905–1910   Minstrels in Hot Springs, Arkansas, 1913.   Photos courtesy *wikipedia*

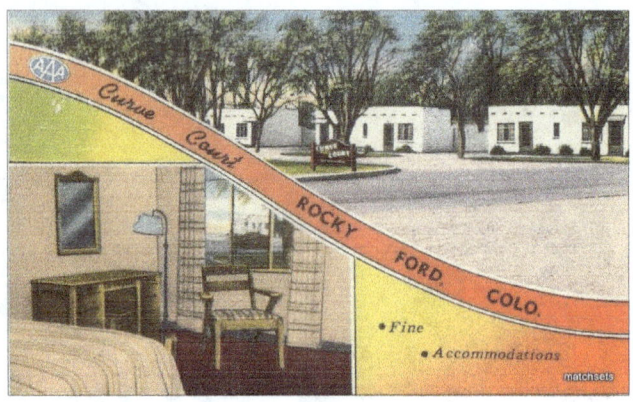

A&M Auto Repair, Eighth Street & Elm Avenue. At left- partial sign- was the third site of Bill & Bob's Auto Repair at 810 Elm Avenue.
Photos courtesy *Rocky Ford Public Library*

Curve Court was listed in the 1945-1948 city directory as **Curve Enterprises & Motel**, operated by RE and Josephine Carder, owner and manager (in succession).
Post card photos *c 1949*

Auto Clinic eventually located here at Eighth Street and Elm Avenue.

Sign at right stood at the entrance of Curve Motel, 1500 Elm Avenue on US Highway 50.

A Walk Past Local Businesses

Watermelon Day, September 5, 1901
  Courtesy *Rocky Ford Public Library*

Colorado Governor William E. Sweet and friends, below, wait for the governor to carve and pass the melon. His attendance at the Fair was during his tenure, January 9, 1923 to January 13, 1925.
  Courtesy, *History Colorado, Subject File Collection, 10044484*

Many photos exist of this celebration since a wagon load was served at the first celebration in 1878. Several show barriers aiding in safety and fair and timely distribution of melons. The first visitors attending in 1878 were served by one person, the founder Mr. GW Swink, who in his words told of "... not more than 25 persons being present ... ." Since then the number of attendees at Watermelon Day has grown to thousands.

Photo above, shows a substantial barrier which also served as table and cutting board. Many city officials and pioneers attended the Fair and Watermelon Days in fine dress.

Three Rocky Ford boys harvest melons, 1910.

Photo courtesy *Rocky Ford Public Library*

Watermelon Day c 1915–1918   Courtesy, *History Colorado, Denver Post Historical Collection, 10027865*

Watermelon Day 1893 photographed by JE Orr who had a studio at Ninth Street and Walnut Avenue. He prepared this *carte de visit*, French for visiting card. A larger cabinet card portrait was also made of an albumen print, a thin paper photograph mounted on a thicker paper card. Backs of the cards and borders were used for the photographer's advertising.

Courtesy *Rocky Ford Public Museum*

Watermelon Day c 1900, among the trees of GW Swink's former timber claim. *Do you see twins?*
Photos courtesy, *Rocky Ford Public Museum*

The 1911 melon pile is incomplete. Workers rest and wait for the next wagon load.

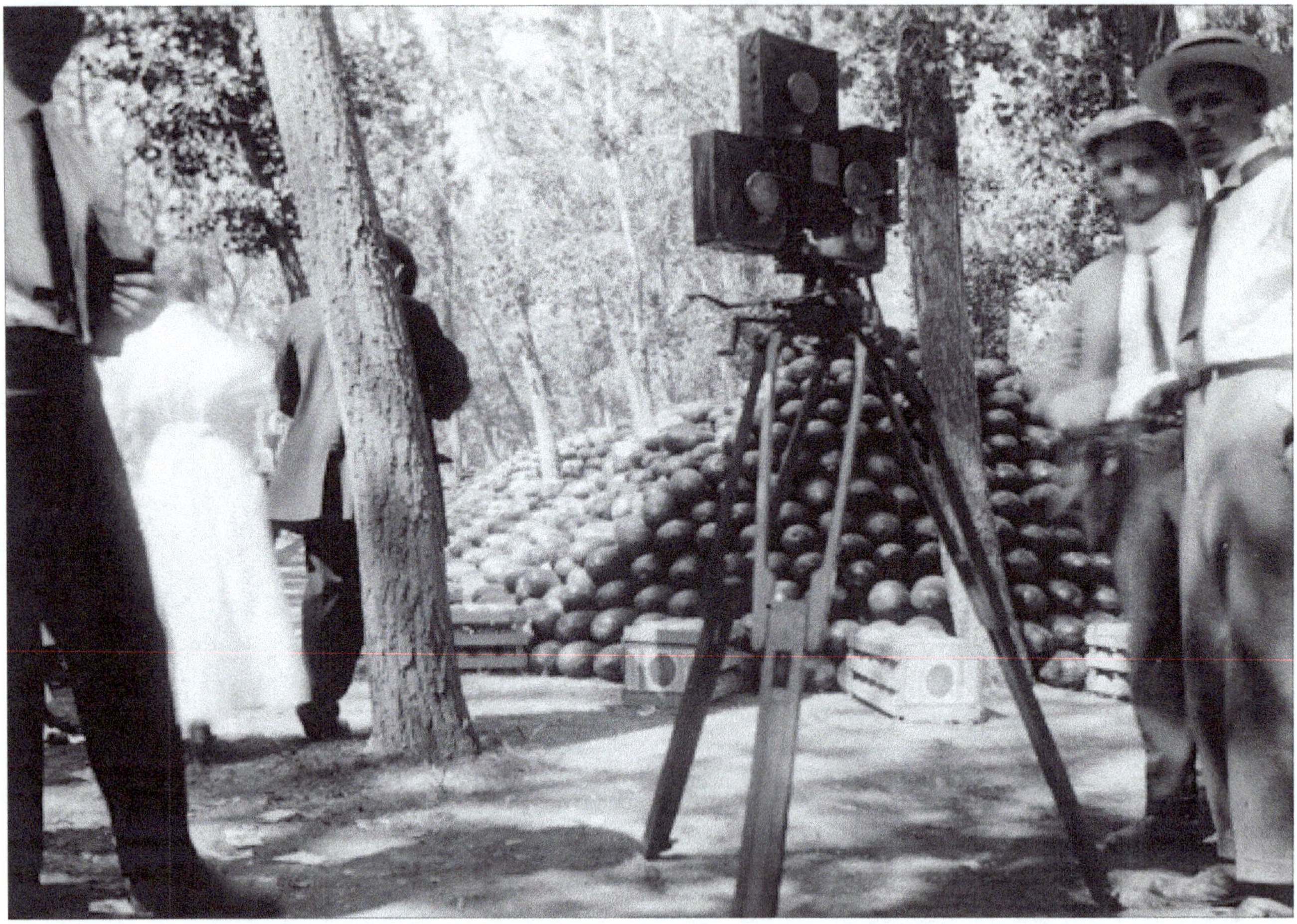

Watermelon Day Photographers c 1910–1920. The camera appears to be for motion pictures. Cantaloupe shipping crates of the era are on display at the base of the watermelon pile.

Courtesy, *History Colorado, Original Photograph Collection 10045159.*

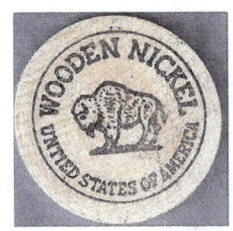

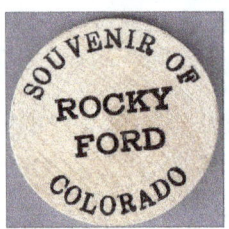

Souvenirs were distributed at fair time, two surviving ones shown. The *Nickel* was actually made from wood. One at right was printed on a stiff fabric like oilcloth.

Pin-back lapel buttons were popular as were banners in 1910.

ebay.com

WOODEN NICKEL
72nd Annual
WATERMELON DAY
Rocky Ford, Colorado
— ALWAYS —
FIRST THURSDAY IN SEPTEMBER
WOODEN NICKEL

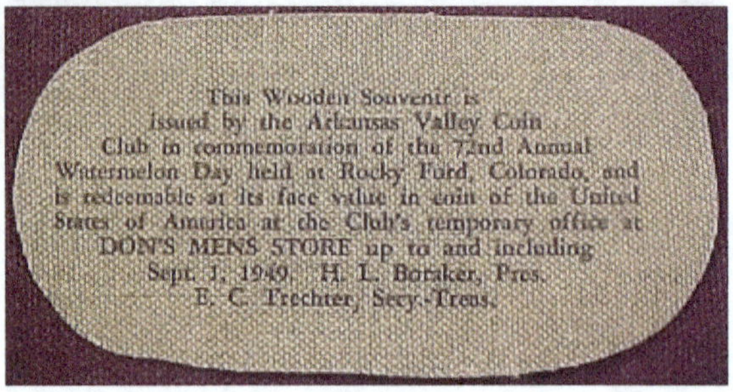
This Wooden Souvenir is issued by the Arkansas Valley Coin Club in commemoration of the 72nd Annual Watermelon Day held at Rocky Ford, Colorado, and is redeemable at its face value in coin of the United States of America at the Club's temporary office at DON'S MENS STORE up to and including Sept. 1, 1949. H. L. Boraker, Pres. E. C. Trechter, Secy.-Treas.

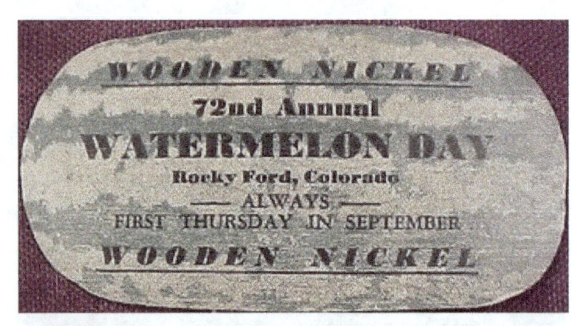

A Walk Past Local Businesses

Watermelon Day workers took pride in their work. Melons were placed so each layer dispersed weight from those above, protecting all from being crushed. Large, dark-rind melons were a favorite for Melon Day many years. Fair officials offered Fair-goers a choice by providing cantaloupe whose smaller stacks resemble those of Civil War cannon balls, as in the 1920s below.

Courtesy, *Denver Public Library, Original Photograph Collection, 10044483*

Melons often were 12 tiers high and neatly stacked.

Courtesy, *Rocky Ford Public Museum*

Watermelon Day 1894. Photo is among the earliest of those researched, printed by *Orr and Anderson* as a cabinet photo. The growth of trees in GW Swink's former timber claim are here young and numerous compared to later photos of this celebration.

The *cabinet photo* or *card* was a style of photograph widely used for portraiture after 1870. It consisted of a thin photograph mounted on a card of varying dimension, commonly 108 by 165 mm (4¼ by 6½ inches).

A different Watermelon Day pile, date unknown. Most melons had been a large, dark-rind variety. They are in recent years varied and have been placed in a covered area in the open ground of the Rocky Ford High School outdoor track.   Photos Courtesy *Rocky Ford Public Museum*

A Walk Past Local Businesses

Rocky Ford Garage interior. Location and date of this photo are not known. Rocky Ford Garage was at times at 406 N Main and 419–421 S Main Street, in the Cheek Building. (See note p. 303 for another possibility.)
Photo courtesy *Rocky Ford Public Museum*

Dog House at 403 and **St. John Building** at 401 Main Street, once occupied by Bible Book Store. Both buildings have been razed.
Photo courtesy *Rocky Ford Public Library*

Two houses, on factory grounds, were at the west entrance across CR 19 from two others. Company housing was also built on Chestnut and Swink Avenues east of Fourth Street to the east side of Second Street except for two privately owned. All were rented and later sold to employees.

Encore, a special events business is now in the building at 400 Chestnut Avenue. The former ACSC office and clubhouse, served factory workers and were connected by a lattice-covered breeze-way, below.

Photos, c 1970s courtesy, *Rocky Ford Public Library*

American Beet Sugar Co. provided some housing for their workers. Oxnard Construction Co. built six houses on Chestnut Avenue and the office building. Some houses were two-story brick, others one-story frame.

North American Dehydrate Company drying plant and storage bins on the west end of factory grounds, c 1978. ACSC provided cossettes, raw, wet, spaghetti-like beet slices for drying. The NADCO end product was a compressed, dry pellet, bagged and sold as pulp.

Photos courtesy *Rocky Ford Public Library*

A Walk Past Local Businesses

Fred Blackford in 1927 with a *Star* automobile near the **Ada** and **Robert M. Adams** house at 423 S Main Street. **Blackford & Boughman Garage**, in the background, is in the Cheek building at 419–421. Both Adams house and Cheek Building are extant.

Roy Taylor in the *Star*.

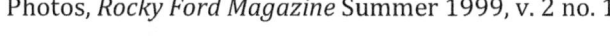

Photos, *Rocky Ford Magazine* Summer 1999, v. 2 no. 1

Block 300 S Main reveals the front of the 1890s **Land Office** building at 305 between trees at left. Large windows and doorways appear as earlier when trees had been recently planted. **St. James Hotel** at 300 S Main at this time retains its ornate parapet clearly in rear view at right. The hotel appears in red brick until painted later to match the **Cantaloupe Café** next door.

Rocky Ford Magazine, Summer 1998, v. 1 no. 1

Fiesta Café at 204 S Main Street. This 1898 building was once the location of Govreau's Grocery and Meat Market-page 21.

Rocky Ford Magazine, Summer 1998, v. 1 no. 1

Fiesta Café closed on Main Street, moved to 400 N Eleventh Street and reopened as **Fiesta Restaurant** in a new building.

Courtesy *facebook.com/FiestaCafeRestaurant*

A Walk Past Local Businesses

Reynolds Metals Building was redesigned for **Discount Tire** c 1998. Discount Tire moved from 402 Elm to this location at 1601 Elm after a design was accepted incorporating much of the former Reynolds building above.

The concept, above right, became reality in photo below showing major addition of office and showroom. Left end of photo above left is enlarged below left to show the angular canopy supports on the facade of the former **Wright Motor Lines.** *Rocky Ford Magazine Summer 1998, v.1 no.1*

Rocky Ford Magazine Summer 1998, vol.1 no.1

Expanded from top left photo.

Rocky Ford Magazine Summer 1998, v.1 no.1   Courtesy *Rocky Ford Public Library 1958*

EDCO occupied the former Law Motor Lines building at 1315 Elm Avenue. (See also p. 272 the seed-cleaning and elevator business of Francis H. and Elva Clute, Ed Clute's parents.)

Rocky Ford Federal Savings & Loan, 801 Swink Avenue. In the absence of a photo of this business the street sign will identify this site to many. An earlier location was in the Gobin Building at 900 Elm Avenue. Lower Arkansas Water Management Association later occupied 801 Swink Avenue.

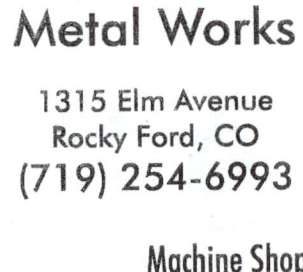

EDCO Metal Works
1315 Elm Avenue
Rocky Ford, CO
(719) 254-6993

Machine Shop
Heating & Air Conditioning

ED CLUTE
Owner

Ad from *Rocky Ford Magazine* vol. 2 no. 1 Summer 1999

Peggy's Café 1701 Elm Avenue occupied the former Polly's Café, see p. 152 and p. 215 top photo for the building.

Ads, *Rocky Ford Magazine*, vol. 1 no. 1 Summer 1998

Johnson & Govreau Coal, Grain, Transfer, & Water business was located in the area behind 110 N Main Street extending east along Railroad Avenue and Santa Fe tracks.

An incongruity in such a place is presented by the tidy unidentified worker in his coat, collar, tie and cap standing in the shed.

Later businesses at this site were Jackson & Lawson, Claude Silvers Coal, Frank G. Hough & Company Beans, and Heil Bean, Inc.

An earlier coal business once located at this site. People's Transfer and Coal, organized in 1902 with CW Albert as bookkeeper, mined coal south of Bloom, Colorado but because of poor quality the business did not thrive. Jackson & Lawson were local distributors of the product. Shack, top photo, with its window and door is visible at lower left of this photo.

Photos courtesy, *Rocky Ford Public Museum*

Donk's Variety Store in 1949 at 207 N Main.

JC Penney Company in 1949, at 305, and **Evalynn's** at 307 N Main Street. Athalie's later occupied the JC Penney site at 305 and Western Auto occupied 307 after Evalynn's.

Braden's Drug Store in 1949 at 209 N Main before a move to Elm Avenue. The large sign—DRUGS—visible above two photos has also been moved to the Elm Avenue site.

Southern Colorado Power Company, 1949, at 301 N Main Street. SOCOPOCO once occupied 307 N Main and operated a new generating station on the 200 block of S Eleventh Street. The Barber Pole at left was front of Calvin A. Aulgur's Barber Shop at 954 Elm Avenue.

Photos courtesy *Doris Baublits*

A Walk Past Local Businesses

Fraser Dry Goods, 1949, at 309 N Main Street in the Bernard-Cover Building, adjacent **Don's Mens Store** at 311. Fraser's and former Western Auto at 307 were later occupied by Harris Pharmacy.

Love's Shoe Store, 1949, at 313 N Main Street, SW corner of Main Street and Swink Avenue. **Cartwright Building**, below c 1950s, at 421 N Main Street.

Businesses in 1950s include **Smith's Department Store**, center, at 309 N Main Street, **Athalie's,** 305 at far left, **Southern Colorado Power Company** at 307 and **Don's for Lad and Dad** at 311.

Lee's Barber Shop occupies the left store room at this time.

[*Marks could not be removed without further damage. Photo of LEE'S BARBER SHOP is the only available*].

Photos courtesy *Doris Baublits*

North Side Cut-Rate & Package Liquor Store at 423 N Main Street in 1949, occupied by Hernandez Pool Hall in 1940s–1950s. Site was the original J Wood Peery Cash Grocery.

Kaplan Mercantile Co. 208 N Main Street in afternoon sunlight, 1949. Charles J. Wanger proprietor, Harry R. Wanger, manager. Building was formerly occupied by Mint Saloon.

Hesteds Store at 304 N Main Street. Parking was on the north of this business at left. Part of Hesteds adjoining the parking area was the original Safeway Store in the 1940s. Carousel, p. 187 in 1950s, *occupied* 304–312 followed by Duckwalls. Global Treasurez currently occupies this site.

Kaplan's Clothing at 208 N Main Street, 1970, is adjacent Phil's Hardware in the former Hardt location at 206. A prominent elevated sign indicates the way to Play Park. Note changes in building front above since that in 1949, including name. Photos courtesy *Doris Baublits*

A Walk Past Local Businesses

Beman Building, 300 N Main Street, 1949, at this time was likely the site of the Studebaker agency. Known originally as the Godding Block, at 300–302 N Main. La Frances Dress Shop was at this address sometime before First Industrial Bank.

Gambles store at 204 N Main Street in 1949. Visible at right is part of the building at 200 N Main, future site of Fashion Center and Walker's Men's Wear. A consignment shop later would occupy 200 N Main Street.

Hardt Hardware at 206 N Main Street in 1949. Ritthaler Bakery operated by Lee and Josie Ritthaler occupied 206 in the 1940s. Curtis-Erickson Carpet occupied in the 1970s.

Photos courtesy *Doris Baublits*

St. James Hotel, 300 S Main Street, the original occupant. Appliances appear in the street-level window, indicating business in the absence of a sign. **Army Navy Store** is next door right at 302 under the awning. The workman is servicing a street light.

Army-Navy Store, left, adjacent the former Cantaloupe Café, 306 S Main Street, center, with current business unidentified in this photo. The white brick building remained unchanged in appearance until the east side 300 block S Main was razed. **Stauffer Food Company,** right, occupied S Main 306–310 beginning 1914. Construction of McClain's Super Foods proceeded after closing of Rhoades Food Center.
Photos courtesy *Rocky Ford Public Library*

Though not quite a match the composite below shows **P&M Café** at 915 and **Karl's Café and Liquor** at 917 Elm Avenue in 1949. Alleyways divide the 900 block on Elm Avenue between Ninth and Main Streets and Main and Tenth Streets. Main Street bisects the entire 900 block of Elm between Ninth and Tenth Streets. These businesses were between an alley, left, and Main Street.

Photos courtesy *Doris Baublits*

A Walk Past Local Businesses

Trail Café, above in 1949, advertises "Good Coffee, Steaks and Chops."

[Location of this business at publication not confirmed.]

June Chevrolet at 966 Elm Avenue in 1949 was earlier at 404–406 N Main Street.

June Chevrolet Used Cars, below, at 101 N Tenth Street. South side of the building faced Elm Avenue.

View is from below George B. Nelson's Conoco station sign on the SW corner Tenth Street and Elm Avenue, in 1949.

North Tenth Street 101, above, was eventually site of Ark Valley Memorial Company, owned by Mike and Suzanne Donelson.

Photos courtesy *Doris Baublits*

Standard Credit Company, in 1949 on Elm Avenue.

Motor [*Supply*?] **Co.,** 1971
[*Location of this business is not verified.*]

Clute Manufacturing Co. of Francis H. and Elva Clute. Seed cleaning equipment and elevators were manufactured in this building before it was destroyed by fire. The building was located south of Hopkins Avenue on the east side of SH 71 (S Twelfth Street) facing west, c 1949.

Nikkel's Superior Service operated here, later **Johnson's Superior Service,** 116 Elm Avenue–US 50.

Super Bronze and *Super Ethyl* were available for a great price at this station in 1949.

Photos courtesy *Doris Baublits*

[*Ink marks could not be removed without further damage.*]

A Walk Past Local Businesses

Rocky Ford Pump House, c 1908   Courtesy *Rocky Ford Public Library, 12x28, V.S. Colo.-3, 4/16/31*

Narrative by DK Spencer:

It is a railroad maintenance shed for section gang motor cars and working gear. Enlarging the photo shows regular RR track at the bottom. Each door has wooden 'tracks' from the iron tracks to the doors of the shed for the motor cars. My guess is the house standing alone in the background belonged to the foreman and the longer house in the background is for the gang.

I understand there was such a setup off of the 7th street crossing last occupied by Goodner Pump and Supply Co. Another typical RR item is the sign outlined against the side of the foreman's house [far right]. They were made to last using 4x4 or 6x6 lumber, with edging of iron.

Not sure about the water tank, but assume the photo was taken from the south side, facing north. The tank may have been used to fill the locomotive tenders. However, it lacks a necessary swing down crane that was used to fill the tenders. Maybe it had been removed by the time this picture was taken. However, it seems to me that at one time, there [were] two tanks here, the other being close to the 10th Street crossing just west of Swink's store which was the first depot. It may have been the one with the crane. I assume it must have been for the section gang's use ?? If so, the gang would have 10 or 15 men, so along with families they probably would use a lot of water. Not sure what the initials V.S.* would stand for unless it was Vroman School?

DK Spencer, Rocky Ford and Santa Fe Railroad historian, email 7-1-2014.

Courtesy *Rocky Ford Public Library*

Hawley Store, a rural gas stop at the crossroads of SH 10, foreground, and SH 71, at left. This store was a familiar sight for many traveling La Junta to Walsenburg and points west. Undated photo shows the store open for business. Property was once owned by Charley and Elma Black.

Photo c 1930s courtesy *Doris Baublits*

Airplane Inn on US 50, to left, current site of Grace Baptist Church, near Crooked Arroyo west of La Junta, CO. Many in the Arkansas Valley were familiar with this bar and dance hall just before, during, and after WWII. West-facing front is shown. Though not in Rocky Ford, both these businesses were familiar to many people of the Arkansas Valley.

A Walk Past Local Businesses

Southeastern Colorado Exposition
AUGUST 31, SEPTEMBER 1, 2, 3, 1926
Rocky Ford, Colorado

THE FINEST EXPOSITION BUILDING IN THE WEST   Photo courtesy *Rocky Ford Public Library*

"85x135 feet in dimensions with no posts in interior–Fire proof built of Fabricated Steel, Brick and Cement. Don't miss this exposition and Fair. It is the show window of what is produced in the greatest agricultural section the SUN shines on. One hundred thousand people will be in attendance."

Caption and description below photo were printed in the *Enterprise*. Building probably was located on the American Beet Sugar Company grounds, but does not appear on a map of the succeeding American Crystal Sugar Company grounds made in 1951. Building exhibits similar architecture as other factory buildings and may have been converted to other use.*

An accompanying note attached to the above newspaper article and photo, apparently added by an archivist, refers to another news article: "Read March 21, 1924 to learn more about the Fair Association in American Beet Sugar Co. History."

*Factory records archived at *Minnesota Historical Society*, mnhs.org

Baker Jewelry at 205 N Main would at another time occupy a site in the Gobin building at 920 Elm Avenue. **Holland Drug** at 203 N Main remained at site with periodic store-front updates.

Todd Airfield was on the prairie 2.5 miles S of Rocky Ford near County Roads DD and 18. At least three other airfields at one time located in Otero County near Rocky Ford. Cottonwood Airfield, SE Rocky Ford, Zimmerman Airfield near Dye Reservoir, as well as Melon Field, located on CR 21 SE of Rocky Ford.

Photos courtesy *Rocky Ford Public Library*

A Walk Past Local Businesses

People at the Fair
Watermelon Day was originally celebrated on the first Thursday in September.

10045156

10045154
Photos c 1920s-1930s
Courtesy *History Colorado, Original Photograph Collection.* Call numbers adjacent photos

10045158

10045155

People at the Fair always dressed well. Hats are worn by every individual, young and old. Dusty shoes and stockings were the norm and at least one woman, far left photo, holds a paper fan mounted on a small wooden handle. September was usually warm.

Rench Grocery at 303 N Main Street c 1900 adjacent the 1895 Hale Building. Canned items are visible, sacked items are displayed outdoors. Unidentified items are displayed behind three men.

Photos courtesy *Rocky Ford Public Museum*

Rumsey Grocery and Bakery 417–419 N Main Street directly adjacent north of the future Masonic Hall in 1902, lot here vacant at left.

This building is extant, partially visible, pp. 107, 110 bottom photos at far right. Building is visible p. 144 at the Cut & Style location.

House and delivery wagon to the right are signed **Home Bakery**, apparently supplier and delivery service for the grocery. The house at right is adjacent the future location in 1910 of the Cartwright Building to the north. N Main at 419 would eventually house Henry's Cleaners where the house is in this photo.

A Walk Past Local Businesses

Hale Building, built in 1895 at 401 N Main Street. Adjacent buildings north eventually would have second stories visible in photograph below. Photo above is dated 1900 when ditches yet watered some of the city's 3000 Cottonwood trees planted in 1888. Function of the small building behind the baby pram is not known.
Photos courtesy *Rocky Ford Public Library*

Rocky Ford Garage at 406 N Main Street was the business of James K. Lumbar who would eventually move to 419–421 S Main, the Cheek Building.

June Chevrolet Co. would locate here from 1936 to 1939. Building preceded construction January 4, 1900 of 400 N Main to be adjacent the house. Donk's Furniture occupied 406 N Main years later.

House at 404 N Main—marker above—was home of Mrs. Effie Hall who rented rooms to five individuals in 1911. Her home-site years later would become McClelland Motor Parts.

Rocky Ford Auto Co. garage site several years later is enhanced by maturing trees. The era of automobiles is reflected in the sign addition.

Mrs. Hall's house at 404 N Main has been removed reflected by the space between 406 and the building now at 400 N Main, behind water truck, below.

Garage above, year and men are not identified. Several locations likely, possibly an automobile agency. Photo known to be taken in Rocky Ford.
Courtesy *facebook.com/Rocky-Ford-Colorado*

Occupants of the buildings at 406 and 400 N Main Street at the time of this photo are not known. Stepped facade of 406 is visible in all three photos above. The 1919 city sprinkler is cleaning a paved Main Street, indicating c 1921 or later. [City Council had authorized the Main Street Paving District January 25, 1921].

Three photos above courtesy
Rocky Ford Public Museum

Children of Rocky Ford School District No. 4   Photo courtesy *Rocky Ford Public Museum*

Children are on the racetrack at the fairgrounds, near the grandstand for exercises. Year is not known but such an event in early springtime was part of the author's experience in the 1940s as a student at Washington School. Event location was the same area as above.

A teacher at right operates a phonograph on a small table, apparently playing music for those in the circle. Caption for the near circle is '1st Grade.'

A clear view of the west grandstand shows persons occupying some of the box seats below the supporting columns and the extensive bleachers from center to right distance. The Agriculture Building and two others are visible behind the bleachers. The livestock barn with its gambrel roof is the last at far right.

Everson Tabernacle, October 20, 1929.　　　　　　　　Courtesy *Doris L. Baublits*

This photo presents a mystery. People appear well-dressed, prepared for the October weather, apparently sitting in a large meeting hall. Group appears anticipating an event for several in the front are attracted to something or someone at their left. Somber congregation might be part of a revival meeting such as one at the location depicted p. 13. Several gatherings attended revival events in town over the years.

　　Time must have been running on. Three young men—*box*—seem to have mastered the art of sitting-up asleep. The bearded man at their front appears to have joined them.

Research for *Rocky Ford, Colorado—A Walk Past Local Doors* has taken more than three years. Many places searched for vintage photographs and facts about the businesses in town eventually left the inevitable unknowns. Pages 25, 271, 272, and this one have photos of unidentified location, people, or year of event. There are, no doubt, many more.

　　　　　　　　　　　　　　　　　　　　　　　　　　　　　　　　　　　　　　Author

Postscript: Life of a Building, and of a Town

Longevity of a building was not always considered when pioneering a new town out West. The entrepreneur drew a chance in a lottery or bought a lot at the town lot auction expecting quickly to set up his home or shop in a tent, adobe, or wattle-and-daub structure with thatched, sod roof.

Design was not really important, except for size, nor was a master plan for the future. Only expedient and immediate protection from the elements or hostile human or threatening animal contacts. The goal; get the house or business started.

Materials on location were used in construction. Not until years passed could buildings be designed and erected with locally-made bricks or milled lumber. Utilities were not available until water systems, electricity generators and distribution systems, telephone lines, and sewer systems were developed. The rudimentary building could then be equipped with some amenities.

An electric light franchise was granted in 1896 and the Rocky Ford Electric Company was provided permit to distribute light and heat to citizens in 1897. Southern Colorado Power opened offices in 1929. When gas for heating and lighting came into use in Rocky Ford April 1929, it was after a pipeline brought it from Texas. Some houses in this country were already lighted by a home gas-production system requiring tanks periodically recharged with calcium carbide and water. The acetylene gas produced was piped to lamps controlled by valves at each use site.

With utilities, planning and maintenance became important. Buildings eventually reached limits of usefulness until space was added, with some attention to esthetics. Owners of buildings and proprietors of businesses began to think of preservation to extend longevity, and the cost was greater in the process.

Early in the days when buildings went up fast, corners may have been cut. Construction budgets limited what was designed into a building. Inevitably this reflected on its life and the likelihood an owner could profitably upgrade, renovate, add on or sell to someone who could do something with the structure.

Without these refinements, the ultimate stage in the life of many buildings is deconstruction. Unfortunately, we see that happening in many places, not only in Rocky Ford. Many would say there is merit to erecting the new building with all its technological improvements.

Local economy had a great influence on what happened in the past. Rocky Ford streets, homes, and businesses were quite different because of the many jobs that accompanied a vigorous sugar economy. Even more benefits came from dozens of peripheral businesses and service providers that were needed then. Even so, without them citizens today are conscientiously working toward longevity, not only of remaining city buildings, but life of the city.

Afterword: Observations on Watermelon Day

Many involved with fair activities, especially Watermelon Day, wondered what to do after it was over. Since the first 25 or so people served by George W. Swink at the establishment of the celebration in 1878, the numbers have soared.

Tons of donated melons, later bought from farmers, were arranged in a long pile among the trees of GW Swink's former Timber Claim. Early in its history at an appointed hour the gathered crowd was unguided and unrestrained to approach the melon pile. Some concern followed. Many melon-fanciers took more than one, if they could carry them under each arm, and with family or friends helping. Some even pulled their red *Radio Flyers* and pushed baby prams to transport their melons. A few individuals, regrettably, suffered crowd abuse.

Following years required that a limit be set, one to a customer. The melons were passed to the people who gathered at an enclosure, sometimes over a counter, sometimes through a gate. In the late 1800s and early 1900s that enclosure kept order around the pile. Helpers in the distribution of the melons actually carved them open for those wanting to eat them on site. There were cutting boards and long tables for the purpose. Early photos show aproned men in shirt-sleeves, ties, and hats doing this, with long knives. Some melon recipients did their own carving a few yards away from the milling crowd. Others carried theirs to their buggy or wagon, and in later years, to their auto for a ride home (see note p. 303).

Many tons, 80 some years—100 in 1955—were given away to those who eagerly opened them for the heart, leaving the rest on the ground producing an unsightly, wasteful scene. In little time, flies were everywhere, drawn to the sweet remains in the summer heat. Negotiating a path through yards of many spoiling rinds was tricky. Photographer PE Kennedy recorded the scene, pp. 65, 238.

Reacting to the aftermath, some suggested animals could graze on what was left. Goats were brought in but they did not eat just anything, as thought. It seems they are selective about eating spoiled food and are sensitive to molds and *Listeria*. Another time, swine fed there among the trees. They did a better job of eating the remains. However, the fly problem was worse, especially after the pigs left. In the end, cleanup crews with shovels, rakes, and trucks produced a far safer, healthier, and more thorough outcome than what had been tried.

For the future, the presence of so many thousands of visitors to the Fair, especially on Watermelon Day, required that no melons be eaten on premises. With all its challenges and changes, this great tradition has survived the years. Apart from the celebration of it, I still enjoy a melon taken directly from the vine in the coolness of an evening when no one else is around.

The Author

Dave and C J Muth
February 12, 2012

David J. Muth was born November 30, 1936 on a farm near Rocky Ford, Otero County, Colorado. He moved with his family to East Ranch of the American Crystal Sugar Company in 1938.

He and his siblings, Dorothy, Kenneth, and Vernon attended Washington Elementary and Rocky Ford High School. After graduation David enlisted in the US Army, 1954–1957, then attended Otero Junior College in La Junta 1957–1959. At Colorado State University in Fort Collins he studied the Biological Sciences 1959–1962 and Immunology as a graduate student, 1972.

In 1962 he began a 32-year federal civilian career diagnosing viral diseases in the laboratories of the Centers For Disease Control and Prevention. Dave and CJ's son Michael lives in Loveland and is a rural mail carrier for the USPS. He owns Blue Mountain Lawn Care. Their daughter Mary travels the US and sometimes other countries in her profession as a software installation and training specialist for companies preparing for financial planning and growth. She and husband Clay Crist own CNC Technical Services of Aurora, aiding businesses to improve electronic communication.

After CJ's retirement from the Poudre Valley Hospital Pathology Department, she and Dave moved from Fort Collins to the mountains near Livermore, Colorado in 1997. Dave has been writing family history until this latest effort at some history of his home town, Rocky Ford.

Publications in Retirement:

Arnpriester Family History: *From the Bergseite Colony Rosenberg of the Russian Volga Province Saratov and the United States.*, Ruth Muth Grenard, Archival Contributor and Editor, published privately: Glacier View Meadows, Livermore, Colorado, 2010.

Maintenance Manual: *Procedures for Inspection and Seasonal Maintenance, Peace With Christ Lutheran Church, Fort Collins*, Colorado. Edited by Board of Trustees, published privately: Fort Collins, Colorado, 1997.

Muth, Red White Blue and Gray: *Soldier Muth in the American Revolution and the War Between the States.* A monograph published privately: Glacier View Meadows, Livermore, Colorado, 2012.

Our Muth Family History: *From Germany to the Volga Kanton, Russia and the United States.* Ruth Muth Grenard, Archival Contributor and Editor, published privately: Glacier View Meadows, Livermore, Colorado, 2007. Re-edited with supplement 2011.

Our Spate Family History: *From Germany to The Volga Provinces, Russia and the United States.* Ruth Muth Grenard, Archival Contributor and Editor, published privately: Glacier View Meadows, Livermore, Colorado, 2008. Re-edited with supplement 2011.

The American Beet Sugar Company, 1899 to American Crystal Sugar Company, 1934–1979. Part I Photographs of the Beet Sugar Industry; Part II East Ranch Memories. A monograph published privately: Glacier View Meadows, Livermore, Colorado, 2010.

Publications in Career:

Twenty-five articles were co-authored with fellow researchers for various journals during a 32-year career in public health. Address of work site: *Division of Vector-Borne Infectious Diseases, National Center for Infectious Diseases, Centers for Disease Control and Prevention, Public Health Service, U.S. Department of Health and Human Services,* Fort Collins, Colorado.

Acta Virologica. 1984 Mar; 28(2): 148-51.

American Journal of Epidemiology. 1966 Jul; 84(1): 67-73.

American Journal of Tropical Medicine and Hygiene. 1977 Sep; 26(5 Pt 1): 997-1002.
Ibid. 1980 Jul; 29(4): 624-34.
____ 1980 Nov; 29(6): 1428-40.
____ 1981 Mar; 30(2): 490-6.
____ 1983 Mar; 32(2): 424-31.
____ 1983 Jul; 32(4): 877-85.
____ 1986 Mar; 35(2): 429-43.

American Journal of Veterinary Research. 1986 Jun; 47(6): 1296-9.

Bulletin of the Pan American Health Organization. 1980; 14(4): 386-91.

Canadian Journal of Microbiology. 1978 Apr; 24(4): 422-6.

Epidemiology and Infection. 2000 Aug; 125(1): 181-8.

Journal of American Veterinary Medical Association. 1983 Aug; 15183(4): 438-40.

Journal of Clinical Microbiology. 1981 Aug; 14(2): 135-40.
Ibid. 1984 Oct; 20(4): 784-90.
____ 1985 Oct; 22(4): 566-71.
____ 1986 Feb; 23(2): 369-72.
____ 1986 Apr; 23(4): 667-71.
____ 2000 May; 38(5): 1823-6.

Journal of Laboratory and Clinical Medicine. 1970 Mar; 75(3): 457-62.

Journal of Wildlife Diseases. 1989, Oct; 25(4): 481-9.

Lancet. 1987 Jan; 17;1(8525): 165-6.

Southern Medical Journal. 1980 Nov; 73(11): 1548.

Transactions of the Royal Society of Tropical Medicine and Hygiene. 1981; 75(2): 282-6.

Titles and articles may be accessed through the National Center for Biotechnology Information,

National Library of Medicine, National Institutes of Health on their web site by entering author's full name: http://www.ncbi.nlm.nih.gov:80.

Appendix A

A Chronology to the Centennial Year 1987

	1869	Kansas Pacific Railroad reached the eastern boundary of Colorado Territory.
	1870	A spur of the Kit Carson Trail came west from Kit Carson, namesake of the frontiersman, in eastern Colorado Territory and went southwest toward the Spanish Peaks. The trail crossed the Arkansas River at a *rocky ford*. The trail at this crossing went south toward the Santa Fe Trail and another spur west to Pueblo.
	1871	GW Swink and Asa Russell built their first trading post.
Dec 1	1871	Post office established at original site of Old Rocky Ford on the Arkansas River.
	1873	John Swift, James Lowe, and Andy Nichols arrived and among them built a blacksmith shop, boarding house, and a log ferry for wagons and teams. William Matthews and James Lowe surveyed and built the first three miles of the Rocky Ford ditch. AT & S Fe RR reached ten miles into Colorado Territory. A school district was organized, then in the western part of Bent County.
	1874	AT & SF construction to La Junta meeting The Pueblo & Arkansas Valley RR.
May 14	1874	Rocky Ford Canal was decreed, first irrigation canal in Otero County.
	1875	GW Swink and Levi Beghtol filed claims near railroad survey.
Jan 5	1876	Santa Fe Railroad arrived in the Arkansas Valley.
Jul 4	1876	First town plat by William Matthews.
	1876	GW Swink built an adobe store near RR crossing and Kit Carson Road.
Aug 1	1876	Colorado Territory became the state Colorado.
	1877	First school built in July of adobe south of Swink's timber claim, later boarded, painted white, known as *The Little White School*.
Sep 5	1878	GW Swink began Watermelon Day with 25 persons in attendance.
	1879	The first camp meeting ever held in the Arkansas Valley in Swink's factory at 100 S Twelfth Street.
Jan 11	1882	GW Swink completes artificial lake near east end of Maple Avenue.
Apr 12	1887	Rocky Ford platted for second time, legally filed. Sale of town lots held.
Jun 2	1887	The Rocky Ford Enterprise of HV Alexander first published.
14	1887	The State Bank of Rocky Ford was organized.
23	1887	McKay's Turf Exchange served free beer.
24	1887	The State Bank of Rocky Ford was incorporated.
Jul 13	1887	Commissioners, appointed by court published notice of election for incorporation as a town.
28	1887	Construction began on the State Bank building at 201 N Main.
Aug 6	1887	Electors voted for incorporation of Rocky Ford as a town.
10	1887	Incorporation papers filed in Bent County Court, Las Animas.
19	1887	Rocky Ford incorporation papers were recorded in Denver.
Sep 3	1887	The mayor and six trustees were elected.
25	1887	Construction of Holbrook Ditch; decreed 155 ac. ft water Sept. 25, 1889.
29	1887	Bd. of Trustees passed ordinance; *Ordinance Concerning Ordinances*.
Oct 5	1887	Group met to begin the work of the Methodist Episcopal Church in Rocky Ford.
25	1887	Marshal appointed at salary $40.00 per month. Committee appointed to find site for town jail.
Nov 3	1887	GW Swink received Timber Culture Certificate No. 1, now part of the Arkansas Valley Fairgrounds.
Dec 15	1887	First issue Rocky Ford *Enterprise*.
Jan 15	1888	The Presbyterian Church was organized.
	1888	First bridge [wooden] over the Arkansas built a mile east of the original ford.
	1888	First Catholic Mass held in the Little White School.
Feb 18	1889	St. Johns Lodge No. 75 Ancient, Free and Accepted Masons [AF&AM] organized.
	1889	High Line Canal Company founded.
Jan 20	1890	Rocky Ford Lodge No. 87, Independent Order of Odd Fellows [IOOF] was organized.
Jul 31	1890	The city reservoir was completely cemented.
Dec 20	1890	The First Baptist Church was organized.
Mar 5	1891	Violet Rebekah Lodge No. 3, [ladies associated with IOOF].
Feb 23	1892	Second US Timber Culture certificate issued to Isaiah Dennes.
Apr 6	1892	Arkansas Valley Fair Association organized.
Sep 7	1893	Watermelon Day special trains from Canon City, Pueblo, Monument, other cities.

Chronology to the Centennial Year 1987

Oct 5 1893		Race track and horse barns had been built as first improvements of the fairgrounds.
Dec 3 1884		Catlin Canal Company received priority decree of 248 second feet of water.
Jan 9 1894		CM Miller petitioned commissioners for bridge between Rocky Ford and Swink.
Mar 12 1894		The canning factory began accepting contracts for the season.
Apr 13 1894		FY Hauck Hose Company organized, LR Fenlason chief, FY Hauck asst chief.
1894		Steel truss bridge replaced the original wooden structure of 1888.
1894		First Christian Church organized in *small adobe building* 300 block S Main.
Apr 21 1894		The Golden Rule Department Store opened in the Odd Fellows Building 200 S Main.
July 8 1894		Dedication of first Catholic Church.
Sep 6 1894		Third annual fair & Watermelon Day sponsored by Ark. Valley Fair Assoc.
Sep 27 1894		Swink Hotel was sold to JP Salls and Charles Chandler of Colorado Springs.
Oct 23 1894		The Arkansas Valley Irrigation Society organized in La Junta.
29 1894		Rocky Ford Camp 195 Woodmen of the World organized with 59 charter members.
Nov 5 1894		BU Dye stocked 100 black bass in his lake across the river.
10 1894		The river bridge was completed on the road to the Holbrook area NE of town.
Jan 3 1895		The Swink Hotel at 300 S Main was sold to JS Seeley.
Mar 8 1895		L. Anderson purchased the Photograph Gallery from JE Orr.
Jun 26 1895		The Cretcher and McMurtry Lumber Yard began stock with four carloads.
Sep 2 1895		The [first] artesian well was connected to the town's piping system.
Oct 21 1895		Valley Lodge No. 98, Knights of Pythias [K of P] organized; chartered Sep. 10, 1896.
Apr 9 1896		Bridges over Rocky Ford Canal on Main and Ninth Street completed.
Apr 30 1896		South Main Street opened with walnut trees planted both sides.
Aug 11 1896		An electric light franchise was granted JB Downey.
Sep 10 1896		WF Stark opened a store for new and second hand goods of all kinds.
Jan 8 1897		WN Randall surveyed the streets to establish a sidewalk grade.
Jan 15 1897		JS Scott took possession of BF Knause's barber shop.
Jan 27 1897		Fred Cheek began construction of Rocky Ford Creamery at 1300 Elm Avenue].
Jan 31 1897		Mrs. NC Young and Mrs. JC Kain opened the recently purchased Swink Hotel.
May 9 1897		First services at new Baptist Church; dedicated June 6, 1897.
Jun 7 1897		First 275 pounds of butter produced at the Rocky Ford Creamery of LW Babcock.
Jun 18 1897		The Public Grocery and Market opened at 302 S Main.
Aug 13 1897		The Harlan Thomas Camp No. 18, Sons of Veterans organized with 30 members.
14 1897		The Otero Co. Veteran's Assoc. of Blue & Gray tented at the AV Fairgrounds.
Oct 14 1897		BG Wilson & Co. received contract to furnish 420 for Recker's Hall.
23 1897		The Rocky Ford Women's Club organized at Mrs. Godding's home.
Nov 6 1897		NW Terry laid out Ellingwood and Hauck's 30 x 80 ft. warehouse on Main Street.
2 1897		Rocky Ford Electric Co. received permit to furnish light and heat to citizens.
Dec 27 1897		Stockholders of Rocky Ford Ice & Storage Co. set by-laws and elected directors.
Jan 8 1898		Meeting at Masonic Hall to discuss organization of a lodge of the Eastern Star.
Jun 1 1898		The Rocky Ford Church of The Brethren was organized.
8 1898		Acacia Chapter, No. 38, Order of Eastern Star was chartered.
16 1898		The Opera House Pharmacy opened on SE corner of the Recker-Hagen block.
July 2 1898		The Arkansas Valley Sheep Feeder's Association was organized.
Aug 25 1898		A saloon license was granted JJ Gholson.
Sep 1 1898		Hay Palace was replaced by a frame structure in a dense grove.
Apr 22 1899		Farmer's & Merchant's Bank opened at 301 S Main, moved 208 N Main.
May 4 1899		Colorado Telephone Co. completed a line from Pueblo to Rocky Ford with offices rear of Price and Lance's Store.
Jan 4 1900		Modern Woodmen Camp No. 7473 chartered. George Higgins built a large brick Livery barn 400 N Main Street west of the new Liberty School on Tenth Street.
Feb 14 1900		Construction of the American Beet Sugar Company factory began.
15 1900		Colorado Telephone Company organized a joint Rocky Ford-La Junta exchange.

Rocky Ford, Colorado, A Walk Past Local Doors

Jun 27 1900	Foundation work started for the TE Godding block at 300-302 N Main.
Oct 5 1900	New hotel plans [El Capitan] at NW corner Main and Chestnut were presented.
13 1900	Republican Club met in uncompleted K of P building 401 N Main.
Feb 12 1901	The telephone company added new phones to some residences.
Jun 5 1901	The Rocky Ford Fire Co. elected officers, chief, captain, treasurer, and secretary.
Mar 28 1902	The Rocky Ford Town and Investment Company dissolved.
Apr 9 1902	People's Transfer & Coal Co. incorporated.
23 1902	Park Addition was annexed to Rocky Ford.
Jun 28 1902	Voters approved enlarging Washington School and funds for Lincoln School.
July 1 1902	Free mail delivery started in Rocky Ford.
5 1902	Contract to Rocky Ford Brick & Tile Co. for addition to Washington School.
Aug 4 1902	Ordinance 94 created the Rocky Ford Fire Department.
5 1902	Grand Opera House opened.
Sep 20 1902	Ninth annual Blue & Grey Encampment, two days, at the fairgrounds.
Nov 6 1902	Rocky Ford Masonic Hall opened.
8 1902	Dedication of Masonic St. John's Lodge No. 75.
Jan 7 1903	An overheated flue caused some fire damage at the depot.
Sep 17 1903	A Chapter of the Royal Arch Masons of the New York Rite was chartered.
Oct 18 1903	Christian Church was dedicated.
Jan 1 1904	Rocky Ford Christian Science Society was organized.
Jan 2 1904	First National Bank of Rocky Ford chartered, opened at 201 S Main. Bank later moved to 301 N Main.
Jul 27 1904	Fire damaged the outbuilding at Washington School.
Aug 29 1904	The Daily Gazette began delivering to subscribers.
Nov 3 1904	Piper Brothers contractors began work on the city sewer system.
Nov 23 1904	Rocky Ford Trading Company and ER Cook Implement consolidated.
Dec 3 1904	WL Jackson's bowling alley opened.
Dec 12 1904	The WE Clark Meat Market opened in the Barrow Grocery Store.
Jan 12 1905	Ford J. Steward reopened his plumbing shop.
Jan 25 1905	The First National Bank opened at 201 S Main Street.
Apr 1 1905	Rocky Ford Creamery incorporated.
Apr 5 1905	Western Union Telegraph Office opened at 110 N Main Street.
Feb 10 1905	Dr. Fisher Smith sold City Hospital to Mr. And Mrs. Frank Miller. WR Dye purchased The Little Cash Grocery at 409 N Main Street.
Mar 11 1905	GP Randall opened The Gem Grocery Store.
Aug 2 1905	Bartow Consolidated Canning Company opened their new plant.
16 1905	GW Lewis, WD Lewis, and JA Johnson purchased Dawley-Wilson Hardware and Furniture Company and opened Aug. 29, 1905.
Sep 8 1905	The Abe Lincoln Mines and Milling Company organized in Rocky Ford.
Nov 11 1905	Rocky Ford Gazette was sold to WH Butterfield.
1906	St. Peter's Ev. Lutheran Church organized with 60 adult members.
Jan 4 1906	City took possession of a new fire wagon.
17 1906	The Valley Trading Company sold to A. Stoop.
Jul 6 1906	Nelson and Winters opened a new cash grocery store.
Feb 1 1906	The Arkansas Valley Railroad was incorporated; (Pueblo and Arkansas Valley Railroad).
Mar 21 1906	The Palmer Dry Goods Company opened.
Apr 4 1906	Construction started for Cover-Hale-Kimzey block at 307-309 N Main Street.
May 1 1906	Cornerstone laid for new Methodist Church.
Aug 1 1906	BF Baker purchased the Gem Restaurant from HL Nichols.
Sep 11 1906	Rocky Ford Cement Brick & Tile Company made first cement blocks at 209 S Twelfth Street.
Oct 11 1906	All Rocky Ford saloons agreed to close for good.
Nov 29 1906	Brick laying began on the new Presbyterian Church.
Dec 2 1906	Brick laying began on the new Santa Fe Depot 105 N Main Street.

Chronology to the Centennial Year 1987

Dec 14 1906	Immanuel Congregational Church organized.
18 1906	Cornerstone laid for the new Presbyterian Church.
Jan 29 1907	Old adobe landmark building at Maple Avenue and Main Street was taken down.
Feb 2 1907	The Opera House Meat Market opened at 403 S Main Street.
18 1907	Work began on the new Express Office at 100 N Ninth Street.
21 1907	City tested successfully a new pumping plant for fire hoses.
Apr 5 1907	Construction began for the Walter Cheek building at 415-417 S Main Street.
Oct 3 1907	Anderson Brothers Clothing Store opened at 312 S Main Street.
Oct 10 1907	Empire Theatre opened in the new Gobin block on Elm Avenue.
Dec 26 1907	Dickinson & Davis Grocers on Railroad Avenue closed.
Dec 31 1907	Council passed ordinance granting Library Board a lease on part of City Park.
Mar 10 1908	Peoples Home Bank opened at 301 S Main Street.
Apr 27 1908	Rocky Ford National Bank chartered and opened for business at 201 N Main Street.
May 7 1908	Contract let for the Carnegie Library.
Jun 20 1908	The new high school building opened.
Aug 29 1908	WH White opened Photography Gallery at 411 ½ S Main Street.
Oct 3 1908	JL Bonta Mercantile Company opened at 200 S Main Street.
4 1908	Fire destroyed JD Herring's carpenter shop on N Ninth Street and damaged Mrs. Berry's candy store on S Main Street.
Nov 2 1908	CL Govreau Grocery & Market at 204 S Main Street became Govreau Brothers, adding CB Govreau.
Dec 21 1908	There was a small fire in Atterbury's tailor shop.
6 1909	City Park, Central Park, and South Park are so named.
7 1909	The Rocky Ford Gazette was resurrected by JB Lacy and FA Dislow.
9 1909	Fire with heavy loss, Sever & Culp Stationers and Tobacconists at 308 N Main Street.
Apr 8 1909	Rocky Ford BPOE Lodge 1147 chartered.
26 1909	The Sanitary Bakery opened at 406 S Main Street.
Jun 24 1909	The Carnegie Library opened.
Aug 9 1909	The Fulton Meat Market opened at 415 N Main Street. HM Minor, lawyer and notary public opened office at 307 ½ N Main Street.
May 1910	St. Paul's Ev. Lutheran split from German Ev. Lutheran Immanuel Church.
Sep 24 1910	Sen. GW Swink, Rocky Ford founder, died at his home 401 N Ninth Street.
Jun 3 1911	The Star Theatre opened at 409 N Main Street.
12 1911	David Downer sold the Rocky Ford Garage to FW Bell and HR Sunday.
Oct 19 1911	WH Allen bought the Rocky Ford Dairy from E. and GL Windburn.
Jun 10 1912	FW Welland bought the New Method Laundry from Fred Polhemus.
11 1912	Harry Swink moved pool hall from Weid building to room near Sanitary Bakery.
Jan 26 1914	The Farmers and Merchants Bank was liquidated.
Mar 4 1914	The Kimzey-Cover Block on N Main Street west side was destroyed by fire.
Dec 9 1914	John R. Maring purchased JS Denny's interest in Denny & Lopez Grocery Store.
Dec 15 1914	Stauffer Market, new packing plant opened.
20 1914	Rear of the Holsun Grocery at 310 S Main Street damaged by fire.
Jun 19 1918	David Stanbridge Post No. 8 American Legion chartered at 966 Walnut Avenue.
Sep 28 1918	American Legion Post named in honor of Pvt. David M. Stanbridge, Inf., MIA.
1918	Pythian Sisters organized.
Jul 15 1920	Rocky Ford Lions Club received their charter.
Jun 4 1921	Arkansas River flood claimed eight lives.
May 1 1927	Airplane field established near Dye Reservoir, later named Zimmerman Field.
Jul 17 1927	The JB Byers Company moved to a new location at 305 N Main Street.
Aug 18 1927	Art Goebel, formerly of Rocky Ford, won the Honolulu Airplane Race.
Jan 4 1928	Johnson Hardware and Furniture Store sold at auction.
6 1928	JC Vaughn Transfer & Transportation Co. and Jackson Transfer Co. received permits to operate on eastern slope of Colorado.

Rocky Ford, Colorado, A Walk Past Local Doors

Jan 7 1928	City Drug Store opened at 200 N Main Street.
May 6 1928	Post office temporarily moved to Knights of Pythias building for remodeling.
Aug 27 1928	Arthur Johnson, delivery agent for American Railway Express Co. retired 'Old Dobbin' and began driving a new truck.
Oct 25 1928	The City Drug Store was sold to the Maltby Drug Company.
Jan 30 1929	George W. Grenard purchased The Toggery from WF Woodside and George Forbes.
Apr 8 1929	Natural gas piped from Texas oil fields first used by consumers in Rocky Ford.
Sep 8 1929	American Legion dedicated the Earl Zimmerman Airport near Dye reservoir.
Oct 5 1929	Mountain States Telephone and Telegraph converted to automatic power from wet cell batteries.
Oct 26 1929	The Southern Colorado Power Company opened new offices at 301 N Main Street.
Nov 26 1929	Burrell Seed Growers Co. purchased Cheek Block at 417 S Main, then occupied by Blackford - Baughman Motor Company.
	Art Black opened Ideal Market, a self-serve store.
Jan 2 1930	Spencer Chevrolet became General Chevrolet Company under Arnold Groth.
Mar 1 1930	Bandstand in Railroad Park was demolished.
Jul 26 1930	Shamrock Service Station opened at the corner of N Main and Chestnut Avenue.
Sep 30 1930	The Stauffer-Marsh Food Company purchased the Valley Food Store.
Oct 6 1930	Construction began on O-Boy Cabins of Paul Gobin and George R. Cameron, NW corner Eleventh Street and Elm Avenue.
Oct 27 1930	Fred R. Kelly, former cashier at Rocky Ford National Bank, took charge of Fenlason Realty Co.
May 8 1931	Fire damage reported at the Great Western Poultry Farm.
Jul 22 1931	Fred Knaus' real estate and insurance business consolidated with Fenlason Realty Company.
Oct 2 1931	Arrangements made for door-to-door freight delivery by Santa Fe Railroad contract with Amos Bish.
Nov 16 1931	Economy measures agreed by local businessmen; to open from 7:30 AM to 5:00 PM.
Nov 30 1931	Fire destroyed the JB King service station.
Dec 27 1931	LE Stevenson, Red Cross Pharmacy purchased stock of Palace Drug and moved to 313 S Main Street.
Apr 18 1932	Work began on two tennis courts at 500 S Main Street.
Mar 22 1932	JC Braden moved the Rexall Drug Store to 921 Elm from 209 N Main Street.
Apr 23 1932	Frank Gandara began business at 914 Front Street after purchasing a billiard parlor from Harry Asakawa.
May 24 1932	Merchant's softball league organized at the fairgrounds.
Jun 21 1932	City Council repealed blue laws pertaining to Sunday amusements.
Sep 14 1932	The season's first celery crop came on market by Horace Yeater & McAfee.
Dec 11 1932	Freight office moved from the old depot west of Ninth Street to west end of passenger depot.
Jan 3 1933	Billy Smallwood and Woodrow Hayes purchased Bill Smith's restaurant at 206 S Main Street.
Nov 7 1933	City council arranged for completion of paving US 50, Elm Avenue.
17 1933	The automatic stoplight at intersection of Main and Elm was installed.
May 29 1934	Roxy Theatre opened at 421 N Main.
Jun 22 1934	Fire destroyed the Grand Theatre.
30 1934	The south wall of the Grand Theatre gave way to strong wind.
Aug 3 1934	Three wells at the tennis courts at 520 S Main Street were completed.
Oct 22 1934	Amanda Funk and Evelyn Campbell purchased Mrs. GM Baker's equipment from the Stitch Shop, opened a needlework shop in south side of Starky building
30 1934	Triangle Café east of Rocky Ford on US 50 started dances on Tuesdays, Thursdays, and Saturdays.
Jan 22 1935	HE Fly opened his public sale ring east of the Santa Fe Stock Yards.
24 1935	Work started on the new Grand Theatre building.
Feb 27 1935	Oran Dowlers opened Dowler's Fashion Shop, ladies clothing on S Main Street.
Mar 23 1935	Gamble Store opened at 207 N Main Street by WP Hardt.
May 1 1935	New Grand Theatre opened.
11 1935	Dedication of Highway 71 and river bridge connecting Otero and Crowley Counties.
Jul 14 1935	A man and two women were arrested at 206 ½ S Main Street with 9 cases of home brew.

Chronology to the Centennial Year 1987

Aug 17 1935	Tommy Thompson opened his Sweet Shoppe adjoining the Grand Theatre.
Sep 19 1935	Contractor George Teats began work preparing Grand Theatre for a new screen and sound system.
Oct 12 1935	Grand Lodge of Masons laid post office cornerstone at 401 N Ninth Street at 3 PM.
Nov 8 1935	Park Hotel at 200 S Ninth Street was razed, moved and rebuilt on Recker's property.
19 1935	City council purchased a new Chevrolet fire truck from Nelson-June Company.
Mar 13 1936	The new Post Office was opened at 401 N Ninth Street.
16 1936	John Lohmier opened Economy Clothes Shop at 404 N Main Street.
Jun 13 1936	The Dairy Shop opened at 406 N Main Street.
29 1936	Everett Marshall of La Junta won World Heavyweight Wrestling Championship.
Nov 27 1936	Fraser Dry Goods Store grand opening.
Dec 14 1936	Film ignited causing slight damage to projector at the Roxy Theatre.
Feb 24 1937	Additional land purchases from Mrs. Janes increased golf course to nine holes.
May 12 1937	Workmen began oiling streets at railroad on Ninth Street south to city limits.
Jun 3 1937	Junior Chamber of Commerce chartered.
	RFHS class of 1937 donated tennis court to school district, constructed behind RFHS, west of bus barn. A metal dedication plaque was set in court surface.
Mar 17 1938	City approved building improvements and new adobe barns for fairgrounds.
Apr 2 1938	Mrs. Bertha DeFreese opened Bertha's Lunch at 310 Elm Avenue.
26 1938	Police radio receiving and broadcast set installed.
Sep 2 1938	The Rex Theatre opened with a matinee.
Jul 24 1939	Fire damaged the Ritthaler Bakery at 206 N Main Street.
1940	Organization of Rocky Ford Archaeological Society.
May 30 1941	The first swimming pool in Rocky Ford opened.
May 1 1946	Catholic Church dedicated.
Sep 12 1949	The Empire State Bank opened.
Mar 17 1950	Rocky Ford Enterprise ceased publication; began as Rocky Ford Daily Gazette-Topic And Enterprise.
Apr 3 1950	Groundbreaking for Southern Colorado Power Plant on S Eleventh Street.
Jul 12 1953	Fire Chief Clyde Summers and volunteer Martel Lueker died in a rescue attempt during a flood.
Apr 16 1954	The Rocky Ford Daily Gazette-Topic And Enterprise renamed The Rocky Ford Daily Gazette.
Aug 23 1954	The Pioneer Memorial Hospital was dedicated.
Jan 20 1965	The First Industrial Bank opened at 917 Railroad Avenue.
Aug 21 1965	Watermelon Day, always the first Thursday of September, was moved to a Saturday for the first time.
Feb 5 1968	Don Ahlers sold Don's Mens Store to Otis Love and Don Gause.
Mar 20 1975	Kitch Pontiac building at 1014 Elm was destroyed by fire.
Dec 4 1977	Firemen battled six hours fighting four fires set by arsonists.
Aug 5 1983	TE Hanson purchased the Gambles store.
Nov 4 1983	Grand opening of the Rocky Ford Inn.
May 3 1984	Frozen Foods began processing onions from Texas.
Oct 9 1986	Wrangler Foods opened at 800 Chestnut Avenue.

In 1987 and 1988, special editions of the *Daily Gazette, Rocky Ford Centennial Recollections* appeared. Photos of businesses, new and old, were included. Many are in *A Photo History* of this book.

Rocky Ford Centennial Committee of the Rocky Ford Chamber of Commerce provided most of this chronology, published in *Calendar of Historical Interest.* Herman L. Boraker, committee member, commended the following for assistance and information: Dee Henderson, Eleanor Lacy, Homer Mackey, Pauline Morgan, Mrs. John [Elizabeth] Muth, Greg Smith, Rex Sprinkle, Mrs. Stipe, Gary Ratliff, Martin Andrew of La Junta, Jerre Swink, George Boraker, and JR Thompson.   November 1, 1986

Information in the chronology is supplemented with data from newspapers and John Doll's book, The History of Rocky Ford, published in 1987. Author

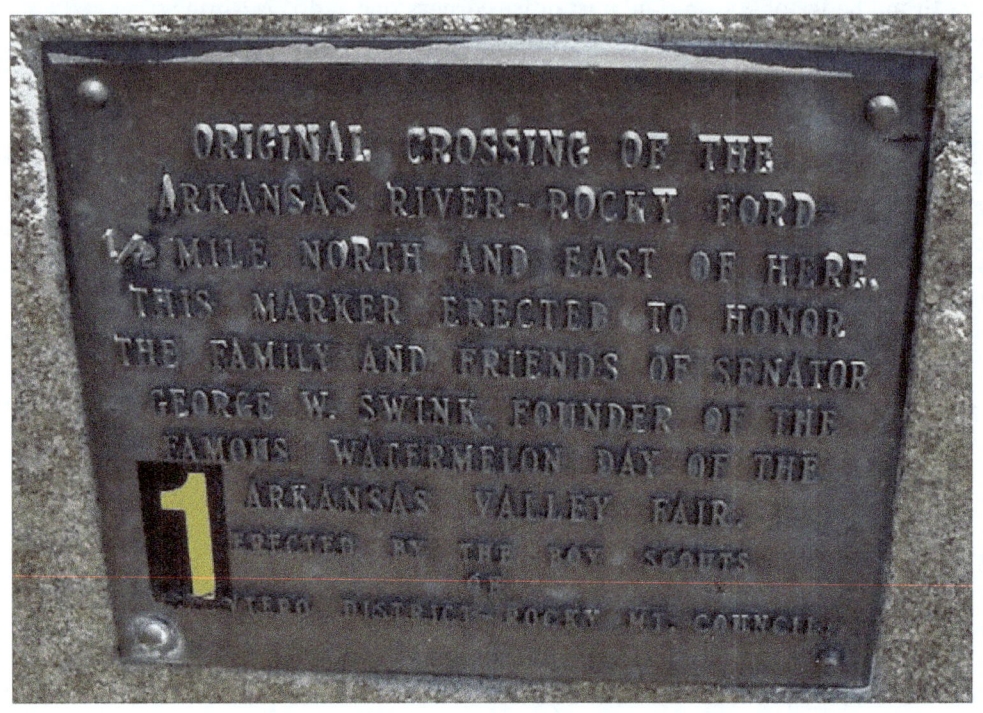

Photo courtesy *C J Muth*

**ORIGINAL CROSSING OF THE
ARKANSAS RIVER - ROCKY FORD**
1/2 MILE NORTH AND EAST OF HERE.
THIS MARKER ERECTED TO HONOR
THE FAMILIES AND FRIENDS OF SENATOR
GEORGE W. SWINK, FOUNDER OF THE
FAMOUS WATERMELON DAY OF THE
ARKANSAS VALLEY FAIR.
ERECTED BY THE BOY SCOUTS
OF OTERO COUNTY—ROCKY MT. COUNCIL.

Appendix B

GW Swink: Founder of Rocky Ford

In brief, George Washington Swink:

    Was born June 30, 1836 in Breckinridge County, Kentucky;
    Moved with his family to Schuyler County, Illinois when he was 4;
    Worked in a sawmill there as a young man, then farmed and began merchandising in Bardolph, Illinois;
    Married Mary J. Cook in 1855 and eventually they raised six boys and five girls;
    Moved to Bent County, Colorado in 1871 where he established a store and cattle business with partner Asa Russell at *Old Rocky Ford* on the Arkansas River;
    Began a canal system for irrigation with first excavations of the Rocky Ford Canal in 1873, also assisted the development of the Catlin and High Line Canals;
    Served as first postmaster in 1875, moved store and goods to the *new Rocky Ford* in 1876;
    Was selected first station agent in Rocky Ford when Santa Fe tracks arrived in the Arkansas Valley in 1876;
    Began Watermelon Day in 1878;
    Received first Timber Culture Claim from the US government in 1887;
    Participated in sale of town lots before Rocky Ford was incorporated in 1887;
    Was a three-term mayor beginning the first in 1887 and ending his last term in 1903;
    Served two terms as Colorado State Senator 1892-1900;
    Died in 1910.

Among the several interests of Mr. Swink, beyond cattle-raising, was the development of agriculture in the Arkansas Valley. He established honey bee culture in 1878, watermelon, and cantaloupe industries and began his first alfalfa crop in 1879. He was an early supporter of the sugar beet industry and aided the establishment of American Beet Sugar Company, later to be known as American Crystal Sugar Company.

    The 1904 world's Fair in St. Louis, Missouri hosted the agriculture and horticulture display from Colorado under the direction of GW Swink. He was greatly concerned about the means of delivery and availability of water for agricultural development in the Arkansas Valley.

Swink's Artificial Lake

Lake Avenue appears on the eastern-most edge of the William Matthews 1876 plat of the town site, p. 64. GW Swink appears to have had the construction of his lake in mind six years before the actual construction of it and Lake Avenue was named in anticipation of the future.

The concern of GW Swink over water was evident early in his helping to plan a canal system and delivery to users. The first trees planted in new Rocky Ford benefitted from open ditch delivery down each of the early streets from the supply south of town called Rocky Ford Canal. Soon after incorporation on August 10, 1887, city council voted to plant 3000 cottonwood trees. These were placed three blocks each direction from Main Street and the railroad. Other trees were planted as the town expanded on other streets.

Ditches were already carrying water to each lot during the town lot sale April 12, 1887. These ditches eventually were to water future homeowners' lawns, fruit trees and flowers, and eventually provide for some cattle, horses and other backyard livestock.

Important, but somehow escaping much notice in newspaper accounts and city council proceedings, at least as to discovery of record, was Mr. Swink's personal decision to provide for water storage. He decided to build an impoundment that would come to be known as Swink's Artificial Lake or Swink's Lake.

Mattie (Swink) Lamon, a daughter born at the site of Old Rocky Ford June 1, 1874, was interviewed by the *Rocky Ford Daily Gazette* January 26, 1981. In her recollection one of the few known references to the lake is made. *"Since there was no electricity or refrigeration, Mr. Swink had an ice pond at the present site of Stauffer pens* [corrals at east end of Maple avenue for livestock processing in Stauffer's abattoir]. *When the pond was frozen solid, a mule team would be driven on it with a device to mark off squares. The three foot blocks would be sawed from the pond by hand, loaded into box cars, and brought to the ice house* located west of Swink's store. The ice pond was great fun to skate on, Guthries, Maltbys and Darings were among the best skaters, for they came from Ohio and Wisconsin, where there was ice."*

*Swink's ice house was between Main Street and Swink's store on Tenth Street near the railroad crossing. Ice was stored in sawdust and sold, sometimes being shipped to other towns. Mrs. Swink made gloves of Canton flannel for men to use in handling ice.

Another reference to Swink's Lake is in *The Story of Early Rocky Ford (Rocky Ford, Colorado)* by author John Doll. It is from an *Enterprise* article March 10, 1898.

> The Rocky Ford Ice and Storage Company is building a store house for the ice from Swink's Lake, south of the railroad on 10th.

A further reference to the lake is found in a Denver paper:

> Mr. G. W. Swink of Rocky Ford, Las Animas County* has just completed one of the finest artificial lakes in the State. It covers an area of 20 acres, and has an average depth of ten feet."
>
> *Rocky Mountain News*, Wed. 11 Jan. 1882

*Parts of Bent and Las Animas Counties were restructured, placing Rocky Ford in the new Otero County.

About Swink's Lake

The description or any mention of the *artificial lake* is found in few places. Especially interesting is its reported size in one reference. The area where the lake was now reveals no evidence of such a large impoundment. Earthen dikes, dams, or control gates are not found but Mr. Swink evidently chose the site below the Rocky Ford Canal from which the impoundment received water. Railroad tracks on the north along Railroad Avenue—original Main Street— facilitated the delivery of ice to storage places, as Mrs. Lamon said in her interview.

Location: The area at the east end of Maple Avenue was once the site of NW Terry Brick Yard. This business was firing bricks beginning October, 1894 and supplied many bricks in the replacement of most wooden frame buildings on Main Street and housing in other parts of town.

Stauffer pens, referred to by Mattie Lamon, and Valley Concrete were on the east Maple property years after Swink's Lake. The area has since been developed by other businesses on a relatively level surface, removing any suggestion of a depression or former location of a lake.

The lake was completed as reported in the *Rocky Mountain News* January 11, 1882 indicating the enterprise was producing ice approximately 12 winters prior the brick yard business.

Storage: Ice was being stored both in the Swink ice house between Main and Tenth Streets as well as in an ice house on Tenth Street just south of the railroad in 1897–1898. Rocky Ford Ice and Mercantile Company opened business there in 1905 with ice-making machinery thereby reducing the need for Swink's Lake ice.

Size: The *Rocky Mountain News* article reports the lake dimensions "20 acres with average depth 10 feet." The 20 acre surface is similar to 15 football fields and considering the reported depth, a significant water impoundment project attributed to the area.

Some speculation: The reference to the lake may have acquired embellishment either through a typographical error in the Denver newspaper account of 1882, or exaggeration by its reporter who was resident in Rocky Ford. A lake in the area is plausible if actually a two acre lake, a size more descriptive of a "pond" given by Mattie Lamon, p.298, and would have been easily accommodated in the area off east Maple Avenue. A 20 acre body of water would have been larger than the community of Rocky Ford in 1882, five years before the town lot sale in 1887.

Note: See p. 303 about existence of another pond.

This *militia* of mirthful *meloneers* banded together in 1898 apparently to aim their **Siege Gun** humorously, but with purpose.

Exaggerated subject post cards like this were produced by photographers to promote the town, the Arkansas Valley, its crops, and the Fair. *'Gun'* appears to be on a platform near railroad tracks and depicts a large melon, a trick of the photographer.

Courtesy *Rocky Ford Public Museum*

Swink Ditch and Irrigation Company: Swink Reservoirs 1-6

George Washington Swink family formed this company to further develop agriculture supplied with irrigation to areas of the prairie, the interest of GW Swink since his arrival in the Arkansas Valley. Work on a canal from the Apishapa River to Reservoir 1 began in 1901. Forty miles of interconnecting ditches were eventually built to flow into six reservoirs. Reservoirs 2, 3, 4, and 5 were completed but number 6 was never started. Current online records list only Reservoirs 1, 2, 5, and undeveloped number 6. Reservoir 3 is not currently listed and site names have been removed from some geographic atlases.

Swink Reservoirs 1, 2, 5, and 6 are on ranch property southeast of Fowler, CO but the reservoir sites lay south of Manzanola, SW of Rocky Ford, and NW of Timpas. Author and historian, John Doll, lived in a dugout as a young man near one of these reservoirs southwest of Rocky Ford where his father was homesteading in 1910. Crop failure and grasshoppers forced the family to move nearer the west side of town where they were able to farm in a more hospitable environment.

The reservoirs are classified *cultural features* because they were man-made, listed currently inactive structures which physically exist but with no diversion decrees. The Apishapa River from which water was to be taken begins on the slope of East Spanish Peak in Huerfano County and flows 139 miles (224 km) through Las Animas and Otero Counties to the Arkansas River east of Fowler. The Swink company had a decree only for flood water from the river and its drainage.

A reservoir for additional storage in the system was built in 1910 about 25 miles east of East Spanish Peak in Las Animas County called Seven Lakes, existing on current maps. The design was to hold runoff from a large area of prairie to add to the Apishapa by canal to supplement the river when needed.

The death in 1910 of GW Swink probably influenced the eventual transfer in 1914 of the Swink family interest to their stockholders, who in turn, sold to a Denver investment group. The Denver group had some interest in completing the ditch and reservoir system but found the supply of water from the river unreliable to support it. The reservoirs and the ditch system are gradually filling with wind-blown soil and prairie vegetation. Much as the Santa Fe Trail, they have become remnants of industrious, arduous activity.

This water project and others GW Swink was involved with exhibits to some extent his energies and dedication to promotion of agriculture in the Arkansas Valley, and especially of Rocky Ford.

Five artesian wells were opened beginning 1895 in and near the town. They were the direct result of his efforts in investment of time and finance and his persistence and accomplishments are evident today in the functioning 1874 Rocky Ford and 1889 Rocky Ford Highline Canals.

Intertwined with his water and agriculture projects GW Swink found time to serve his community and state as three-term mayor of Rocky Ford 1887–1892, 1893–1894, 1901–1903 and as two-term state senator 1892–1900.

Notes on Text

p. 2   Council minutes indicate *Curbs and Gutters* were taken up July 18, 1919 and paving Main Street taken up as the *Main Street Paving District* January 25, 1921.

p. 8   The Berkeley was razed; El Capitan and its annex, the former Pollock's Hospital, are extant.

p. 16   Don Gause recalled the *'man with the turban'* was *'either from India or another Asian country who owned farmland north of town'*. He would often hire laborers from the group gathered near the corner of Railroad and Main, either at the Rocky Ford National bank 201 N Main or Frank Boraker's shop across the street. The man with the turban eventually *'sold his farms to Mr. John Law'* and was seen no more.

          DK Spencer related that the corner of Railroad Avenue and Main Street where potential laborers gathered was also the site where an evangelist would often appear.

          "This does bring to mind a character that 6 days out of week had him pulling a little red wagon around to the grocery stores for scraps to feed to animals at his home place on US 50 West. He usually had an older looking lady with him that we took to be his wife, however in later years we found out she was his sister. On Sundays he dressed in his suit and he would stand on the corner near Frank Boraker's news stand, and beat a big bass drum calling the sinners to repent and mostly caused a bunch of kids to show up and harass him. He tried to set up a church at his home place, but doubt if many ever attended. I later found out that he was at one time a rodeo cowboy that had a relationship with rodeo greats such as Tom Mix and his ilk. He once showed [me] some 8X10's glossy photos of him and Tom. No remembrance of what happened to him or his sister". Don Gause recalled the man described by DK Spencer was a *Mr. Proctor* but could not relate him to the present family well-known in the Rocky Ford area.

p. 17   Roman and chariot races were a feature of the August 31–September 1–3, 1926 fair.

p. 18   William L. Gobin Community Center, c 1990s, is now on the site of former Railway Express Agency.

p. 48   Interest in Roy Taylor's Conoco Service relates to the business site of the first hotel on the first Main Street of the new town, now Railroad avenue. A frame hotel of Andy Nichols was built there c 1876, replaced later by the De Seeley Hotel in the 1880s.

p. 50   Businesses nor residences were numerous east of Main Street. Hall Motor Freight Co. is the final business our walk encounters on Elm Avenue in the 1914–1915 directory. Rapidity of change and appearance and disappearance of businesses precludes inclusion of every enterprise that opened for business in a changing business environment. Some apparently were not open long enough to advertise or identify their site by sign.

p. 63   Typhoid fever was prevalent among Rocky Ford citizens using *'raw water'* from ditches or canals. Physicians warned the populace to boil water, advice often ignored for the effort that took. Rudimentary filters of sand and charcoal were used in some households (p. 36 of John Doll, *The Story of Early Rocky Ford*) but this only cleared some of the turbidity.

          State Board of Health requested the city discontinue the disposal of sewage into the river, read in council May 1, 1934. Outdoor toilets were recognized as a health problem to be regulated after a July 7, 1934 council discussion. Garbage collection was authorized as a city function June 18, 1920. Council on November 30, 1900 dealt with diphtheria, scarlet fever, and small pox by authorizing the design and construction of a *'pest house'* to isolate disease cases. Design was completed but the *'house'* was never built. Instead, cases were isolated by *quarantine* in home until such time as a health officer determined the crisis past. To wit, the author's 1885 boyhood home of soft red brick at 810 S Thirteenth Street was pockmarked with numerous conical-shaped holes left of the front door made by nails, some yet in place in 1942 when my family moved there. Stucco c 1950s, for us, covered this remnant of past quarantine and presumed reproach felt by many.

p. 67   William B. Gobin residence at 400 N Ninth, was across the street from the home of GW Swink. Judge Gobin, at one time before many trees were large enough to block his view, was able to look out his 2nd floor window and see Washington School at Twelfth and Washington. *July 2013 conversation with Carol and Don Gause.*

p. 97   The *Kit Carson Road* west of the terminus of the Kansas Pacific railroad at Kit Carson, Colorado was the path to Taos and Santa Fe through Rocky Ford on current Tenth Street.

Notes on Text

p. 98   *Houses and first structures* were rudimentary. GW Swink and partner, Asa Russell, investigated possibilities of starting a cattle business. Instead, they built a shelter of cottonwood posts with a post and brush roof and opened a store. In time they built an adobe structure with a more substantial roof depicted on p. 86. In the new Rocky Ford, having bought out Asa Russell, Swink built a general store of adobe on railroad land.

   First residents built a community with materials on site using poles, logs, branches, grasses, and adobe. The first substantial business *building* at the Old Rocky Ford in 1871 was built using adobe with a very low-pitched roof and rough-cut lumber supports, photo p. 86. Homesteaders near the store used poles to form walls, brush and earth for roofs to provide their shelters.

   Brick buildings were replacing adobe and frame buildings in the early 1880s and more so after the NW Terry brickyard opened in 1894. The Cement Stone Company did not begin manufacture of large blocks until 1906. The De Seeley Hotel bricks are described as 'adobe' by townspeople but in photos appear of more sophisticated construction than the earth-colored kind that we usually see.

p. 99   'Cal' Seeley apparently was a nickname of JS Seeley. John Doll used the nickname on p. 15 of his book. A descendant, also named Cal Seeley, once owned Polly's Café circa 1950s–1960s with Pauline (Polly) Aston.

   Circa 1870 *emulsified asphalt* was being used in roads, brick, and adobe to provide cohesiveness and water-resistence. Asphalt-containing bituminous rock was mined in several places in the US for these purposes. Stronger, more uniform brick and larger block were made, possibly accounting for the regular and dark appearance of De Seeley construction. I find no commentary in the town's archives about local production of this kind of material.

p. 106 German POWs were marched from the railroad depot north on Ninth Street toward the fairgrounds on a day the author was on the sidewalk near Martel Lueker's Sinclair station. Approximately 30 were in uniform, a few carrying extra clothes. All were billeted in the adobe horse stalls or camped on the fairgrounds. Eventually they were to number 225, temporarily employed in farm labor during their stay in Rocky Ford.

p. 259 Arched door with arched windows on either side are reminiscent of Main Street and Chestnut Avenue entrances of Cartwright building although addresses are not known among those Rocky Ford Garage used.

p. 284 References in *Afterword: Observations on Watermelon Day* are from personal recollections of my family members. I was able to find one record of March 12, 1986 dealing with dispensing melons and public health concerns, although there likely were many.

   The Fair Committee minutes "**Suggested we start meeting the needs of the rest of the public. Serving watermelon slices throughout the entire fair instead of just watermelons on Watermelon Day. Providing a rest area (tent) with tables and chairs in the shade to serve watermelons. Report on giving away sliced watermelons instead of whole melons. As long as there is chlorine put in the water to store the melons and the area kept clean there would be no problem with the Hralth** [sic] **Department.**"

p. 299 City of Rocky Ford once created a small pond for ice skating just south of the railroad tracks near the Rocky Ford Canal, possibly in the area formerly Swink's lake.

Undated photo, courtesy, *Rocky Ford Public Library*. Note on reverse, **Watermelon Day at Rocky Ford ... nothing like it ... was 19 years ago.**

303

Sources

Bollacker Keck, Frances, general information of Rocky Ford in *A History of Otero and Crowley Counties Colorado*, 1999.

Denver Fire Journal, information of *Clyde F. Summers* and *William M. Lueker*, in *denverfirejournal.com*.

Directory, *Colorado Business, Rocky Ford, Otero County, 1911, The Gazetteer Publishing Co.*, in *ftp.rootsweb.com*.

Directory, *Rocky Ford City, 1914-1915*, F.A. McKinney in *coloradoplains.com*.

Directory, *Rocky Ford, Colorado, c. 1945-1948*, by *The Rocky Ford Tribune*.

Doll, John, *The Story of Early Rocky Ford (Rocky Ford Colorado)*, Rocky Ford Archaeological Society, 1987.

_____:, *George Washington Swink Story*, unpublished, August 2, 1977, Rocky Ford Public Museum.

History of Otero County in *coloradoplains.com* and links.

Le Cantaloupe, That Wonderful Year, published privately, Rocky Ford High School class 1961.

McFarland, Blanche, *History of Rocky Ford by the Schoolchildren*, 1925.

Officer Down Memorial Page, ODMP Remembers, information of officers *Jesse B. Craig, Sr., Jacob A. Kipper*, and *Louis Box* in *odmp.org*.

Otero County, Colorado History in *cogenweb.com* and links.

Denver Public Library, *Rocky Ford Aerial View 1936*, in *denverdigitallibrary.org*.

Rocky Ford Daily Gazette, City Well, Friday, February 7, 2003.

_____:, *Rocky Ford Centennial Recollections*, pp. 3-16 April 10, 1987; pp. 50, 60, 82 January 5, 1988 interviews of pioneer descendants.

Rocky Ford Magazine, vol.1, no.1 for information of, Main Str. 1905, Watermelon Day 1916, Ark. Valley Fair Gate, 300 Block S Main, summer 1998.

_____:, vol, 2 no. 1 for information of *Smith's Café, Roy's Conoco*, summer 1999.

Spencer, D. K., in *Rocky Ford Daily Gazette, Remembering Frank Boraker* (date missing).

_____:, for general information of Santa Fe Railway, *atsfrr.com/resources* and links.

Swink, G. W., *Brief history of the Arkansas Valley Fair and Watermelon Day*, *arkvalleyfair.com*.

Special thanks to:

Rocky Ford Public Library personnel who graciously contributed copies of many historic building photos and businesses by download from library CDs.

Rocky Ford Public Museum personnel for allowing access to and reproduction of many vintage photos in their collection.

Woodruff Memorial Library staff in La Junta, Colorado who made available extended use of reference room materials, especially notebooks of vintage photographs compiled by Doris L. Baublits and Merle L. Baublits.

Name Index

Most names are from the early years of Rocky Ford during the nineteenth and twentieth century. Some current names are also listed to show involvement in business enterprises as they are at publication but not all are included if advertising was not available. Frequent change in enterprises and their proprietors was accompanied by failure to thrive for some.

A

Abert
  Donna L. vii, 5, 137
Adams
  Ada B. 26, 121, 123, 261
  Robert M. 26, 121, 123, 261
Adcock
  Otis E. 41
Ahlers
  Don 295
Albert
  C. W. 265
Aldis
  George 10
Alexander
  Harry V. 52, 290
Allderdice
  H. E. 20
Allen
  W. H. 293
Altheide
  Roxaena (Swink) 166
Amerine
  Dale 50
Amos
  George 86, 93
  Horace 9
  Linn 9
  S. Anne 9
Anderson
  A. F. 20
  Jonas 45
  L. 289
  Nannie I. 45
  W. L. (Sid) 56
Andrew
  Martin 295
Appleman
  Bob 149
Arnold
  Hobart M. 34
  Myrtle E. 34
  Oliver F. 34
Asakawa
  Harry 294
Ascherman
  Harry E. 37
Asher
  Florence A. (Mrs.) 25, 72
Aston
  Pauline (Polly) 303
Athey
  Myrtle (Mrs.) 11
Attorneys
  Beall, (?) 20
  Guyton, Elizabeth L. 26, 56
  Minor, H. M. 293
  Todd, Joel W. 123
Aulgur
  Calvin A. 32, 47, 266
  Gabie L. 32, 47
Aylesworth
  Barton O. 28

B

Babcock
  Robert T. 33
  L. W. 50, 154
Baca
  Fred 55
Bailey
  C. S. 10
  J. Edd 10
  Rosa 10
  H. A. 10
Baker
  B. F. 292
  G. M. (Mrs.) 294
Barker
  James 7
  Sylvia A. 7
Barnes
  Harry 145, 248
Barnett
  Daniel 4
  Lizzie S. 4
Barrow
  Frank M. 5
  G. E. 29
  Nell F. 5
Bass
  J. L. 19, 39
  Nora 39
Bates
  Peggy 215
Baublits
  Doris L. vii, 53, 135, 244, 267, 268, 269, 270, 271, 272, 282
  Merle vii
Beaty
  Robert R. 26
Beck
  D. F. 36
Beeks
  Bertram xiii
  Maude xiii
Beghtol
  (Mr.) 40
  Levi 97, 290
  William 97
Bell
  F. W. 293
Belle
  M. 36
Ben Hur 17
Berry
  (Mrs.) 293
Beymer
  Arthur S. 10
  Emma J. 10
Billy 27
Bingham
  Grace S. 26
  S. 26
Bish
  Amos 294
  W. R. 115, 118
Black
  Arthur W. 22, 294
  Charley 274
  Elma 274
  Eva A. 20
  Harry J. 20
  May N. 22
Blackford
  Fred 261
Blakely
  G. A. 20, 178
Blinn
  J. J. 14, 47
Boggs
  Canna 39
  Emery R. 39
Boley
  Dora 43
  Ephraim M. (dec.)
  Fay Ellen 43
  Lou 43
  Martha (widow of Ephraim M.) 43
Boraker
  Frank H. 16–17, 81, 302
  George 295
  Herman L. 295
Bonta
  Carrie 21
  John L. 21, 293
Booth
  Ives 29
Box
  Louis 73
  Mathilda (Hilda) 74
Boyd
  Charles B. 35
  Pearl A. 35
Braden
  J. C. 14, 47, 109, 294
Brannan
  Charles O. 35
  Effie Z. 35
Breitenfeld
  Walter 128
Brown
  Clay D. 44
  Crystal 20
  Eliza Jane (widow of George M.) 44
  George M. (dec.) 44
  Nellie O. 44
  Ralph A. 44
  Walter G. 20, 25, 72
  William J. 10
Bruenger
  Rev. A. P. 44
Bruse
  Henry 13
  Katherine 13
Bryant
  Elva M. 30
  G. E. 6, 30
  George E. 19
  George 19
  Mabel M. 19
Buckwalter
  Harry H. 238
Budge
  Mike 49, 68, 77, 78, 126, 209
Buis
  B. R. 16
Burchett
  Lester W. 9, 206
Burke
  C. F. 10
Burnett
  Carrie C. 15
Burrell
  Delavan B. 10, 26, 59
Buis
  B. R. 16
Burchett
  Lester W. 9, 206
Burke
  C. F. 10
Burnett
  Carrie C. 15
Burrell
  Delavan B. 10, 26, 59, 107, 123
  Maude 10
Bushey
  A. H. 22
Butler
  Walt 221
Butterfield
  James 29
  W. H. 292
Byers
  J. B. 291

Name Index

C

Cadwallader
  Bob 201
  E. Elizabeth 36
  Elmer E. 36
Cameron
  Jenny Gobin 53, 57
  George R. 50, 151, 294
Campbell
  Evelyn 294
Capitan
  F. J. 235
  Carmon (horse) 28
Carder
  Josephine 252
  R. E. 252
Carroll
  C.E. (Mrs.) 7
Carrillo
  Richard F. xiii
Carson
  Kit 290
Cartwright
  Charles 9
Caruthers
  (ball player) 31
Casebeer
  E. W. 11
Chandler
  Charles 291
Chavez
  Leanna vii
Cheek
  Fred W. 33. 130, 235, 291
  Nellie Macklin 33
  Walter 26, 126, 198, 293
Childs
  Arthur 75
Chiropractors
  Schuth, C. R. 26, 155
  Van Antwerp, H. E. 26
  Van Antwerp, H. S. 26
Chritton
  James M. 20
  Mary 20
Clark
  Bill 177, 318
  C. O. 20
  Leo 177, 318
  W. E. 292
Cleveland
  E. Faye 26
  Grover (Pres.) 66
Clifford
  Norman 130
Cline
  Ella 13

Clute
  Ed 264
  Elva 264, 272
  Francis H. 264, 272
Coffman
  C. C. 22
  T. E. 22
Cole
  Patricia (Gerlock) 74
Conklin
  Henry H. 43
  Rhoda A. 43
Conquest
  Nellie (Mrs.) 47, 135
Cook
  E. R. 292
  George T. 39
  Mary F. 39
Coon
  Arthur D. 32
  Harry J. 44
  Helen C. 44
  Hiram J. (dec.) 44
  Lois L. 32
  Sarah A. (widow of Hiram J.) 44
Cope
  Sally vii
Corcoran
  Alvia (Mrs.) 22, 71
Cover
  Charles 34
  Durbin 34
  Edith 34
  Hunter 34
  Lee H. 34
Corwin
  R. W. 28
Craig
  Jesse B., Sr. 73
Cramer
  Ben 7
  Temperance 7
Crans
  Bartholomew M. 35 (dec.)
  Harriet (widow) 35
Creagor
  A. W. 26
Creo
  Jose 86, 93
Crist
  Clay 285
  Mary E. vii, 285
Crowel
  Nora 83
Crowl (sic), see Crowel
  J. Frank 83
  Nora B. 83
Curran
  F. G. 130

D

Daring
  Ada 33
  Charles, Sr. 40
  George R. 22, 33, 72, 122, 237
Davenport
  Blanche W. 6
Davy
  Thomas A. 8, 71
Dawley
  Earl A. 29
  H. A. 19, 29, 111, 156, 205
  Myrtle B. 29
  Richard S. 29
Day
  Frank 35
Deal
  Vitula 34
  W. N. 34
Dearing
  Jesse M. 29
  Leona 29
DeBolt
  Virgil V. 8
DeFreese
  Bertha (Mrs.) 295
Dennes
  (Isaiah) 22
Denson
  Mark 75
Denny
  J. S. 25, 72, 293
Dislow
  F. A. 291
Dentist
  Samuel, J. H. 12
DeWeese
  (ball player) 31
  Edwin 56
Dietrich
  Jacob S. 44
  Hattie G. 44
Dobbins
  Robert Gaston 8
Doll
  John ix, 39, 60, 64, 93, 95, 96, 97, 98, 223, 295, 298, 302
Donk
  Ellen (Bradshaw) 53
Dowlers
  Oran 292, 294
Downer
  David 293
Downey
  J. B. 291

Downing
  Carl D. (Pug) 84, 241
  Vera 241
Dubois
  Harry 29
Dye
  Addie (Mrs.) 15
  B. U. 27–28, 31, 69, 88–89, 97, 99, 101, 102, 121, 243, 291
  J. K. 58
  Will 89, 97, 98, 243
  W. R. 292

E

Edwards
  Alfred Augustus 28
  Paul P. 14
Eichelbeger
  Lila M. (Mrs.) 69, 71
  William S. 69
Eichler
  Elizabeth (Betty) 204
Elder
  Belle 44
  John H. 44
Elser
  LeRoy 40, 98
Ellis
  Ira B. 30, 178
  Mae 30
  Maedene 30
  Rex 178
Enderud
  A. G. 38
English
  R. W. 19, 29, 114, 232, 233
Eppinger
  Ted 32

F

Farris
  Dick 8, 47
  Ed 10
  John 10
  R. and Mrs. R. 10
  Viola (Mrs.) 8, 71
Fenlason
  L. R. 20, 45
  Nonette S. 45
Fenton
  Nannie A. 10

309

Ferril
C. Otto 22
Fielder
S. L. 20
Findlay
L. 202
Fleak
Daisy 30
Dennis L. 30
L. D. 14
Fleet
Eve 8
Fly
H. E. 294
Forbes
George W. 36, 294
Frame
Olive B. 38
Owen L. 38
O. L. (Mrs.) 15, 38
Frantz
Claude 26, 56
George 75
O. C. 85
Funk
Alice J. 12
Amanda 294
Henry 12

G

Gacy
J. C. 21
Gandara
Dolores 54
Frank R. 54, 142, 294
Garity
Audrey J. 22
Francis E. 22
Garwood
H. D. 14, 29
Gauna
Maria vii
Gause
Carol vii, 302
Don vii, 83, 295, 302
Gerbing
Emma P. 44
Fannie (widow of Gustav T.) 44
Gustav T. (dec.) 44
Leota 44
William F. 15, 44
Gerst
Mame 40, (Mrs. Ed. Smith) 49
Gibeson
Mina E. 29

Gibson
John B. 43
Vena 43
W. R. 10
Giffen
L. C. 32
Gilbert
G. K. 63, 90
Gilmore
T. R. 25, 72
Ging
Gee 188
Gobin
E. C. 40
Paul I. 50, 151, 294
William B. 85, 97, 224, 235, 302
William L. 302
Godding
(Mrs.) 291
T. E. 205, 292
Goeringer
Albert 14
Goebel
Art 291
Gonzales
Jerre 84
Gorsuch
Della 11
Eula 11
Lucas B. 11
Govreau
A. Gertrude 39
Alice M. 21
C. B. 17, 291
Charles L. 21, 39, 291
Graves
E. Louisa 9
John D. 9
Greer
John B. 43
Hattie E. 43
Gregory
Joan vii
Gregg
Carl 48
Grenard
George W. 294
R. J. 36
Ruth Muth vii, 106, 286
Griffin
J. I. 56
Grimsley
'Fly' 230
Harry 37
Grossarth
Etta S. 20
William 20, 178
Groth
Arnold 294

Gunther
A. 11

H

Hagan
H. Hart 13
(Hart-Magann, 13)
Hagen
H. F. 120-121, 132, 146-147, 209, 234
Susan L. 29, 71, 120
Hahn
Celia L. 44
Lottie M. 44
Hale
Alberta 204
Haley
Clay 4
Walker 4
Hall
Effie (Mrs.) 11, 198, 280
Flora J. 45
Gilbert M. 45
Lurana B. 38
Melvin W. 38
Ruth E. 21, 38
Hamilton
Ann 225
Larry 225
Hamm
Rayna 220
Hamman
Ashley J. 44
Jesse B. 44
Hammond
Virgil 204
W. Lawrence 30
Hannon
Joseph 25
Mary Anna 25
Hanson
T. E. 294
Harada
Family 220
Kazuko (Kaz) Harada
Hardey
Henry 12
Hardt
W. P. 292
Harris
Robert (Bob) 73
Harrison
M. R. 38
Harter
H. G. (Mrs.) 69
Haslett
Artis P. 36
John W. 36

Hawthorne
E. A. 50
Hauck
Frank Y. 98, 235, 291
Hayes
Frank, Jr. (signature) 84
Maud S. 44
Woodrow 83, 292
Heckman
David J. 31
Henderson
Dee 295
Hendricks
(ball player) 31
J. M. ix
W. S. 86, 93
Henry
Enlo 41, 43, 241
Sheila vii
Hernandez
Raul 10
Sam 163
Zack, Jr. 10
Herring
Anna E. 45
John D. 45, 293
Herz
M. J. 14
Heskett
C. A. 54
Higgins
George 11, 245, 289
Hill
Ella L. 22, 29
Graham 10
J. T. 132
Thomas J. 22, 29
(ball player) 31
Hindu
The (See Indian) 16
Hodges
Bill vii
Holmes
Anna L. 44
Holsclaw
Susan Brown vii, 138
Hooper
Granville M. 25, 34, 72
Mary Anna 72
Hoover
Diana 6
Delbert J. 6
Frank B. 6
M. Ella 6
Ralph W. 6
John 6
Hopper
Bert W. 31
Caroline E. 30
Luta 30
Ona P. 31

Name Index

Roland A. 30
V. 30
Horn
 Coleman 11
Hough
 Frank G. 17, 265
Huguein
 Lena 123
Hull
 Edith 21
Hur
 Ben 17

I

Igo
 J. H. 129
Indian
 The (See Hindu) 16
Irvin
 Martha 204
Isherwood
 A. D. 22

J

Jackson
 A. M. 63
 C. W. 36
 R. M. 63
 W. L. 292
James
 R. H. 13, 25
Jameson
 H. I. 78
Janes
 (Mrs.) 295
Jaramillo
 Fred vii
Jefferson
 Elsie 6
Jennings
 Chester L. 75
John
 Frank 30
Johnston
 Fred L. 17, 38
 Jessie K. 38
Johnson
 Arthur 294
 A. S. 13, 111
 F. S. 45
 J. A. 108, 292
 Judy vii
Jones
 Debbie 173
 Dick 173
 Eva F. 22

Jordan
 W. 71

K

Kain
 J. C. (Mrs.) 291
Kearney
 (ball player) 31
 (mascot) 31
Kelley
 F. R. (Mrs.) 30
Killian
 Carolyn 33
Koontz
 Jessie J. 11
 Mary 11
Kaplan
 Anna 6
 Nathan 6
Karpe
 A. H. 75
 Fred A. 75
Keck
 C. F. (Bus) 230
 Emma I. 11
Kelly
 Fred R. 294
Kelso
 Lawrence M. 39
Kerney
 Rae C. 47
 S. Abbie 47
Kienitz
 Helmut 171
King
 J. B. 294
Kipper
 Jacob A. 73
Kitch
 Arlyn Samuel 43
 Paul 128
Knaus
 Eva L. 47
 Fred 47
Knause
 B. F. 291
 Fred 47, 294
Koonce
 O. D. 55
Kraig
 Kay 55
Kreider
 Emma C. 15
 Eugene T. 15
Krueger
 Owen 37

L

Lacey
 Eleanor 295
 J. B. 26, 293
Lamon
 Mattie (Swink) 90, 98 298
Lance
 H. W. 17
 Ione C. 17
Langford
 J. H. 26
Laramore
 Mrs. 7
Laurent
 Christine 242
 Mike 242
Law
 John 302
Lawrence
 B. L. 15
 C. L. 11, 26, 123
Lawton
 W. 237
Lawyer
 Bert L. 34
 Helen N. 34
Leeman
 Carl 4
Leesing
 J. W. 21
Lewis
 G. W. 108, 111, 292
 G. W. (Mrs.) 33
 J. E. 35
 R. D. (Banana Lewis)151
 W. D. 108, 111, 292
 W. D. (Mrs.) 13
Lincoln
 Abe 292
Lindahl
 Kevin 14
 Norma 14
Linn
 Lewis C. 39
Loback
 John H. 22
 Hattie M. 22
Lofgren
 Keneth 185
Lohmier
 John 295
Long
 C. H. 26, 34
 Esther J. 47
 Frederick C. 47
Longden
 William 8
Lopez
 S. A. 25, 72

Loring
 Mary C. 47, 53
Love
 Allie E. 36
 Glen 47, 55
 (ball player) 31
 Otis 9, 295
 Thomas W. 36
Lowe
 James 290
Lowther
 Anna 26
 W. A. 26
Lucero
 Juan 22
Lueker
 Ethel 75
 William Martel 45, 73, 75, 135, 196, 295
Lunquist
 Carl 75
Lumbar
 James K. 11, 26, 128, 198, 280
 W. D. 11
Lusk
 Truman 37
Luth
 L. W. 11
Lyon
 Charles R. 29
 Edna 29

M

Mackey
 Homer 295
Macklin
 Barbara 219
 Jerry 219
Maes
 Heather vii
Maier
 Matilda E. 15
Maltby
 R. C. 15
Maring
 John R. 293
Marlow
 William 6
Marsh
 L. L. 25
Marshall
 Everett 295
Martin
 I. G. 71
 Le Roy 5
 W. H. 36

Mathews
  C. G. 75
Mathewson
  Suzie 138
  S. A. 17
Matthews
  William 61, 64, 95, 97 166, 290
Maxwell
  George 15, 17
  H. I. 14, 235
  W. M. 14
Mazulla
  Fred 130
McCart
  R. A. 29
McColm
  Edward B. 25, 70, 72
McDermid
  Alex 21
  M. Elizabeth, (Mrs.) 26, 123
McDowell
  Archie (dec.) 31
  Beulah (widow) 31
McGee
  James M. 11
  M. Mabel 11
  Mary E. 11
McKenzie
  Frank W. 8
  George 29, 220
McKinney
  F.A. 1
  Jennie B. 47
  William B. 47
McCormack
  A. 33
  George A. 36
McMahan
  Edith M. 25
  Frank H. 25
McMorris
  M. J. 123
McVay
  Charles 63, 90
Mendenhall
  H. B. 38
  Matt 49, 68, 77-78, 126, 209
Meyers
  Mary E. 47
Middleton
  Dick 247
Miller
  C.A. Arnold 29, 71
  C. M. 291
  Cora F. 9
  Frank 292
  (Mrs Frank.) 292
  Jacob L. 9, 10

Kate (Mrs.) 45
Mike 57
Minor
  Earl V. 20
Mitch
  John 58
Mitchell
  B. E. 37
Mix
  Tom 302
Monkman
  W. R. 45, 47
Montgomery
  Jim 170
  J. K. (Mr. & Mrs.) 25
Moody
  A. L. 12, 15, 47
Moore
  Al 6
  Alfred L. 6
  (ball player) 31
  Carl 6
  Eliza J. 6
  Garry 176
  Merle, (Mrs.) 11
  Ralph B. 8
  V. A. 243
Morgan
  Pauline 295
Morris
  Anderson E. 29, 180
  Dub 214, 221
  Elmira E. 25
  Nancy E. 29
  Newton C. 25
Morrison
  Ruth Ellen 223
Morse
  Harry C. 12, 110
  Monnie E. 12
Muth
  Carol J. vii, 96, 204, 285, 296
  David J. iii, 204, 285
  Dorothy E. 285
  Elizabeth (Mrs. John) 295
  Kenneth J, 285
  Michael D. 285
  Vernon J. 285
Myama
  M. G. 25

N

Nagel
  Bob 153
  Esther 153
Neenan
  Fr. W. S. 223

Nelson
  Anton 204
  George B. 228, 271
  Lloyd 50
  R. J. 43
Newberry
  Beulah A. 43
  William W. 43
Nichols
  Al M. 11
  Andy 88, 89, 93, 95, 97, 98, 99, 290
  George W. 98
  H. L. 292
  J. B. 20
  Thomas C. 33
Nishimura
  Sam 13, 127, 236
  Shizu 13
North
  Paul M. 12
  Stella G. 12
Northen
  T. Y. 31

O

Obermiller
  Jeff 226
O'brien
  Neil 251
O'Bryant
  H. W. 110
Orr
  J. E. 231, 254, 291
Orrell
  W. 30
Optometrist
  Burnett, Erwin F. 15
Osteopathic Physicians
  Hull, W. N. 9
  Kellogg, Seay Moore 20, 132
Otwell
  Annie E. 29
Overbagh
  Henry A. 13
  Georgia B. 13

P

Palmer
  Belle L. 36
  Hillie (Mrs.) 11
  Walton L. 36

Parr
  Corrinne (Posey) 204
  R. L. 30
Payne
  (ball player) 31
Peery
  Anna L. 10
  J. Wood 10, 11, 53, 112, 143, 268
Perry
  C. A. 123
Petersen
  Emma E. 36
  August H. 36
Peterson
  Lottie F. (Mrs.) 5
  James Oscar 5
Phillips
  George (dec.) 31
  Lulu (Widow) 31
Physicians
  Barbour, Llewellyn P.
  Blotz, B. B. 8, 210, 246
  Blotz, B. F. 8, 246
  Fenton, W. C. 10, 12, 235
  Larson (?) 185
  Lawson, John A. 14, 34, 47, 109
  Lovejoy, H. E. 26, 123
  Maier, Frank W. 15
  Martin, Ted E. 231
  McKittrick, Roy 231
  Morgan, E. L. 185, 190, 200
  Pollock, Lloyd R. 46
  Pollock, Robert M. 8, 18, 19, 79, 112, 122, 168, 235
  Savage, S. Hubbard 20, 30
  Shima, R. T. 231
  Smith, Fisher 292
  Wolfe, Roy E. 32
Pierce
  James 6
Polhemus
  Fred 293
Poole
  Frank J. 4
  G. Arzo 4
  Minnie 4
Potter
  D. D. 26
Powell
  B. F. 45
Price
  Carrie E. 12
  Etta 4
  John R. 4
  Joseph H. 12
Proctor
  (Mr.) 300

Name Index

R

Randall
  G. P. 292
  W. N. 291
Ratliff
  Gary 295
Ray
  (ball player) 31
Recker
  Charles 14, 60, 132, 146, 234
Reeves
  Bud W. 7, 47
  Mabel 7, 47
Reifel
  P. J. 26
Rex
  J. W. 21
  Katherine 21
Reynolds
  Clara E. 32
  Howard E. 56, 178
  John F. 32
  Loren A. 32
  W. I. 32
Richert
  John 20
Rickey
  Rebecca J. 5
  William B. 5
Rider
  Lloyd 193
Ritter
  J. B. 78
  Ritthaler 295
  Josie 269
  Lee 269
Roach
  Hettie 56
Robards
  Perry 237
Robb
  (Colonel) 236
Robbins
  Charles 40
Robinson
  J. C. 56, 219
  Lawrence 55
Rockafellow
  B. F. 28
Rodeck
  Louis L. 10
Rogers
  Lynn H. 12
  Rose A. 12
Rohn
  Capt. 40
Roosevelt
  Franklin D. (Pres.) 208

Rosson
  (ball player) 31
Rowe
  Almira 5
  Thomas 5
Royal
  Frank 239
  Herb 239
Runt 27
Russell
  Asa 86, 93, 104, 290, 303
Ryan
  Kathleen 204

S

Salls
  J. P. 291
Sanders
  Myra (Mrs.) 29
Savage
  Bertha 20, 30
Scammon
  Mr. (?) 221
Schooley
  Dave 203
  Hazel 203
Scott
  J. S. 291
Scribner
  Jerry B. 26
  Nora H. 26
Seeley
  J. S. 291, 303
  Cal 89, 99, 303
  Polly 215
Segar
  E. C. 84
Sexton
  Bob 44, 55, 152
Shaw
  Florence C. 20
  James H. 20
Shelton
  E. C. 15
  Edwin C. 38
  Edwina 38
  Effie M. 38
  Garland M. 38
  Gene 9
  G. M. 15
Sherman
  Henry C. 26, 123
Siders
  John K. (dec.) 30
  Mary L. (Widow) 30
Silvers
  Claude 17, 265

Smallwood
  Billy 83, 294
Smirl
  Callie E. 34
  Emma A. 34
  I. L. 34, 53
  Letha 34
  Ralph 34
  R. J. 22
  T. J. 22, 34, 53
Smith
  Annie, (Mrs.) 4
  A. P. 75
  Bill 178
  Bill (Mr. & Mrs.) 83
  Bob 178
  Ed. 40, 49
  Elizabeth B. 4
  Ernest 4
  E. F. 46
  Greg 295
  Joan 14
  Martin 4
  Mame (Mrs. Ed. Smith) 49
  Roy 201
  William 4
  W. L. 20
Snider
  A. Nora 6
  Ed 6
Snow
  Cecil V. 25
Spencer
  D. K. vii, 13, 16, 273 302
Sylvan
  (Cecil Spence) 20
Sprinkle
  Rex 85, 295
Stafford
  Claralee 138
Stanley
  Bryan 25, 38
  Dean 25, 38
  Int 25, 38, 72
  L. Theirs 38
  Nora L. 38
Stanbridge
  David 138, 293
Staples
  A. 71, 72
Stark
  W. F. 291
Stauffer
  Ben 161
  O. B. 161
Steele
  William C. 40, 164
Steir
  J J 22
Stephenson
  Charles 11
  Dessie 11

Stevens
  Hazel 149
Stevenson
  L. E. 294
Steward
  Ford J. 292
Stipe
  (Mrs.) 295
St. John
  A. P. 36, 123
  M. L. 56, 123
Stockstill
  Edna 4
  John A. 4
Stoop
  F. D. 31
Stratton
  T. H. 14
Stout
  Pete 191, 211
Sturges
  Lois 225
Summers
  Clyde F. 19, 54, 73, 75, 117, 295
  Sylvia 75
Sunday
  H. R. 293
Sutherland
  Rudy 22
Sweet
  William E. (Gov.) 253
Swift
  John 97, 98, 290
Swink
  G. W. ix, xi, xii, 1, 2, 32, 37, 40, 63, 66–67, 89, 92, 93, 95, 97, 101, 118, 131, 159, 166, 202, 253, 255, 258, 284, 290, 293, 297, 298–299, 300, 303
  Harry 293
  Jerre 95, 295
  Mary J. (Mrs. Swink), 296

T

Talhelm
  H.P. 10, 112
Taylor
  Bessie N. 34
  Charles W. 21
Taylor, cont.
  Clara B. 21
  George H. 34
  Roy 48, 93, 261
Teats
  George O. 48, 89, 93, 148, 295

Terry
　N. W. 72, 99, 235, 290, 299, 303
Tewes
　William H. 44
Thatcher
　M. D. 20
Thiers
　Int L. 25
Thomas
　Bill 221
　Harlan 28, 291
　W. W. 20
Thompson
　J. R. 295
　Laura vii
　Tommy 295
Tindall
　Charles 55
Toad 27
Todd
　J. W. 26
Torgler
　Shannon 173
Tracey
　Jay W. 57, 115
Truman
　Harry S. (Pres.) 74
Tucker
　Frances I. 45
　Walter C. 45
Turley
　Rachael T. 7
Tyler
　Claude 22, 23

U

Umbarger
　Clyde S. 38
　J. E. 10
　May E. 38
Ushiama
　Aki 221
Ustick
　Carl M., Sr. 47, 54, 120, 162
　Millicent 120, 162

V

Van Antwerp
　H. E. 26
　H. S. 26
Van Buskirk
　H. 26

Vaughn
　John C. 19, 293
　Mattie 19
Van Skike
　Nackie R. 12
　Richard H. 12
Veal
　Howard W. 56
Vickers
　David 166
Veterinarians
　Cleveland, W. J. 26, 123
　Keck, Paul P. 11
Voegtle
　Mabel 33
　Robert 33

W

Walker
　Bonnie 53
　Doc 53
　Ginger 53
　R. T. 118
Wanger
　Charles J. 268
　Harry R. 268
Warner
　Rev. S. B.
Washburn
　C. C. 40
Weid
　Karl 119
Weigand
　Robert W. 204
Weir
　Addie 29
Weiss
　Carol 19
Weist
　Philip J. 33
Welch
　Tom 96
Welland
　F. W. 293
White
　W. H. 293
Whitlock
　D. Thomas 33
　Lulu M. 33
Wilkins
　Don 153
Will
　Bill 221, 225
Williams
　C. S. 219
Williamsom
　Oliver M. 20

Wilson
　B. G. 291
Wimpy
　J. Wellington 84, 241
Windburn
　G. L. 291
Winiger
　Flossie A. 21
　Joseph 6, 21
Winsor
　Betty (Gobin) 150
　Howard vii
Wolf
　J. D. 188
Wolfe
　Jane M. 32
Wolfmeyer
　Emmet A. 174
　Fannie 174
Wood
　George T. 15
　Maggie 15
　Walter A. 88
Woods
　Alfred W. 7
　Marion Alta 7
Woodside
　W. F. 294
Woodward
　W. L. (Mrs.) 71
Wright
　George 194
Wyatt
　John H. 4
　Mary J. 4

Y

Yeater
　Horace 294
Yoder
　Joe 149
Young
　N. C. (Mrs.) 291
Youngblood
　Darla 138

Z

Zavala
　Cecil 234
Zimmerman
　Earl 82

Rocky Ford City Directory
c 1945–1948
Author's Collection

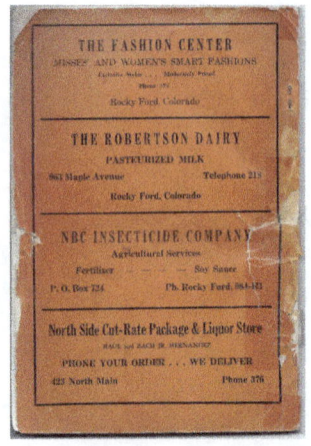

General Index

Businesses and buildings they were in—or are in to date—are listed in this section. A few buildings with their occupants from first to the current are indicated among foregoing pages. For some buildings, succession of one occupant to the next was influenced by local economy, business failure or closure, resulting in vacancy or demolition of the building.

Current addresses of businesses were not always listed in available directories because of frequent moves. Many businesses are without photo, some without address. Undoubtedly some photos exist but were not discovered. Numerals in bold print indicate an illustration.

A

Abe Lincoln Mines & Milling Co. 292
Absolute Automotive 17
Adams House, Ada & Robert M. 121, 123
Affiliated Foods 173
Agriculture Building **281**
Airplane Inn **274**
Aldis Food Market 216
Al's Goodie Shop 14, 19
Allis-Chalmers, Farm Equipment **170**, 230
Alta Vista Camp 82, 142
A&M Auto Repair **252**
Amarine Radio Service 44
American Beet Sugar Co. (ABSC) 4, 43, 72, 102, **207**, 260, 275, 291
American Civil War 27
American Crystal Sugar Co., ACSC 43, 54, 142, **207**, **260**, 275, 285
American Fruit Growers, Inc. 14
American Legion David Stanbridge Post No. 8 138, 139, 293
American Railway Express 294
Amos Co. (Hardware) 9, (11)
Ancient Free & Accepted Masons (AF & AM)
   St. John's Lodge No. 75 290
Anderson Brothers Clothing Store 293
Anderson Motor Co. 56
Anti-Saloon Party 20
Apishapa River 300
Aragon's Tavern 138
Arch Inn 50
Archie's Diagnostic Center **125**
Arkansas River 63, **82**, 86, 285, 290, Flood 293
Arkansas Valley 67, 274, 299, 300
   Broom Factory 50, **57**, **150**, 151
   Business & Chance Collection Agency 20
   Fair 66, **80**, **81**, 106, 116, 157, 296
   Fair Association 46, 275, 290, 291
   Fair Exposition Building **106**
   Fair Grandstands 32, **202**, **281**
   Fairgrounds 238, 281, 290
      Adobe (Horse) Barns **106**, 291
      Adobe Walls **105**
   Fair parade 1900, 116
   Fair Racetrack 31, **32**, **281**, 291
   Irrigation Society 289
   Memorial Co. **134**, 154, 198, 271
   Railroad; see Pueblo & Arkansas Valley Railroad 292
   Railway Light & Power Co. 46
   Seeds, Inc. 53, **149**, 231
   Sheep Feeder's Association 291
Arlington Café 25, **34**, 70, 72
Army Air Force Base 81
Army-Navy Store 57, **269**, **270**
Arnie Olson's TV Repair 14
Asakawa Billiard Parlor 294
AT & SF Railway 17, 290, Depot **130**
Artesian Well, First 1895, 14, (Water) **62**–**63**, (**90**), 291
Athalie's Dress Shop 12, **140**, 141, 249, **267**

Atterbury's Tailor Shop 293
Alta Vista Camp, Mercantile **54**
Aubert Eye Clinic 125
Aulgur's Barber Shop 266
Auto Baggage Truck No.1 14, 47
Auto Clinic **252**
A&W Root Beer 68, 123, **137**, 251

B

B&AIE Center 11
Babcock, LW, Creamery 50, 53, 154, 291
Bailey & Umbarger 38
Baker's Drug Store 46
Baker's Jewelry 14, **171**, **276**
Ballot issue, 1896 20
B&M Implement Co. 11, **128**, 221, 245
Bandstand, Railroad Park 294, Cemetery 80
Banta-Smith Auto Co. 11, **126**
Barrow Amusements 29
Barrow Grocery Store 292
Bartow Consolidated Canning Co. 292
Bass & Summers Transfer & Storage 19, 39
Bauer Home **246**
Baughman's Garage 9
Bay Station, L Findlay 202
B&B Liquor; Nite Club **179**
Beauty Nook 123, 197
Beek's Grocery 30, 56, 164
Beet Pulp 43
Before The Feast (Watermelon Day) **65**
Beman Building 13, 53, 108, **145**, 195, **205**, **213**, **269**
Beman, Inc. 110
Bender's Clock & Lock **144**, **197**, **222**, 240
Bennett's Liquor Store 46
Bent County 118, 164, 297, Court 290
Bent's Old Fort 95
Bernard-Cover Building **110**, 133, **140**, 267
Berry's Candy Store 293
Berry's Super Service 50, **151**
Bertha's Lunch 43, 295
Betry Printing Co. 47
Bible Book Store 171, 259
Big A Auto Parts **136**
Big Four Cash Grocery 21
Bijou Amusement Hall 26, 71, 123
Bill & Bob's Service 21, 45, **178**, 222, **226**, 252
Bill Will's Fruit Stand 225
Bish Brothers Co. 19, 114, 232, **233**
   Lumber Warehouse **156**, Feed Store **229**
Bish, WR, Hardware & Furniture Co. 17, 57, **136**
Blackford & Baughman Garage **261**
   Motor Co. 294
Black's Jewelry 20
Blacksmith & Repair Shop **88**
Block (definition) 20
Bloomfield Usher Dye (house) 27, 29, 31, 121
Blotz Seed & Produce Co. 55
Blue & Gray Encampment 291

Blue Stamps 173
Blue Mountain Lawn Care 285
Bloom, Colorado 265
Boardwalk/s **25**, **125**, **127**, 181
Board sidewalk 164
Bob's Food Products, Valley Chip & Supply co. 57
Bonta Mercantile Co. 21, 293
Book Stationery Store **127**
Boompa's Country Seconds **12**
Borden's Plumbing & Heating **180**, 220
Bostwick Brothers, Confectioners 22
Boys & Girls Club 78
Boy Scouts, Rocky Mountain Council 296
BPOE Lodge 1147 **49**, 54, 79, 196, 293
    Trade tokens 49
Braden's Rexall Drug Store 14, 57, **199**, 210, **266**
Bradshaw's Emporium 53
Brandt Blacksmith Shop **153**
Brewer Construction Co. 158
Brick Kilns, Fred Cheek 101, 130
Briscoe Staples & Fancy Groceries **119**
Brown Studio **190**
Bruse's Variety Store 12-13, 128
Buck & Pap Grocers 15
BU Dye Blacksmith & Repair Shop 1888 **88**, 243
BU Dye Livery Barn **88**, 97-99, **101-102**; House **121**
Buick (auto dealership) 9, 112
Burrell Seed Growers Co. 10, 59, **107**, 126, 292
Business Men's Party 20
Butterfield's Hardware & Furniture 120

C

CA Heskett Produce Co. 54
Cabbages (1908 postcard) **36**
Cabinet Photo (see carte de visite) 254, **258**
Cad's Cleaners 146, 201, 202
Calaboose 22
Campers, **238**, Campground 88
Canon City, Colorado 290
Cantaloupe Café **24**, 25, **70**, 72, 139, **262**, 270
Canterbury Barber Shop 47
Carman & Sons Plumbing & Heating 22, 23
Carmax 216
Carmon (horse) 28
Carnegie Library 293, architectural style 77
Canning Factory 1, 95, 231, 291, 292
Carousel 13, **187**, 268
Casa Luz **203**
Carte de visite (see Cabinet Photo) **254**, 258
Cartwright Building 9, 53, **112**, **143**, **144**, **267**, 278
Carquest 17
Casebeer Produce Co. 10
Catholic Church, St. Peter Parish 172, **223**, 290, 295
Catlin Canal Co. Ditch 46, 63, 82, 291
Cement Stone Co. 72, 95, 102
Cemetery 166
    Valley View Cemetery 27
Centers For Disease Control & Prevention 285
Central Liquor **193**

Central Meat Market 10
Central Park (Railroad Park) 14, 229, 293
Central Shoe Repair-Service **126**, **146**, **147**, 205, **234**
Chamberlain Realty 22, **212**
Chamber of Commerce 63, 117, **180**, **220**
Champlin Oil 178
Chase Auto Repair 50, **179**
Cheek's Kiln (Brick Yard) 235
Cheek, Walter, Building / Block **126**, 146, 198, 205, 259, **261**, 280, 291, 293
Cherry Corner 155, **169**
Chevron Service **191**
Chic Paree 26
China Kitchen 50
Chrane Service Station 56
Christine's 241, **242**
Christmas Decorations **117**
Christian Church, (Disciples of Christ) **222**, 291
Christian Science Reading Room 22, 212, 290
Chuck Wagon (County Road Crew) **239**
Chuck Wagon 44, 55, 152
Church Furniture by Woodcraft **188**
Church of the Brethren 291
Children of Rocky Ford School Dist. No. 4 **281**
Cigarette Tax Stamp **145**
Citizen's Utilities Co. 25, 161, **196**
City Administration Building 132, 147, **209**, 234
City Drug Store 14-15, 34, 58, **81**, **113**, **127**, 155, 236, 294
City Dump **82**
City Engineer, Harry Barnes **145**, 248
City Hall **208**, **209**
City Hospital 292
City Ice Service 50
City Map **61**
City Park 293
    Reservoirs 116, 290
    Water Works 39, 82
Clark's (Leo & Bill) AG Food Market **176**, **177**
    Grocery & Camp 54, 176
Clark Music Co. 20
Claude Silvers Coal 17, 265
Claude's Shoe Shine Shop 22, **23**, 212
Clute Manufacturing Co. **272**
CNC Technical Services 285
Coca Cola Bottling Co. 42, 57, **184**, 221
Coffea Shop 14, **109**
Colorado A & M horse barn **28**
Colorado National Guard Armory 5
    Rocky Ford Unit 81
Colorado Preservation 106
Colorado Springs, Colorado 82, 291
Colorado State Highway no. 10 274
    State Highway no. 71 93, 112, 274, 294
Colorado State Penitentiary 73
Colorado State University 285
    Library Archives 97
    Extension Service 11
Colorado Telephone Co. 7, 292
Colorado Territory 290
Community Banks of Rocky Ford 14
Continental Oil Co. 55
Continental Trailways Bus Lines 155

Control Panel (Sugar Factory) **207**
CO-OP 202
Cork Brothers Liquor 191
Corrals, stockyards, feed lots 43
Cossettes 260
Cottonwood Airfield 276
County Commissioners 164
Cover-Hale-Kimsey Block 292
Cowboys, ABSC Corporate 43
Cox's Daylight Donuts **211**
Craig Meat Market 132
Cretcher & McMurtry Lumber Yard 291
Crooked Arroyo 75, 274
Crossing Signs **18**
Crosswhite Realty 14, 171
Crowley County, Colorado 294
Crutchfield & Woolfolk 36, 46
Crystal Springs Bottling Co. 12
CS Williams Co., Onions **219**
    Feed & Agricultural Chemicals 219
Culligan Soft Water Service 11
Culling's Hill **116**
Curtis-Erickson Carpet **179**, **212**, 269
Curve Enterprises & Motel, (Court) 50, (**252**)
Curve Liquor Store 95, **151**
Cut & Style 10, **144**, 278
Country Kitchen 43

D

Dairy Bake (Shop) 25, 161, (295)
Dairy Treet 57
Dale's Texaco Service 50
Daniel's Bicycle Shop 132
Daring Agency, Real Estate, Insurance 57, **199–200**, 202
Daughters of the American Revolution (DAR) 138
Dawley, HA, Hardware, Furniture, Undertaking
    & Embalming **110**, 111
        Hardware, Warehouse 156
Dawley-Wilson Hardware & Furniture Co. 108, 111, 292
Daylight Donuts 205
Decoration Day 80
Delmonte Grocery 70, 72, 161
Denny & Lopez Grocery Store 293
Denver, Colorado 207, 288, 238; *Denver Post* 89, 104
Department of Employment 205
Diamond Mine Jewelers **226**
Dickinson & Davis Grocers 293
Discount Tire 194, 225, **263**
Dobbs & Lyons Furniture & Undertaking 120
Doc & Bonnie's Café 22, **53**, **125**
Dodge Brothers Garage 11, **128**, 198
Dog House **259**
Donk's Furniture 11, 198, 245, 280
    Variety & Radio 14, **81**, **266**
Don's Bar **226**
Don's For Lad & Dad 33, **141**, 202, 267
    Mens Store 12, 33, 57, 83, **140**, **267**, 295
Double A Heating & Air Conditioning 196
Double R Automotive 17

Douglas Markets **174**
Dub's Superior Service **214**, 227
Duckwalls 187, 268
Dugouts, (family of Jose Creo) 86, 93
Dutch And Dutchess Motel **192**
DV Burrell Seed Growers Co. 59, 123
Dowler's Fashion Shop 294
Dye Livery Barn, c 1877 243
    Reservoir **82**, 276
Dysentery 285

E

Earl Zimmerman Airfield 82, 276, 293, 294
Earl's Barber Shop 171
Easley Service Station 45
East Ranch, ABSC, ACSC 285
East Spanish Peak 300
Easy Wash, *auto*, 214, 227; Laundry 42
Ebbert Seed Co. 10, 123
Economy Clothes Shop 295
    Variety Store 12, 15, 47, **107**, **140**, **249**
Econo-Wash 22
EC Shelton & Son 38
EDCO Metal Works **172**, 264
Edwards Rexall Drugs **210**
Electric Shoe Shop 10
Elks Club (BPOE Lodge 1147) **49**, 54, 71
Ellis Auto Service 30
E & M Music Co. 54
Empire State Bank 133, 295
Empire Theatre, in Gobin Building 293
Emulsified asphalt 89, 303
ENCO Station **178**
Encore 260
Engle Grocery 54
Entablature, IOOF building **78**
ER Cook Implement Co. 292
Erlinda's Beauty Salon 14, 47
Evalynn's Dress Shop 12, **140**, 249, **266**
Evan's Jewelers **140**, **141**, **180**, 216, 249
Everson Tabernacle **282**
Exposition Building **275**

F

Facade 20, 48, **68**, **78**, **93–94**, **96**, **99–102**, **108**, **156**, **187**,
    227, **263**, 280
Fairbanks scale **88**, **102**
Fairchild Floral 45, 47
Family Dollar 173
Family Health Center, LLC 50, 243
Family Worship Center 124, 210
Farm Bureau **142**
Farm & Home Supply 54
Farmer's Department Store 120
    Insurance Group **224**
    & Merchants Bank 22, 291, 293
Fashion Center 15, 57, **157**, 269

Fenlason Agency **193**
   Realty Co. 56, **187**, **195**, 294
Fenton Drug Co. 10, **107**, **109**
Fiesta Café 21, 78, **262**, Restaurant **262**
Finley Motor Co. 43
Fire Hose Pumping Station 132, 293, Hydrants 132
Firemen **73–75**, **329**
First Baptist Church 290
   Christian Church 291
   Christian Science Church **244**
   Industrial Bank 13, 53, **187**, **213**, 269, 295
F & J Scaff Brothers 57
First Methodist Episcopal Church 46, 49, **79**, 134, 185, **199**, **203**
First National Bank, Rocky Ford 20, 133, 292
   Ordway, Las Animas 13
First Prize Foods **136**
Flagman Station, (The Transfer Man) 19
Fleak Clothing Co. 14, **113**
Florence, Arkansas 251
Fly Harness **36**
Fly Public Sale Ring 294
Foerster Refrigeration Service 56
Food Bank 78, Food Stamps **173**
Ford J. Steward Plumbing 292
Ford, The, (original rocky ford river crossing) **87**
Fort Collins, Colorado 285
Fowler, Colorado 300
Frame's Studio 15, 38
Frank Day Farm **35**
Frank G. Hough & Co. Beans 17, 265
Frank H. Boraker's Shop **16**, 81, 302
Frank's Garage 42, Garage (unknown) **280**
Fraser Dry Goods 12, 216, 249, **267**, 295
Freddie's Corner **186**, **193**, 196
Freeman's Fine Pastries 27, 123, 146, 155, 202, **205**
Frozen Foods 295
Fulton Meat Market 293
Funk's Soda Fountain 12, 107, **249**
FY Hauck Hose Co. 291

G

Gambles 15, 202, **236**, **269**, 294, 295
Gandara Mercantile **142**
Garden Place 14, 30, 63, 72, 98
Garry Moore Texaco Service **176**
Garwood & Butterfield Hardware & Furniture 29, **120**
G & K Co, (Grimsley & Keck) 54, 139, 170, Onions 54
Gem Grocery, Restaurant 292; Theatre **24**, 70–72, 161
General Chevrolet Co. 198, 245, 292
George Aldis Food Market 10
George Maxwell Clothing 15, 17
George McKenzie Music & Furniture Co. 29, **121**, **220**
George E. Bryant Coal 19
George Nelson's Conoco **228**, 271
George O. Teats, General Contractor 93, 148
Gerbing Meat Market 15, **109**, 113
Gibson Lumber Co. 60, **116**, **122**
Gibson & Fenlason Realty 132

Gibson's Racket Store 10
Ging Hand Laundry 188
Ginger's Café 53
Global Treasurez 13, 187, 268
Gobin Billiard Hall 47
Gobin Block (Building) **45**, 47, 71, **134**, 135, 171, 194, 220, **224**, 226, 264, 276
Gobin Bookkeeping Service 44, Gobin, Inc. 171, 210
Gobin Community Center **44**
Godding Block 71, **108**, 269, 290
Goeringer Realty 14, 19, **169**
Golden Rule Department Store 14, **113**, **129**, 291
Golf Course 82, 295
Goodner Iron & Pump Works; Mfg. Co. 44, 54, 56, 273
Gorsuch Cleaning Shop 53
Govreau Grocery & Meat Market **21**, 53, 78, 262, 293
Government Printing Office 90
Grady's Grill **53**
Grand Beer Tavern 68
Grand Opera House 68, **123**, **250**, **251**, 292
Grand Opera House Ticket Booth **250**
Grand Theatre 27, **68**, **157**, **250**, 294, 295
Grace Baptist Church, La Junta, Colorado 274
Grapette Beverage Agency 55
GR Daring Transfer & Coal Co. 122
Great Western Poultry Farm 294
Green & Babcock, Inc. (Lumber) 54, (**158**)
Grenada, Colorado 104
Griffin, Holder, & Thomas Onion Shippers 50
Grimsley & Keck Co. **170**, 230
Grimsley, White & Co. 53
Guynn Mercantile Co. 15

H

H & B Seeds, Inc. 55
Hagen, HF, Block (Building) 29, 71, **120**, **121**, **132**, **146**, **147**, 209, 234
Hagen Furnished (Modern) Rooms 29, (**120**, 220)
Hagen-Recker Block (Building) 20, 71, **114**, **119**
Hair Affair 10
Hale Building (Block) **110**, 124, **133**, **329**, 278–**279**
Haley's Texaco Service 45
Halle's Dress Shop **226**
Hall Motor Freight Co. 50
Hamilton's Variety & Gift Store 14
Hancock Real Estate & Insurance 169, **210**
Hancock's (Men's Wear) (25, 53), **139**, **160**, 202
Hand pump (Hotel De Seeley) **94**, 95
Harada Farms Daily Fresh Market **220**
Hardey Dry Goods Co. 12
Harding Electric Co. 55
Hardt Hardware 15, 212, **236**, 268, **269**
Harris Pharmacy 12, 141, 216, 267
Harrison's Variety Store 53
Hawley Store **274**
Hay Palace (Ark. Valley Fairgrounds) 291
HD Garwood Seed Co. 14
Heil Bean, Inc. 17, 265
Help-UR-Self Laundry **197**, 231

Hendricks Brothers Building **129**
Hendrix Auto Repairing 55
Henry's Cleaners 10, **144**, **189**, 278
Hernandez Pool Hall 268
Herring's Carpentry Shop 293
Herring & Griffin Garage 95
Hested Stores 13, **268**
Hetty Roach Beauty Shop 56
Highbe Popper 119
High Chaparral Inn & Restaurant **215**
High Grade Work Clothes 13
Highline Canal Co. (Canal) 46, (116), **187**, 300
Hi-Way Liquor Store 47, 55, **226**
Hoff Plumbing & Heating 10
Holbrook Ditch 290
Holder's Service Station 43
Holland Drug Store 14, **81**, **157**, **276**
Holsun Grocery 22, 33, 70, 72, 293
Home Bakery **278**
Home Finance Co. 47
Home Realty 22
Homestead Act, 1862 66
Honolulu Airplane Race 293
Horse stalls **106**, 303
Horton's Market **57**, 189
Hotels, apartments, rooms
   Amos Flats 71
   Berkeley 8, 71, 142
   Best 29, 71, **120**, 202
   Bolton 71, **134**
   Central 15, 71, 109, 211
   De Seeley 48, **88**, 93–95 (Welcome Home 95), 97–**100**
   El Capitan 8, 71, 102, 112, 155, **235**, 246, 292
   Elk 69, 71, **212**
   Longworth 69, 71
   National House 71
   Pacific House 71, **116**, **119**
   Park 53, 60, 295
   Park View 55
   Rector 47, 71
   Rockford (Rocky Ford Hotel) 71, 95
   Royal 45, 71, 134, 135, **194**, **224**, **226**
   St. James **24**, 69–**70**–**72**, 114, **131**, 139, 161, 164, 262, 269
   Swink 69, 131, 291
   West 69, 131
Hot Springs, Arkansas 251
Howard Grocery **55**
Hoyt's O-K Rubber Welders 57; Tire Shop **154**
Huerfano County 300
Huri-Back Lunch (Menu) 42, **83**, (**84**), 152, **241**
Huri-Back Park 85, 149
Huri-Back Service Station 42, 241
HW O'Bryant's Jewelry **110**

I

Ichi Ban Restaurant 13, **127**, 236
IDEA Center 198
Ideal Market 294
IL Smirl's Dry Goods Store 53

Immanuel Congregational Church **244**, 293
Int Stanley & Sons 25, 38, 72
IOOF Hall, Lodge 87 21, 34, **78**, 114, **233**, 290

J

Jackson & Lawson Transfer Co. 15, **17**, 113, **116**, 122, 136, 265
Jackson Transfer & Storage 54, 57, 139, **196**, 291
JB Byers Co. 293
JB King Service Station 294
JC Braden Rexall Drug Store 47, 57, **109**, 113
JC Mercantile 12, 141
JC Penney Co. 10, 12, 140, 141, **180**, **216**, 249, **266**
JC Robinson Seed Co. 56, **219**
JC Vaughn Transfer & Transportation Co. 293
Jenner Plumbing & Heating 22, 53
Jenny Gobin Cameron's Millinery, Ready-To-Wear 53
JE Orr Photography 231, 254, 291
Jess's Barber Shop 15
JH Igo Building **129**
JI Case Farm Implements 128, 285
JI Griffin, Onions 56
Jim Montgomery Auto Sales **170**
Jimbo's Drive-In Restaurant **225**
Joe's Barber Shop 46
Joe's Service **225**
John Deere, agency 89, 93
John Deere Implements 48, 54
Johnny Doll Pine Avenue Garage **96**
Johnny's Auto Service 21
Johnny's Bar 47
Johnson-Ebert Photography **190**
Johnson & Govreau 17
   Coal, Grain, Transfer & Water), **265**
Johnson Hardware & Furniture Store 111, 293
Johnson's Superior Bay Station 53
Johnson's Superior Station 42, (Conoco **184**), **272**
Johnson's Undertaker & Embalmer 132
JT Hill Sewing Machines & Organs 132
June Chevrolet Co. 11, 47, 198, 226, **271**, 280
   OK Used Cars **247**, **271**
Junior Chamber of Commerce 295
Junior Towne Shop 14
J Wood Peery Cash Grocery 10, 53, **112**, 143, 268

K

Kansas Pacific Railroad 290
Kaplan's Clothing **236**, **268**
Kaplan Mercantile Co. 15, 109, 211, **268**
Karl's Cafe & Bar (Liquor) 47, 57, 211, (**270**)
Kansas District Mission Board 218
KAVI Radio 193, 202
Kay Kraig Ceramics 55
Kearby's Pharmacy **109**, 113
Kimsey-Cover Block (Building) **107**, 110, **133**, 140, **249**, 293
King's Ferry (river ford) 87

Kit Carson Road (Trail) 88, 95, 97, 98, 102, 104, (290)
Kitch Feed Lots 43
Kitch Pontiac Agency (Building) 50, 93, 151, **243**, (295)
Klondike (Melon) 59
Knaus Real Estate & Insurance Co. 294
Knights Of Pythias Hall (Building, K of P) **10**, 56, 71, **107–108**, **110**, 169, 216, 290, 294
    Valley Lodge No. 98 291
Kriss Kross Grocery 53

L

La Clinica del Valle 166, 172
La Frances Dress Shop 13, 269
La Junta Air Base Chapel 223
    Army Air Force Base 285
La Junta, Colorado 66, 73, 81, 99, 104, 274
Lamplight Lounge **175**
Land Office **125**, **262**
Langford Used Furniture 123
La Nortena 45
Las Animas, Colorado 104, County 118, 300
Las Animas Leader 95
Latson & Boggs 39
Law Motor Lines 55, 57, **150**, **172**, 194, 264
Lawrence, Charles L. Signs, Wallpaper & Paints 123
Lawrence Robinson & Son 55
Lawrence Warehouse Co. 53
Lee's Barber Shop 10, **267**
Leghorn, rooster, hen **85**
Leroy's Grocery Market 54, 57, 163, Locker Plant 57
Les's Garage 54
Lewis Bros & Johnson Merc. Co. 13, **108**, 111, **205**
Lewis Brothers Hardware & Furniture Co. 111
Lewis Furniture 10, 216
Libby, McNeil, & Libby Canning Factory 95, 231
Liberty School 11, 164, 166, **237**, 291
Library Board 293
Library Park 80
Lighthouse Church 22
Lincoln Park 163
Lincoln School, (Students) c 1943 124, (**163**), 292
Listeria 284
Little Cash Grocery 292
Little White School 11, 12, 97, 164, **166**, 220, 290
Livermore, Colorado 285
Livery Stable, BU Dye & Son **88**
Loaf 'N Jug Food Store **215**, 247
Love Box Co. 37
Love's Café 46, **199**
    Shoe Store 12, 33, **141**, 267
Lower Arkansas Water Management Assoc. 264
Luetcke Pontiac Co. 57, 151
Lyons-Burmood **136**, **148**

M

Macklin Photography 190
Madonna's Towne Shoppe 12
Maltby Drug Store 294
Mameda, Colorado Produce 178
Manzanola, Colorado 300
Mars Nite Club 179
Mart Lueker's Sinclair Service Station 45, **135**, **196**
Mary C. Loring Ladies Wear, (Clothing Store) 47, (53)
Marticia's Gift Shop 47, 57
Ma's Place 25, 70, 72
Masonic Hall
    Lodge 10, 49, 71, **107**, **110**, 144, 278, 292, 295
    Royal Arch Masons, New York Rite 292
Matthews & Sons Electric **176**
Maxwell Block (Building) 71, 113, 116, 136, 155, 157
Maxwell-Fleak Clothing Co. 30
Maytag Appliances **220**
McKenzie Music & Furniture Co. **121**, 153, 234
    New & Used Furniture **220**
McCLain's Super Foods 71, **160**, 161, 197, 240, 270
McClelland Motor Parts 11, 198, **245**, 280
McCoy's Service Station 45
McDougal Farm Equipment 48, **148**
McKay's Turf Exchange 290
Meade Co. 219
    (See Sawyer-Meade Co.) 219
Mehlin & Sons 22, 29, 180
Melon City Royal Service (Conoco) **172**, 227
Melon Day 1904 **60**
Meloneer 182; meloneers **299**
Melon Field (airfield) 276
Memorial Bridge **138**
Meng's Mixed Drinks 50, 55
Merchant's Softball League 294
Methodist Episcopal Church 288, 290
Mexican Cemetery **168**
    Herders 87
Michigan, Alma 76; Ionia 121
Middleton Super Standard Service **247**
Midtown Texaco 176
Milburn, Inc. Beans 55
Millinery Shop (Mrs. Nellie Conquest) **135**
Minstrel Show **251**
Mint Saloon 15, 109, 113, **226**, 236, 268, Mural **108**
Mission Deli **224**, 243
M & O Pawn & Antiques 225
Model (Dry) Cleaners (25), **153**, **160**, 161, **188**, 197, **231**, (**234**)
Modern Woodmen Camp No. 7473 291
Mom & Pop Store 174
Monument, Colorado 290
Monument, Original River Crossing 93, **296**
    Swink Home Site **208**
Moorhead, Minnesota, ABSC Corporate Headquarters 207
Moose Hall, Lodge No. 306 71, 138
Motor (*Supply*) Co. **272**
Mountain States Telephone & Telegraph Co. 46, 294
Movie World 22
Municipal Swimming Pool 248

Music Room, The **146**, **201**
Myrtle Dairy 34

N

Nathan Kaplan Clothing 6, 12
National Automotive Parts Association (NAPA) 151
National Park Service, Register of Historic Places 169
Native Americans 238
Nava Café & Liquor Store **191**
Nava Manor 11, 237
NBC Insecticide Co. 57
Nelson-June Chevrolet Co. 198, 295
Nelson & Winters Cash Grocery 292
Nepesta, Colorado 7
New Method Laundry 293
Newton Lumber Co. 60, 116, 122
Nikkel's Superior Service Station 42, **184**, 272
North American Dehydrate Co., NADCO 260
North Side Cut-Rate Package & Liquor Store
   & Pool Hall 10, 143, **268**
NW Terry Brick Yard 72, 99, 235

O

Oasis, The 9, **144**
Obelisks, Rocky Ford 85, 95, **149**, **151**, **330**
   Architrave 95
   Entablature 95
Oberling Motors **231**
O-Boy Grocery Market & Cabins 50, **150–151**, **174**, 294
OD Koonce Model Shoe Repair 55
Old Republic, The 76
Old Rocky Ford 86
Oliver Steele Manufacturing Plant 63
Onion Growers Co-op 185
Opera House Block 71
   Meat Market 293
   Pharmacy 132, 146, 291
Order of Eastern Star, Acacia Chapter No. 38 291
Oriental Café 221
Otero County 118, 168, 276, 294, 300
   Agricultural Association 9, 10
   Farm Labor Association 56
   Health Department **156**
   Historical Building 166
   Landfill 82
   Veteran's Association of Blue & Gray 291
   Welfare Office 56
Otero Junior College, La Junta, Colorado 285
Otero Tire Co. 43
Otis E. Adcock & Son 42
Otto Clothing 22
Oxnard Construction Co. 260

P

Palace Drug Store 10, **107**
Palace of Sweets 20, 25, 70, 72
Palmer Dry Goods Co. 292
Parapet, ornamental (St. James Hotel) **70**, **114**, 139
Park Addition 292
Park Avenue Barber Shop **175**
Park View Barber Shop **186**, 187, 193
Pat's Beauty Salon 10
Patterson Valley Road, CO 202, CR FF, Walnut Avenue
Paul Lee's Restaurant 53
Peggy's Café 215, 264
People at the Fair **277**
People's Home Bank 22, 293
People's Transfer & Coal Co. 122, 265, 292
Peterson & Beck (contractors) 36
Phil's Hardware 268
Photograph Gallery, JE Orr 231, 291
Photography Gallery, WH White 293
Physicians Hospital 56, **246**
Pickwick Inn Restaurant 56, (Café & Tavern) **193**
Pilgrim Holiness Church 8, 142
Pioneer Memorial Hospital 164, 295
Pioneer Nursing Home 164
Piper Brothers, Contractors 292
Pizza A-Go-Go 189, 221
PJ's Emporium **221**
Plant Food Corporation 57
Plant's Drive-In 43
Play Park Hill, Reservoir Hill 14, 181, 268
Pleasure Time Beverage Co. **142**
Plew's Ford Motor Co. 8, 50, 142, 198
P&M Café **270**
Polar Ice & Locker~Storage Co. 55, 57, **118**, **158**
Police Radio 295
Pollock's Hospital 112, **168**, **235**, 246
Polly's Café **152**, 215, 264
Pop Shoppe, The **215**
Postal-Telegraph Cable Co. 47
Pott Electric Co. 10, 20, 56
Poudre Valley Hospital, Pathology Dept. 285
Poultry 85, 294
POW Cells (WWII), POWs (German) **106**
Presbyterian Church 138, **197**, **206**, 290, 292, 293
Price Dry Goods 12, 216
Price & Lance Dry Goods **109**, 113, 291
Priscilla Stitch & Gift Shop 56, **240**
Proctor Family 221
Public Grocery & Market 25, 161, 291
Pueblo Chieftan 9, 166
Pueblo & Arkansas Valley Railroad 292; (see page 318)
Pueblo, Colorado 104, 290
Pueblo-Rocky Ford Toll Line 7

Q

Quality Market 47, 55, **226**
Quicksand 87, 285

R

Rabbit Ears Brand 231
Railroad Park, Central Park 14, **18**, 60, 63, 80, 116, 168
Railway Express Agency, Inc. 54, 130, **230**
RA McCart Pool Hall 29
Ra-Nels Bowling Lanes 173
Raw water (untreated) 90
Ray's Auto Repair 50
RC Drug Co. 15
RD Lewis Fruit Co. 151
Recker Bakery **60**
   Building (original frame) 60
   Charles F. (brick Building) 132, 146
Recker-Hagen Block 291
Recker's Hall **60**, **116**, **132**, 146, 147, 209, 234, 291
Red Cross Pharmacy 20, 178, 294
Reliance Auto Co. 45
Rench Grocery **278**
REO (auto dealership) 112
Republican Club 292
Republic Motor Truck Co. 76
Reservoir Hill, Play Park Hill 14, 63, **82**, **116**, 248
Rexall Drug Store 294
Rex Theatre 9, 10, 112, 143, 295
Reynolds Machine Shop 194
   Metals Building **263**
   Oil Co. 56
RH James Seeds 13
Rhoades Food Center 131, **160**, **161**, 270
   Meat Processing Department **158**
   Food Store 25
River Bridge, SH 71 294, crossing 290
Road Crew (County Roads) **239**
Ribeye Feed Yard 43
Rice Seed Co. **188**
Richard Van Skike Furniture 12
Ritthaler Bakery 269, 295
Roberta, Colorado 35
Robertson Dairy 56, 153
Rocky Ford Archeological Society 295
Rocky Ford Army Store 135, **194**
   Auto Co. **280**
   Auto Parts 150, 151, 174
   Bakery & Lunch **119**
   Ball Club 31
   Bottling Co. 7
   Cement Brick & Tile Co. 99, 292
   Centennial Committee and
     Calendar of Historical Interest 295
   City Directory 23, 36, 59, 78, 127, 252, **314**
   City Hall, Town Hall 54, 71, **156**
   Club 47
   Concert Band **80**
   Co-operative Creamery **154**
   Creamery (see Babcock, LW Creamery) 291, 292
Rocky Ford Daily Gazette-(Topic) 5, 27, 47, 85, 90, 123, 135, (155), **194**, 205, 292, 295
   Centennial 85, 96, 129, 173
Rocky Ford Dairy 293
   Canal, 1, 27, 31, 46, 63, 79, 90, 138, 174, 290, 300
   Drug Store 22, 53, 125, 202
   Electric Co. 289
Rocky Ford *Enterprise* 46, 47, 98, 132, 166, 188, 235, 275, 290
   Family Health Center, LLC 50, 243
   Federal Savings & Loan **224**, 264
   Feed Store **88**, **94**, 96, **101**
   Fire Co., & (First Hose Co.) (131), 292
Rocky Ford Fire Department 54, **75–76**, 131, **156**, **209**, 292
   Fire Truck **76**, Truck No. 1 **208**
   Fire Wagon **75**, **131**, **132**, **329**
   Food Market **173**, 185
   Floral Co. **56**, **204**
   Garage 11, **126**, 128, 198, **259**, **280**
   Grocery Co. 6, 14, **113**
   Grocery Store No. 2 132
   Hospital Association 112
   High School 54, 185, 285
     Outdoor track 258
     1908 Building 77, **181–182**, 293
     1918 Building 67, **183**
     1963 Building 82, **183**
   Baseball Team, 1912 **182**
   Historical Museum 197
   Ice & Mercantile Co. **118**, 158
   Ice & Storage Co. 289
   Inn 295
   Lions Club 293
   Melon Growers Association 37
   Municipal Swimming Pool **248**
   National Bank 14–15, 107, **117**, **129**, 155, **157**, 293, 294
Rocky Ford, Old 86, 93, 95
   Onion Growers Co-operative Association 57, **231**
Rocky Ford, Otero County, Colorado 285, 300
   Police Department 74
   Police & Firemen 73, 74
   Public Library, 1908 Carnegie Library **77**
   Public Museum, 1908 **77**
   Carriage House 76, 129
   Pump House **273**
   Sanitary Plumbing Co. 32, 47
   School District R-2 124
   Seed House 10
   Service Station 50, 54
   State Bank 14, **15**, 46, **129**
   (also State Bank of Rocky Ford) 129
   Town Co. (See Santa Fe Town Co.) 63, 97
   Town & Investment Co. 292
   Trading Co. 17, 20, **115**, **117**, 136, 292
Rocky Ford *Tribune* 10, 25, 70, 72, 121
   Women's Club 291
Rocky Mountain Lake Park **238**
Rocky Mountain News 9, 118
Rodeck Billiards 10, 22
Rooms, above Arlington Café 72; above Gem Theatre 72
Ross Repair & Machine Shop 42
Roxy Theatre 9, 10, 112, 294, 295
Roy Smith Model Shoe Repair **201**
Roy Taylor's Conoco Service 48, 88, 93, 95
R&R Nite Club 179
Rules for Teachers & Students 167
Rumsey Grocery & Bakery 10, **278**
Rusler Implement Co. 221

Ruth Café 22, 23
RW English Lumber Co. 19, 29, **114**, 232, 233

S

Safeway 67, **185**, 268
S & H Green Stamp Store **191**, 211
Sanders Accounting 200
Sanitary Bakery 293
Sanitary Landfill 82
Santa Fe Depot **14**, 116, 230
    Early sand-colored station 97, 130
    1876 Swink Store & Depot **104**
    1887 wood-sided **19**, **60**, **130**
        Conversion to Freight Depot **130**
    1907 brick **80**, **130**
Santa Fe Railroad 75, 95, 98–99, 104, 273, 290, 294
    Siding tracks 89
    Wagon camp 95
Santa Fe Stock Yards 294
Santa Fe Town Co., also, Rocky Ford Town Co., Railroad Town Co. 40, 97; Lot sale 97
Santa Fe Trail 66, 87, 290, 300
    Garage 95
Sawyer-Meade Co. 219
Schmidt's Conoco Service 50
School District Administration Building **163**
Scribner's School of Dancing 123, 126
Selective Service Office 203
Settling basins 63, ponds 82
7-UP Bottling Co., (sign) 55, (**139**)
Seven Lakes 300
Sever & Culp Stationers & Tobacconists 293
Shaeffers 225
Shamrock Service Station 57, 294
Sharp Image Styling Salon 19, 229,233
Shaw Clothing Co. 20, 119, 132
Shelton Grocers 15
Shoe Shop (first Main Street, now Railroad Av.) **88**, **100**
Shook 35, 37
Shorty's Tavern **155**
Shuey Bakery & Confectionery 22, 57
Siege Gun **299**
Silvers West Side Food Market **179**, 212
Simplot 219
Smirl Shoe & Garment **114**
Smirl & Son Grocers 22
Smith Brothers (see Bill & Bob) 178
Smith's Café 21, **83**
Smith's Corner **184**
Smith's Department Store 12, **216**, **267**
Sonic Drive-In 50
Sons of Veterans, Harlan Thomas Camp No. 18 291
South Park 293
Southern Colorado Exposition 1926 **275**
Southern Baptist Theological Seminary 13
Southern Colorado Power Co. 57, **124**, **140**, **177**, 249, **266**–**267**, 294–295
Southern Colorado-Northern New Mexico League (High School Baseball) 182

Souvenirs **256**
Spanish herders 87
Spanish Peaks 290
Spanky's Bar 47
Speed Queen Laundry 11
Spencer Chevrolet 294
Spencer's Confectionery 53
    Restaurant 20
Spot Café **155**, 218
Standard Credit Co. 272
Standard Oil 57
Star (automoblie) **261**
    Bar (Old) 175, 191
    Café 55, 191
    Theatre 10, 291
Stark Furniture Store 132
Starlite Drive-In Theatre 68
State Bank of Rocky Ford 218, 290
    Board of Agriculture (CO) 28
    Board of Health (CO) 72
Stauffer Food Co. 25, **270**
    Livestock Pens 118
    & Marsh Food Co. 294
    Meat Market 11, 71, 112
    Meats & Grocery **24**
    OB & Ben 161
    Packing Plant 293
Steward Sheet Metal Works 93, **94**, 243
Stitch Shop 294
St. John, AP, Vacuum Cleaning 123
    Body Shop 56
    Building 71, **123**, **171**, 250, **259**
    ML Repairs 123
St. Joseph Hospital (Denver, Colorado) 73
St. Louis World's Fair, 1904 159
St. Paul's Ev. Lutheran Church **241**, **242**, 293
Stout's Skelly Service 57, 191, 211
St. Peter's Ev. Lutheran Church 44, **218**, 240, 292
Studebaker (automoblie agency)108, 110, 269
Sunny Side Pharmacy 232, **233**
Surv UR Self Laundry **139**
Swede's Conoco 50, 202
Swift's Blacksmith Shop 97, 98
Swink Barn **159**
Swink Ditch and Irrigation Company: Reservoirs 1-6 300
Swink Factory 290
    Artificial Lake 97, 118, 290, 298-299
    Ice House 97
    Recreation Parlor 57
    & Russell 1871 Store **86**, 93
    Store (adobe) 1876 **88**, **89**, 93, 97, **104**, 130
Swink Timber Claim 166, 202, 284, 290

T

Tabernacle **13**, **282**
Taguchi Grocery 57
Talhelm, HP Bakery & Grocery 10, **112**
Tank 'N' Tummy 44, 152, 203, 225
Taqueria Mexico 50

General Index

Tastee Freeze 224, **243**
Telephone Offices **195**
Templeton-Bush, Inc., International Harvestor 42
   McCormick-Deering Implement Co. 11, 198
Tennis courts, City 31, 294, Dedication by RFHS 295
Texas Co., Oils 17, 55, 294
Tex's Automagic Service 56
Thatcher, Colorado Clay Mine 99
Thomas Addition 54, 61
Thompson-Claypool Undertaking Co. 10, 33, 108
Thompson Sweet Shop 295
Time capsule, (*a type of,* November 21, 1920) 138
Timpas Creek 1, 35; Timpas, Colorado 300
Tiny Juarez Café **186**, 193, 196
Tiny's Tavern 50, 57
TJ Smirl's Grocery Store 22, 53
Tobacco Unlimited **175**
Todd Airfield **276**
Toggery, The 21, 57, 294
Tom's Service Station 43
Town Commissioners 98
Town Plat 1876, re-plat 1887 95, 97
   Six-block town site 166
      Town Site, 1876 (renamed streets) **64**, 97
         Church Street **64**
         Front Street **64**
         Kit Carson Road (Tenth Street) 102
         Lake Avenue **64**
         Nichols Avenue (Tenth Street) 102
         Park Street **64**
         Railroad Street **64**
         Robinson Avenue (Main Street) 102
         Washington Avenue (Ninth Street) 102
Tom Welch Repair **96**
Triangle Café 294
Trail Café **271**
Transfer Man, The, Flagman Station 19
Trees 113, 122, 129, 181, 202
   American Elm 79, 100, 164
   Cottonwood 79, 86, 88, 94-95, 100, 125, 202, 238, 279
   Walnut 125
Trinidad, Colorado 99
Two-story Privy (St. James Hotel) 69-70
Typhoid fever 63, 302

U

Union Cleaners & Pressers 11
Union Pacific Railroad 63
Unique Cleaners **189**
United States Geological Survey 63, 90
   Old Rocky Ford 86, 93, 290, 297, 303
   Swink 1876 Store **104**
US Army 81, 285
US Department of Agriculture, (USDA) 171, (185)
   Office of Employment **171**
   Department of the Interior 169
   Highway 50 42, 66, 85, 88, 92, 178-179, 252, 294
US Post Office 10, 155, **208**, 285, 295
   in K of P Hall 108, 216, 292

Ustick Undertaking Co. 47
   Funeral Home 54, **162**
US Timber Claim Certificate No.166, 79, 255, 258, 290
   Timber Claim Certificate No. 2 288

V

Vacuum Cleaner, AP St. John 123
Valle Inpredodo (Rock Valley) 87
Valley Ambulance Service **225**
Valley Concrete 56
Valley Decorators & Builders 56
   Farm Market 221
   Food Store 294
   Laundries 56
   Motor Co. 57, 202
   Supers, (Building) **173**, (203)
   Trading Co. 292
   Produce 57
   Supply, Inc. **193**
Valley (Phillips) 66 Service 50
Van Antwerp Sanitarium & Chiropractors 123
Van Buskirk Seed Co. 123
Van Dyk Insurance Agency 48, 50, **94**
Variety Repair & Keys 56
Veatch Market 44, 57, 188, 240
Vencill Leather Shop 50
Veteran's Day 138
Viga, (log roof / ceiling beams) **155**, **157**, **175**
Violet Rebekah Lodge No. 3, (IOOF Ladies) 290
Voegtle's Harness & Shoe Shop 33

W

Wagon Camp 95
Walker's Mens Wear 15, 155, 157, 269
Wallace Oil Co. **203**
Walsenburg, Colorado 274
Walters (Lager Beer) 122
Walt's Place 53
Wards 179, 212
Washington Road 164
Washington School **164**, **165**–166, 238, 281, 285, 292
   Students 1904 **165**
Water, artesian **90**
Watermelon Day **65**-66, 79–**80**, 122, **238**, **253**–**258**, **277**, 284, 290, 291, 295
Watermelon, The 23, 80
WE Clark Meat Market 292
Weicker Transfer & Storage 57, 196
Weid's Bakery & Lunch 53
Weid Building **138**, 139
Well's Confectionery & Lunch 12, 33, 57
Wells Fargo Co. 130
Western Auto Assoc. Store 14, **141**, 202, 216, 249, 267
Western Game & Poultry Co. 37
Western Hardware & Furniture Co. 20
Western Motel (Cabins) **162**, 192, (**217**)
Western Union Telegraph Co. 12, 292

325

Western Wool Processors, Inc. **231**
West Side Farmer's Market 57, **221**
Whittaker Agency 46, 55, **190**
Whittaker Real Estate & Insurance **200**
Wig Wag signals **18**, **89**, 229
Wilkin's Laundromat **153**
Wilson Hardware & Furniture Store 111
Wilson Plumbing & Heating 11, **189**
Wilson's Hardware & Stoves 132
Wimpy's 42, **83–84**, **241**
Winsor Agency **135**, 202, 224
WL Jackson's Bowling Alley 292
Wolfe & Malty Block 20
Wolfe & Smith Block 20, 71
Wolfmeyer Grocery 55, 174
Wolf's Modern Steam Laundry 188
Woman's Club of Rocky Ford 138
Woodmen of the World
   Rocky Ford Camp No. 95 291
Woodside Seed Growers Co. 21, **78**
Works Progress Administration (WPA) 106, 155, 169, 208, 248
Wrangler Foods 53, 67, 185, 295
Wright Motor Lines, Inc. **194**, **263**
W & W Root Beer **68**, **137**
WW I 138
WW II 285

Y

Yoder-Casterline, Inc. 136, **148**
Yoder-Peterson **148**
Young's Soft Water Service & Auto Supply 240

Z

Zimmerman Airfield 82, 276, 293, 294
Zoar Encampment No. 8
   Independent Order of Odd Fellows (IOOF) **78**

Rocky Ford Fire Wagon stands front of 209 N Main Street, far left. Large 1895 Hale Building across Elm Avenue is at 301 N Main in center background. Date of photo is 1908. Firemen L to R are George Frantz, Fred Hendrick, unidentified, Charles Mellon, Sport Wittenberg, Frank Green and Chief Harpie in white gear. Horses are Prince and Alex who were destroyed behind a carpenter shop fire when trapped in an alley between 12th and 13th Streets near Chestnut avenue tangled in barbed wire.

Fire Wagon appears to be different from that depicted pp. 131–132.

Courtesy facebook.com/Rocky-Ford-Colorado

Addendum

Businesses Listed as Internet Service*

AAA Gifts	959 Elm	
Allied Mortgage	207 N 2nd Str.	
Alternative Pharmaceutical Tech., LLC	417 N Main	
American Builders	805 S 12th Str.	
American Family Life Assurance Company (AFLAC	904 Elm	
Arellano Photography	914 Washington	
Arf, Inc.	305 S Main	
Becerra Television Rpr	802 S 14th Str.	
Bridges & Son	505 S 4th Str.	
Canning Line Warehouse	708 Railroad	
C & D Liquors	1504 Elm	
Centennial Family Health Care	1014 Elm	
Ceramic Corner	313 N Main Str.	
Colorado Lift	605 S 6th Str.	
Country Morning Coffee Shop	400 N Main	
Culver William, Atty	410 N 9th Str.	
Daniel R. Hyatt, Atty	512 N Main Str.	
Dave Lewis Trucking	601 S 8th Str.	
Details By Kat	1009 Maple	
Direzza Industrial Svc	100 S 5th Str.	
Divine Creations	962 Elm	
Family Care Center	409 S Main Str.	
Fern's Floral	409 N Main Str.	
Furniture Gallery	408 N Main Str.	
Gary's Sales & Service	309 Elm	
Gateway To Heaven	307 N 2nd Str.	
G-N-C Auto & Truck	511 N Main	
Goff Family Co., Inc.	963 Elm	
Grace Investment Group	311 S Main	
Hancock Froese & Co.	601 S 8th Str.	
Harmony Health Center	1016 Elm Av.	
H & S Enterprises, LLC	100 S 12th Str.	
International Assoc. Machinists & Aerospace Workers	1600 Washington	
Jane's World TLC	950 ½ Franklin Dr.	
Jennifer's Hair & Nail Salon	410 N Main	
Julio & Sons	511 N 12th Str.	
Justin's Paving, Inc.	1707 Swink	
Kelley Global Exchange	800 Ewers	
Kim's Nail Cottage	1120 Elm	
Larkspur, Inc.	801 Swink.	
Lex Nichols Photography	903 S 7th Str.	
McClelland Manor Condominiums Assoc.	805 Chestnut	
McCo Tax Service	301 S 3rd Str.	
	307 N 7th Str.	
McKittrick Manor	806 Catalpa	
McMillian Autobody	402 Elm	
Nino's, Inc.	406 N 2nd Str.	
Norton's HVAC	28235 Manor Str.	
OCD Otero Cars & Detail	301 N 7th Str.	
Otero County Ext. Agt	411 N 10th Str.	
Patterson Valley Water Co.	96 Willow	
Pettie Enterprises	1724 Washington	
Pettie Pub	968 Front Str.	
Pink Pumpkin Patch Fdn	601 S 8th Str.	
Pipe Dragon, Inc.	1315 Elm	
Plaza Nueva	702 Sandia Dr.	
Precision Instruments, Inc.	413 N Main	
Quickees	1207 Elm	
Rocky Ford Ambulance Sv	203 S 9th Str.	
Rocky Ford City Shops	801 Beech	
Rocky Ford Family Chirop., LLC	605 N 9th Str.	
Rocky Ford Floral & Garden Ctr.	207 N Main	
Rocky Ford Housing, Inc.	702 Sandia Dr.	
Rocky Ford Mini Mart	1305 Swink	
Rocky Ford Produce, Inc.	401 N Main	
Rocky Ford Workforce Center	801 Chestnut	
Rocky Ford Worship Center	504 S 10th	
R & P Enterprises	410 N 9th Str.	
Ruben's Body Shop, Ctr	1001 Swink	
Santo Nino Learning Ctr	1209 Swink	
Schollmeyer Electric	210 Elm	
Scissors Plus Styling Salon	1012 Burrell	
Serenity Enterprises	806 Catalpa #15	
Sixty-Six Food Plaza	1207 Elm	
Soco Security Lpa	603 S 9th Str.	
Southeast Regional Clinic	912 Walnut	
Souther Colorado Rural Emergency Medical Services	402 Elm	
Stan Oswald Photography	915 Elm	
Stormy's Snd Hand Store	400 S Main	
Superior Exterior, Inc.	720 S 2nd Str.	
Tabor Accounting Service	963 Elm	
TNM & O Coaches, Inc.	700 Swink	
Tri-County Family Care	512 ½ N Main	
T-Shirt Palace	900 Elm	
Uptown Music & Video	700 Swink	
Valcrete, Inc.	200 S 17th Str.	
Valley Tire	402 Elm	
Valley Wide Health Sys	903 S 12th	
Vbm Contractors, Inc.	963 Elm	
Wadleigh Insurance	515 N Main	
Walter Chiropractic, P.C.	418 N Main	
Weldon's Paint Can, Inc.	1224 Elm	
West Side Liquor Store	216 Elm	
Windstone	208 N Main	
Woodpecker Creations	806 S 5th Str.	
Worship Ctr of Rocky Ford	919 Elm	
Xi-Gua Siamese of Rocky Ford	506 S 9th Str.	
Xochitl's Hair & Nail Salon	102 Elm	

Businesses listed on this page were not included in directory years 1911, 1914–1915, 1945–1948, the scope of this book. They are added to recognize their activity in succeeding years. Some may be inactive, have no current advertising, are dissolved, or are renamed.

* Bizapedia.com identifies information of businesses by using several parameters including state, city, and type of business.

Ad Blocks from 1914–1915

A. McCormack
General Blacksmithing
Plow and Buggy Work

Horse Shoeing a Specialty

RAILROAD AVENUE   PHONE FORD 89

BUCK AND PAP GROCERS

TELEPHONE FORD 17   ROCKY FORD, COLO.

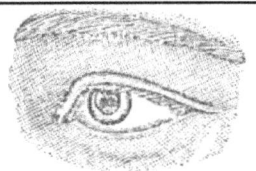

When Your Eyes Need Attention
Consult **E. F. Burnett**
OPTOMETRIST — OPTICIAN
The man with the no-chart method of examining eyes for glasses. Sherman Hotel La Junta, every Friday. National Hotel, Fowler, every Monday.

OFFICES 204 1-2 NORTH MAIN STREET, ROCKY FORD, COLORADO.

Frame's Studio
Mrs. O. L. Frame, Propr.

ALL THE LATEST STYLES IN FINE PHOTOS
SATISFACTION GUARANTEED
Kodak Developing and Printing for Amateurs

204 1-2 NORTH MAIN   ROCKY FORD, COLO.

Mrs. Mary J. Anderson
REAL ESTATE, LOANS AND FIRE INSURANCE
NOTARY PUBLIC

CITY PROPERTY A SPECIALTY

TELEPHONE WEST 522   ROCKY FORD, COLO.

Robt Voegtle — HARNESS MAKER --- SHOE MAKER
First Class Work -- Reasonable Prices
917 Railroad Ave.   Rocky Ford

Hardey's — Dry Goods, Shoes
Phone West 53
Call Us by Phone
ROCKY FORD   COLORADO

NEWLY FURNISHED   REASONABLE RATES
ELK HOTEL
MRS. A. CORCORAN, PROPR.
FIFTY CENTS AND UP
BATHS AND STEAM HEAT
311 1-2 SOUTH MAIN   ROCKY FORD, COLO.
TELEPHONE FORD 121

Grand Valley Livery
R. M. WRIGHT, PROPR.

Horse and Automobile Livery

912 Walnut Avenue   Telephone Ford 84

Bruse's Variety Store

FOR BARGAINS ALWAYS

315 NORTH MAIN STREET
ROCKY FORD, COLO.

Hale Block

Phone Ford 268

Osborn, The Rocky Ford Photographer.

Everything Photographic

Rocky Ford Bakery and Restaurant

Opposite Depot   Short Orders at All Hours   Rocky Ford

Ad Blocks from 1914–1915

The Rocky Ford Sanitary Plumbing Company

DICK FARRIS, PROPRIETOR

PLUMBING, HEATING, STEAM FITTING, TIN AND IRON WORK, TANKS, WIND MILLS

TELEPHONE WEST 249

960 ELM AVENUE　　　　　ROCKY FORD, COLO.

STAR LIVERY

J. H. WINE, PROPR.

FIRST CLASS RIGS AND SADDLE HORSES

Railroad Avenue　　　　　Phone Ford 32

ROCKY FORD, COLO.

The Rocky Ford Land and Investment Company

A. W. WRIGHT, MGR.

Real Estate, Insurance, Loan and Bond Agency

MAXWELL BUILDING　　　　　ROCKY FORD, COLO.

CALL IN THE

VACUUM CLEANER IT EATS THE DIRT

Cleaning of all kinds done at your home, if you have the electric current; if not, I can bring your rugs to my shop

A. P. St. John

801 South Main　　　　　Phone Ford 604

ROCKY FORD, COLO.

THE UNIQUE

L. B. GORSUCH, PROPR.

Dry Cleaners and Pressers

Telephone Ford 55　　　　　975 Railroad Avenue

ROCKY FORD, COLO.

SUTER & COMPANY

General Contracting and Jobbing

Shop Always Open.　Estimates Furnished on Application.
Second Hand Goods Bought and Sold.　P. O. Box 423

900-902 Front Street　　　　　ROCKY FORD, COLO.

W. D. GRISSOM

The Automobile Painter

BEST WORK IN VALLEY

LA JUNTA, COLO.

417 Lincoln Ave.　　　　　Phone East 173

PHONE WEST 505　　　　　ROOMS

The Arlington Cafe

G. M. HOOPER, PROPRIETOR

REGULAR MEALS 25c AND SHORT ORDERS

OPEN DAY AND NIGHT

308 SOUTH MAIN　　　　　ROCKY FORD, COLO.

R. D. Thompson, Pres.　　　　　John R. Schmalzried, Sec.-Treas.

Thompson-Claypool Undertaking Co.

Funeral Directors and Embalmers

Mrs. Nannie Thompson Lady Attendant

CUT FLOWERS AND POTTED PLANTS

917 Swink Avenue　　Phone Ford 617　　Rocky Ford, Colo.

Rocky Ford East Entry

Railroad Avenue, Original Main Street

White leghorns flank a watermelon topped by a sugar beet. Built in 1928-1929.